RED
SHAMBHALA

RED
SHAMBHALA

Magic, Prophecy, and Geopolitics in the Heart of Asia

ANDREI ZNAMENSKI

Theosophical Publishing House
Wheaton, Illinois * Chennai, India

Quest Books
Theosophical Publishing House
P. O. Box 270
Wheaton, IL 60187-0270

www.questbooks.net

Cover image: *Sophia, the Wisdom of the Almighty*, 1932, by Nicholas Roerich, reproduced by permission of the Nicholas Roerich Museum.
Cover design by Drew Stevens.

Library of Congress Cataloging-in-Publication Data

Znamenski, Andrei, A.
Red Shambhala: magic, prophecy, and geopolitics in the heart of Asia / Andrei Znamenski.—1st Quest ed.
      p.   cm.
Includes index.
ISBN 978-0-8356-0891-6
1. Soviet Union—Politics and government—1917–1936.   2. Geopolitics—Soviet Union—History.   3. Shambhala—Political aspects—Soviet Union—History.
4. Prophecies—China—Tibet—History—20th century.   5. Prophecies—Political aspects—Soviet Union—History.   6. Extremists—Soviet Union—Biography.
7. Communisim—Soviet Union—History.   8. Soviet Union—Foreign relations—1917–1945.   9. Soviet Union—Foreign relations—Asia, Central.   10. Asia, Central—Foreign relations—Soviet Union.   I. Title.
DK266.5.Z58 2011
947.084'2—dc22   2010047136

5   4   3   2   1   *   11   12   13   14   15

Printed in the United States of America

Bodhisattvas have no attainment. They depend on and abide by the perfection of wisdom. Because their minds are unobstructed, they are without fear. Having completely passed beyond all error, they go to the fulfillment of nirvana.

—The Heart of Perfect Wisdom Sutra

Contents

Illustrations

Preface

The idea to write *Red Shambhala* developed gradually as a natural off-shoot of my other projects. The first spark came ten years ago when I was doing research for my book *The Beauty of the Primitive*, a cultural history of shamanism. By chance, I found out that in a secret laboratory in the 1920s Gleb Bokii—the chief Bolshevik cryptographer, master of codes, ciphers, electronic surveillance—and his friend Alexander Barchenko, an occult writer from St. Petersburg, explored Kabala, Sufi wisdom, Kalachakra, shamanism, and other esoteric traditions, simultaneously preparing an expedition to Tibet to search for the legendary Shambhala. A natural question arose: what could the Bolshevik commissar have to do with all this? The story of the life and death of the Bolshevik secret police officer Bokii and his friend intrigued me.

Meanwhile, I learned that during the same years, on the other side of the ocean in New York City, the Russian émigré painter Nicholas Roerich and his wife, Helena, were planning a venture into Inner Asia, hoping to use the Shambhala prophecy to build a spiritual kingdom in Asia that would provide humankind with a blueprint of an ideal social commonwealth. To promote his spiritual scheme, he toyed with an idea to blend Tibetan Buddhism and Communism. Then I stumbled upon the German-Armenian historian Emanuel Sarkisyanz's *Russland and der Messianismus des Orients*, which mentioned that the same Shambhala legend was used by Bolshevik fellow travelers in Red Mongolia to anchor Communism among nomads in the early 1920s.[1]

I came across this information when I was working on a paper dealing with the Oirot/Amursana prophecy that sprang up among Altaian nomads of southern Siberia at the turn of the twentieth century. This prophecy, also widespread in neighboring western Mongolia, dealt with the legendary hero some named Oirot and others called Amursana. The resurrected hero was expected to redeem suffering people from alien intrusions and lead them into a golden age of spiritual bliss and prosperity. This legend sounded strikingly similar to the Shambhala prophecy that stirred the minds of Tibetans and the nomads of eastern Mongolia. In my research I also found that the Bolsheviks used the Oirot/Amursana prophecy in the 1920s to anchor themselves in Inner Asia. I began to have a feeling that all the individuals and events mentioned above might have somehow been linked.

First of all, I need to outline at least briefly what Shambhala means. It was a prophecy that emerged in the world of Tibetan Buddhism between the 900s and 1100s CE, centered on a legend about a pure and happy kingdom located somewhere in the north; the Tibetan word *Shambhala* means "source of happiness."[2] The legend said that in this mystical land people enjoyed spiritual bliss, security, and prosperity. Having mastered special techniques, they turned themselves into god-like beings and exercised full control over forces of nature. They were blessed with long lives, never argued, and lived in harmony as brothers and sisters. At one point, as the story went, alien intruders would corrupt and undermine the faith of Buddha. That was when Rudra Chakrin (Rudra with a Wheel), the last king of Shambhala, would step in and in a great battle would crush the forces of evil. After this, the true faith, Tibetan Buddhism, would prevail and spread all over the world. Scholars argue that the paradisal image of Shambhala and the motif of the final battle between good and evil, elements missing in original Buddhism, most likely were borrowed from neighboring religious traditions, particularly from Manichaeism and Islam, which were making violent advances on Buddhism in the early Middle Ages.

In the course of time, indigenous lamas and later Western spiritual seekers muted the "crusade" notions of the prophecy, and Shambhala became the peaceable kingdom that could be reached through spiritual enlightenment and perfection. The famous founder of Theosophy Helena Blavatsky was the first to introduce this cleansed version of the legend into Western esoteric lore in the 1880s. At the same time, she draped Shambhala in the mantle of evolutionary theory and progress, ideas widely popular among her contemporaries. Blavatsky's Shambhala was the abode of the Great White Brotherhood hidden in the Himalayas. The mahatmas from this brotherhood worked to engineer the so-called sixth race of spiritually enlightened and perfect human beings, who possessed superior knowledge and would eventually take over the world. After 1945, when this kind of talk naturally went out of fashion, the legend was refurbished to fit new spiritual needs. Today in Tibetan Buddhism and spiritual literature, in both the East and the West, Shambhala is presented as an ideal spiritual state seekers should aspire to reach by practicing compassion, meditation, and high spirituality. In this most recent interpretation of the legend, the old "holy war" feature is not simply set aside but recast into an inner war against internal demons that block a seeker's movement toward perfection.[3]

Recently it has become fashionable, especially among scholars, to debunk Western spiritual seekers who feed on Oriental wisdom. Anthropologists, cultural-studies scholars, and historians of religion deconstruct this spiritual trend that has been very visible since the 1960s as a naïve "New Age myth" and point out how incorrect it is and how this spiritual romanticism has nothing to do with the "authentic" and "traditional" Tibetan Buddhism of Inner Asia.[4] I want to stress at the outset that my book is not another academic exposure of the Shambhala myth as a Western invention. The reason I am not going to do this is very simple: I am convinced that in matters of religion and spirituality it is pointless to argue what is authentic and genuine and what is not. Incidentally, I adopted the same approach in my previous book, *The Beauty of the Primitive*. So my premise is that in the field of spirituality everything is authentic, genuine, and traditional, including Eastern and Western versions of Tibetan Buddhism along with its Shambhala myth in old and new forms. At the same time, *Red Shambhala* is not a spiritual treatise that calls you to partake of this myth by virtually traveling to the Shambhala land to reach some sort of spiritual enlightenment. Other authors, spiritual seekers, have already done this, the best example being Edwin Bernbaum's *The Way to Shambhala*.

The purpose of my book is different. I want to explore how the Shambhala myth and related prophecies were used in Inner Asia and beyond between the 1890s and 1930s. I draw attention to the fact that the original Shambhala myth with its two sides (the spiritual paradise and the crusade against infidels) and its later versions served different purposes, depending on circumstances and the people dealing with the legend. Some individuals profiled in this book became more attracted to the image of Shambhala as a country of spiritual bliss and the container of superior knowledge. Others turned to Shambhala as a vehicle to bring about a grand Buddhist theocracy in Inner Asia. At the same time, several people were drawn to the old avenging side of the legend and used it as a tool of spiritual resistance. So the story I am going to tell deals with both the peaceful and avenging sides of the Shambhala myth.

As the account unfolds, I will show why Shambhala suddenly became relevant for a number of groups and individuals inside and outside Asia between the1890s and the 1930s. Prophecies usually stay dormant in times of peace and prosperity. Under normal circumstances, few people believe in utopias, share doomsday dreams of the total renewal of the world, or follow political messiahs. Yet in a time of severe crisis or natural calamity, when the established routine of life falls apart and people feel insecure, prophecies, along with messiahs, multiply and come to the forefront. That is when people invoke old myths and legends and cling to various utopias promising ultimate salvation. The period between the 1890s and 1930s was rich in social and political calamities, not only in Asia but all over the world. World War I and the collapse of four large empires (Chinese, Russian, Ottoman, and Austro-Hungarian) followed by bloody revolutions created a fertile environment for various religious and secular prophecies.

Red Shambhala is the first book in English that recounts the story of political and spiritual seekers from the West and the East, who used Tibetan Buddhist prophecies to promote their spiritual, social, and geopolitical agendas and schemes. These were people of different persuasions and backgrounds: lamas (Ja-Lama and Agvan Dorzhiev), a painter-Theosophist (Nicholas Roerich), a Bolshevik secret police cryptographer (Gleb Bokii), an occult writer with leftist leanings (Alexander Barchenko), Bolshevik diplomats and revolutionaries (Georgy Chicherin, Boris Shumatsky) along with their indigenous fellow-travelers (Elbek-Dorji Rinchino, Sergei Borisov, and Choibalsan), and the right-wing fanatic "Bloody White Baron" Roman von Ungern-Sternberg. Despite their different backgrounds and loyalties, they shared the same totalitarian temptation—the faith in ultimate solutions. They were on the quest for what one of them (Bokii) defined as the search for the source of absolute good and absolute evil. All of them were true believers, idealists who dreamed about engineering a perfect free-of-social-vice society based on collective living and controlled by enlightened spiritual or ideological masters (an emperor, the Bolshevik Party, the Great White Brotherhood, a reincarnated deity) who would guide people on the "correct" path. Healthy skepticism and moderation, rare commodities at that time anyway, never visited the minds of the individuals I profile in this book. In this sense, they were true children of their time—an age of extremes that gave birth to totalitarian society.

Much has been written about the appropriation of Tibet and Shambhala by conservative and right-wing "cultural workers." For example, we already know a great deal about Nazi ventures to the Himalayan Forbidden Kingdom that Himmler and his associates envisioned as the motherland of the Aryans.[5] In *Politics and the Occult*, Gary Lachman has pointed out that popular imagination tends to link the occult to the Right, which is not exactly correct.[6] *Red Shambhala* proves yet again that people on the Left were no strangers to the occult, and they were equally mesmerized by the light from the East. In fact, it is more so in our day.

Geographically I focus on Inner Asia, which roughly includes areas populated by people who either belonged to the Tibetan Buddhist tradition (Tibetans, Mongols, Tuvans, Buryat, and Kalmyk) or stood on its fringes (such as Altaians, sometimes called the Oirot people). For the sake of convenience, I call this area the Mongol-Tibetan cultural area. At the same time, I will be making numerous detours to Russia, the United States, Germany, and India.

First, I will introduce the Mongol-Tibetan cultural area along with its deities and situate Shambhala and related prophecies in the historical context of Inner Asia. I propose that Shambhala, rather than being something unique, was part of the prophetic culture of the Mongol-Tibetan world. What made the Shambhala legend stand out were the efforts of the Panchen Lamas, spiritual leaders of Tibet who propagated it beginning in the 1700s, and later attempts of Western seekers to single out this legend and disseminate it in the West. My research into Oirot/Amursana prophecy and insights into the Geser legend popular among the Mongols and Buryat convinced me that we deal here with the same prophetic culture. The legends about Oirot, Amursana, Geser, and Shambhala, which the nomads of Inner Asia frequently conflated, essentially boil down to a story about a heroic redeemer who would appear when the world neared its end, save the righteous from the evil ones, and bring to life a dreamland of spiritual and material prosperity.

Next my attention shifts to Leningrad (St. Petersburg) and Moscow of the 1920s as the Shambhala myth looms in the background. Here, I introduce English-speaking readers for the first time to a fascinating story about the unusual partnership between the esoteric scientist and writer Alexander Barchenko and his patron Gleb Bokii, the chief Bolshevik cryptographer who wanted to supplement a secular utopia (Communism) with a spiritual one (Shambhala). Driven by their desire to construct a new, nobler type of human being—a popular ideological fad among the early Bolsheviks—both wanted to tap into the Shambhala myth and Kalachakra tantra, an esoteric Tibetan Buddhist teaching. The goal was to reinforce the Communist cause by using Asian wisdom.

From Red Russia I shift back to Inner Asia and show how in the first three decades of the twentieth century Shambhala, Geser, Oirot, and Amursana prophecies fed the rising nationalism of the Tibetans,

Mongols, Buryat, and Altaians. I explore the world of Bolshevik revolutionaries and their fellow travelers (Shumatsky, Borisov, and Rinchino) who tried to use popular Buddhism, including the mentioned prophecies, to anchor Bolshevism within Inner Asia. The fact that the Bolsheviks learned well how to massage nationalist sentiments explains why Red Russia was able to sway some indigenous people in this area to its side, at least in the beginning of the 1920s. Here I also discuss Roman von Ungern-Sternberg, a notorious baron with occultist leanings, who briefly hijacked Mongolia in 1921. I propose that both his rise and then quick demise could be attributed to his attitude to Mongol nationalism.

Then from Inner Asia I move to New York City and explore the world of two Russian émigré Theosophists, the painter Nicholas Roerich and his wife, Helena, companions in the quest for Shambhala. In the mid-1920s, Nicholas, along with Helena and their son George, ventured to Tibet, posing as a reincarnation of the fifth Dalai Lama. With equal zeal he courted Red Russian diplomats and spies, American presidents, and Japanese politicians, promoting himself as a cultural celebrity destined to deliver an important spiritual message to humankind. While many present-day Russian seekers treat the Roeriches as patriots and powerful spiritual teachers, American literature portrays them as dangerous gurus who at one point seduced FDR's Secretary of Agriculture Henry Wallace, costing him the presidential nomination in 1948.

My research for *Red Shambhala* at first took me to the Peter the Great Museum of Anthropology and Ethnography (Kunstkamera), where in 2007 I explored archival materials on Oirot and Amursana prophecies. Two years later, in order to better understand how the Bolsheviks used Tibetan Buddhism to promote their agenda in Inner Asia in the 1920s, I visited the Russian Archive of Social and Political History in Moscow. There I mined the papers of Comintern, a Moscow-based organization that had been preoccupied with sponsoring Communism all over the world. Another source, the recently published spiritual journals of Helena Roerich, gave me deeper insight into the minds of the Roeriches.[7]

However, I do not want to create the impression that I am the first trailblazer to touch upon these topics. I have several important predecessors, mostly from Russia, and I drew heavily upon their valuable works. I owe much to the historian Alexandre Andreyev, who was the first to track Bolshevik advances into Tibet.[8] I am equally indebted to another historian, Vladimir Rosov, whose two volumes on Roerich are the most complete biography of this painter and spiritual seeker.[9] I also used Barchenko's correspondence and the records of his interrogation from formerly classified documents first brought to light by Moscow investigative reporter Oleg Shishkin.[10] During the early stages of this project, I also greatly benefited from John McCannon's and Markus Osterrieder's essays, which provide the best overviews of Nicholas Roerich's activities available in English.[11] For thought-provoking ideas that helped me situate Tibetan Buddhist prophecies and Bolshevik relations with Asian nomads, I am indebted to Sarkisyanz and to Terry Martin.[12] Sarkisyanz has not only discussed Soviet Marxism as a form of a surrogate secular religion, but also was the first to show how the Bolshevik prophetic message was customized to the aspirations of traditional and tribal societies in Russia and Asia. Although lengthy and not exactly easy to read, Martin's book provides a brilliant analysis of the Bolsheviks' policies in the 1920s that allowed them to woo to their side various non-Russian nationalities, including nomadic societies of Asia.

The last but not least words of gratitude go to the people who made this book possible. First of all, I want to mention Richard Smoley from Quest Books, who liked the idea of *Red Shambhala* from the very beginning and encouraged me to put it into book form. Sharron Dorr and Will Marsh, two other editors from the same press, made sure that this project was put into good shape. Moreover, Will went as far as immersing himself into my topic and giving me valuable tips that saved me from several embarrassing inconsistencies. I also want to thank the Department of History at the University of Memphis, and especially its chair, Dr. Jannan Sherman, who created wonderful writing opportunities for me, made sure that I had funding for my research, and helped make my first two years in Memphis as smooth as possible. At the final stage of the project, Daniel Entin, director of the Roerich Museum in New York City, generously provided all necessary photographs and copies of rare articles that I urgently needed to complete this book. To be honest, I have never experienced such prompt help in any other libraries and archives. And, finally, I am grateful to A. E. G. Patterson, who suddenly, as if by magic, emerged on the horizon and offered me rigorous editorial assistance in improving the text.

Major Characters

Alexander Barchenko: (1881–1938) Dropout medical student and popular mystery writer. Inspired by the ideas of French occult writer Saint-Yves d'Alveydre, he wants to master the sacred wisdom of the mysterious land Shambhala-Agartha. He believes that by introducing the elite of Red Russia to Tibetan Buddhism and to the knowledge of Shambhala-Agartha, he will be able to make the Communist project in Russia less violent. Barchenko's esoteric quest is sponsored by Gleb Bokii, his powerful secret police patron.

Gleb Bokii: (1879–1937) Marxist revolutionary and one of the spearheads of the 1917 Bolshevik revolution. As chief of the Special Section of the Bolshevik secret police, he creates Soviet ciphers and breaks Western codes. In his work, he also draws upon the help of graphologists, mediums, hypnotists, and esotericists.

Ja-Lama: (1860-1923) Kalmyk native from southern Russia, a spiritual drifter and adventurer who apprenticed a few years in a Tibetan monastery. In the early 1900s, in Western Mongolia, he poses as a reincarnation of Mahakala (an avenging Buddhist deity) and as the grandson of Prince Amursana (eighteenth-century ruler who fought against Chinese domination) to stir nationalist feelings among Mongol nomads and draw them together.

Nicholas Roerich: (1874-1947) Émigré Russian painter and Theosophist. In 1920, he moves to the United States, where, along with his wife, he establishes an art school and himself as an enigmatic and mysterious sage. In the 1920s, upon a call from his spiritual master Mahatma Morya, he ventures to Tibet, Mongolia, and the Altai to establish a Buddhist-Communist theocracy, posing as a reincarnation of the fifth Dalai Lama, who came to cleanse Tibetan Buddhism from modern evils.

Helena Roerich: (1879–1955) Wife of Nicholas Roerich and founder of Agni-Yoga, which merged some Theosophical ideas and her own spiritual insights. She is a constant companion to Nicholas in all his geopolitical ventures. As a spiritual medium, she is in charge of communicating with their otherworldly teacher Mahatma Morya, who guides her, her husband, and other members of their inner circle in all their quests.

George Roerich: (1902–60) Son of Nicholas and Helena Roerich and an accomplished Orientalist scholar, fluent in Tibetan, Mongol, and several other languages of Central and Inner Asia. An expert on indigenous cultures and languages of Inner Asia, he is indispensible to his parents in their geopolitical ventures.

Baron Roman von Ungern-Sternberg: (1885–1921) Russian cavalry officer of Baltic German origin with family roots tracing back to an old lineage of Teutonic knights. He lives by warfare and for warfare and is also fond of Tibetan Buddhism. Harboring a deep hatred of modern Western civilization, Ungern believes that salvation will come from the East. After 1917, he embarks on a utopian project of restoring monarchies from the East to the West.

Boris Shumatsky: (1886–1938) Seasoned Bolshevik of Russian-Jewish origin who grew up in Siberia, where he learned to speak fluent Buryat, in addition to his home-spoken Yiddish and Russian. He is a self-taught worker-intellectual who spent many years in the Marxist underground. After 1917, Shumatsky is the head of the Communist International's Eastern Secretariat, spearheading the Communist gospel in northern and Inner Asia.

Sergei Borisov: (1889–1937) Indigenous intellectual from the Altai who grew up in family of a Christian missionary. After 1917, he becomes a Bolshevik fellow traveler, head of the Communist International's Mongol-Tibetan Section, and then deputy chair of the Eastern Department in the Soviet Commissariat for Foreign Affairs. Along with Shumatsky and Rinchino, Borisov works hard to turn Mongolia Red and later to bring the Communist prophecy to Tibet. In 1925, disguised as a Buddhist pilgrim, he travels to Lhasa, where he tries to sway the Dalai Lama to Red Russia's side.

Elbek-Dorji Rinchino: (1888–1938) Ambitious indigenous intellectual with a law degree from St. Petersburg University; a Bolshevik fellow traveler, and the first Red dictator of Mongolia. He is obsessed with the idea of bringing together the Buryat, Mongols, and all other people of the Mongol-Tibetan culture into a vast pan-Mongol socialist republic that would be a beacon for all people of the Buddhist faith.

Agvan Dorzhiev: (1858–1938) Accomplished Buddhist monk from Siberia and chief tutor for the thirteenth Dalai Lama in the 1890s. In the early 1900s, he is His Holiness's ambassador to the court of the Russian czar. An ardent advocate of the unity of all Tibetan Buddhist people, he dreams about creating a large pan-Buddhist state under Russian protection. After 1917, Dorzhiev sides with Red Russia, naively expecting that the Bolsheviks would help him fulfill his geopolitical dream.

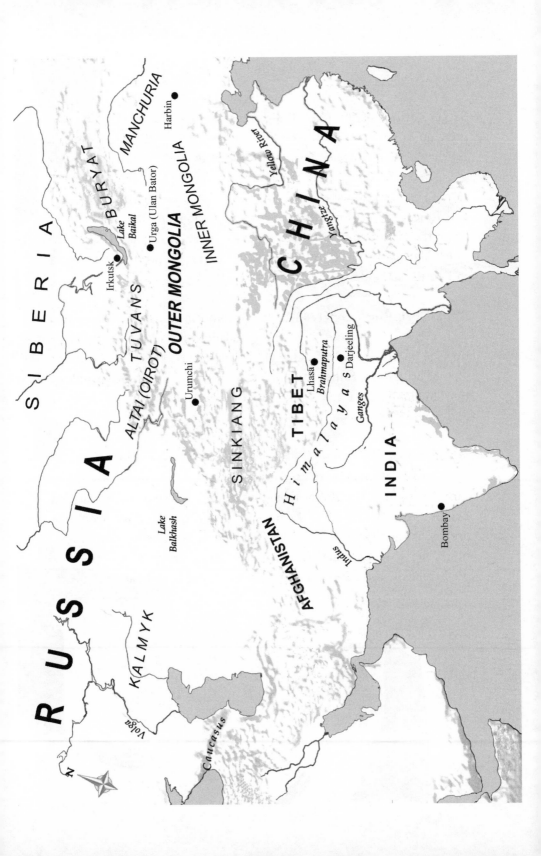

RED
SHAMBHALA

All that we are is a result of
What we have thought.
It is founded on our thoughts
It is made up of our thoughts.
—Gautama Buddha, *Dhammapada*

One

Shambhala, Kalachakra Tantra, and Avenging Gods of Tibetan Buddhism

Somewhere far in the north, goes a Tibetan legend, is the kingdom of Shambhala, shielded from the outside world by mountain peaks as high as the heavens and sharp as the teeth of a tiger. This land has the shape of a giant lotus with eight petals. Those fortunate enough to reach this wonderful place are awed by its beautiful and plentiful lakes, ponds, meadows, forests, and groves. In the middle of Shambhala stands its capital, Kalapa, whose palaces are all made of pure gold, silver, turquoise, coral, pearl, emerald, moon crystal, and other precious stones. Instead of ceilings, these palaces have special circular magnifying crystal spheres through which people can gaze at the gods, the sun, the moon, and the stars, so close that they appear within reach. Window screens are made of sandalwood, and the thrones are all of pure gold. South of Kalapa the seeker will find a special pleasure grove, and in the west one catches a glimpse of the beautiful lake where humans and gods enjoy boat rides together.

The kings who rule Shambhala indulge themselves in sensual pleasures and enjoy their wealth. Despite their pursuit of wealth and pleasure, they strive to be nice to other people and to help them to reach enlightenment and liberation, so the virtues of the royalty never decrease. The people of Shambhala never become sick or old, and they are blessed with handsome and beautiful bodies. The laws of the land

1

are mild and gentle, and beatings along with imprisonments are totally unknown. Last but not least, Shambhala inhabitants never go hungry. All in all, residents of the kingdom are good, virtuous, and intelligent, and capable of reaching Nirvana in their lifetimes. Shambhala's priests are very faithful and humble. They reject material possessions and go barefoot and bareheaded, dressed only in white robes. And, most important, Shambhala is the place where Buddhism exists in its purest and most authentic form.

The way to this land of spiritual bliss and plenty lies through special Kalachakra-tantra practices and virtuous behavior.[1] An old Buddhist parable conveys this idea well: "Where are you going across these wastes of snow," a lama hermit asked a youth who embarked on a long journey to find the wondrous Shambhala land. "To find Shambhala," answered the boy. "Ah, well then, you need not travel far. The kingdom of Shambhala is in your own heart."[2]

The Shambhala legend is the description of the famous Buddhist paradise—the land of spiritual enlightenment and simultaneously the land of plenty that people of the Mongol-Tibetan world dreamed about since the early Middle Ages. The concept of this paradise was absent in early Buddhism; it was introduced later to cater to the sentiments of common folk who could not comprehend some of the abstract principles of the Buddhist faith and needed something "real" to latch onto.[3] Current practitioners of Tibetan Buddhism move back to the original roots of the faith, in some sense, by downplaying the material side of the utopia and putting more stress on its spiritual aspects.

The first to introduce this legend into Western spiritual culture was the famous Western seeker Helena Blavatsky, founding mother of Theosophy, who most likely learned about Shambhala by reading accounts of European travelers to Tibet and hearing about this wondrous land during her brief sojourn to the Tibetan-Indian border. Adjusting the Buddhist legend to the theory of evolution, which was becoming popular at the end of the nineteenth century, Blavatsky argued that Shambhala was the center of evolving superior wisdom—the abode of the so-called Great White Brotherhood located somewhere in the Himalayas. The hidden masters (whom she also referred to as mahatmas) from this brotherhood guided humankind in its evolution away from materialism toward the highest spirituality, which would eventually give rise to the superior sixth race that would replace contemporary imperfect human beings. Such politically incorrect generalizations, especially after what happened during World War II, might offend the sensibilities of current spiritual seekers, yet during Blavatsky's lifetime and well into the 1930s, this kind of evolutionary talk was quite popular among all educated folk who considered themselves advanced and progressive, including Theosophists.

Buddhist Holy War: Shambhala as Spiritual Resistance

Spiritual bliss and plenty were not the only sides of the Shambhala legend. There was another side, which is usually downplayed in current Tibetan Buddhism—spiritual resistance against people who infringed on the Buddhist faith. The story about this aspect of Shambhala, which is an inseparable part of the legend, is not so benevolent and tranquil, but it is no less valid.

The entire Shambhala legend sprang up in northern India in the early Middle Ages, between the 900s and 1200s. Along with the description of Shambhala as the land of enlightenment and plenty, it mentioned that at some point barbarian demons coming from the west would inflict devastating damage on the Buddhist faith. In Sanskrit texts these alien infidels were called *mlecca* people. Tibetan sources referred to them as *lalo*. The invaders, the legend said, would bring misery and chaos, and the whole world would enter *Kaliyuga* (the Age of Disputes), when the true Buddhist faith would decline. The northern Shambhala kingdom would remain the only stronghold of the true faith and would eventually redeem people from this misery.

3

Figure 1.1. Rudra Chakrin (Rigden Djapo), the king of Shambhala, crusading against *mlecca* people, the enemies of Buddhism. From the painting *Shambhala is Coming* by Nicholas Roerich (1926).

To deliver Tibetan Buddhist people from the danger, the last Shambhala king, Rudra Chakrin (the Wrathful One with the Wheel, Rigden Djapo in Tibetan), would enter a trance so that he could see the coming events. Then he would gather a mighty army and launch a merciless attack against the barbarians. In the ensuing horrible, Armageddon-like battle, the infidels would be totally crushed, and the Age of Disputes would be over. After this successful Shambhala war, the true faith (Tibetan Buddhism) would triumph all over the earth. Lobsan Palden Yeshe, the third Panchen Lama, who was considered the spiritual leader of Tibet and who composed a 1775 guidebook to Shambhala, prophesized this final battle as follows:

Thee, great lama, who lives in this paradise land and who is constantly in prayer, shall adopt the title of Rigden Djapo and shall defeat the armies of lalo. Thy army shall include people of many nations. Thee shall have 40,000 large wild elephants, four millions of mad elephants, many warriors, and Thee shall pierce the heart of the king of lalo. Thy twelve powerful gods shall completely destroy all evil gods of the lalo. Thy elephants shall kill their elephants. Thy horses shall smash lalo's horses, and Thy golden chariots shall crash their chariots. Thy people shall tame the lalo's protectors, and lalo's influence shall be totally gone. And then the time shall come when the true faith spreads all over. After many years of preaching the faith, on the 22nd of the middle spring moon in the year of the horse, Thee shall take the seat of the great god and shall be surrounded by mighty warriors and medicine women.[4]

The references to the Age of Disputes and to the king redeemer most likely originated from Hinduism, which had a legend that Vishnu was born in the village of Shambhala. Like Rudra Chakrin, Vishnu was destined to defeat those who stepped on the wrong spiritual path and then to reawaken the minds of hesitant people. Scholars also believe that the apocalyptic notions of the final battle and the idea of the forces of good and evil fighting each other might have penetrated Tibetan Buddhism from Manichaeism and, especially, from Islam. It is well known that in the early Middle Ages, the mlecca people, or people of Mecca, at first mingled with Buddhist communities in eastern Afghanistan and northern India and then mercilessly drove them out.[5]

In eastern Afghanistan under the Abbasid dynasty in the first half of the 800s, Buddhists and Hindus lived side by side with Muslims in relative peace. The Buddhists were even allowed to keep their faith, which opened the door to an exchange of religious ideas. In fact, during this period of peaceful coexistence, to the dismay of the Buddhist clergy, many faithful switched to Islam. Simple and straightforward, the religion of the mlecca people was more alluring to some common folk than Buddhism with its complex and vague principles. In the 900s this multicultural paradise came to an end. The warlike Sunni Turks, new converts to Islam, did not tolerate anyone who did not fit the "true" faith, so they wiped out the Buddhist communities and monasteries in eastern Afghanistan and then advanced farther, taking over Punjab in northern India. When the Muslim hordes tried to seize Kashmir, the Buddhists were able to unite and defeat the intruders, between 1015 and 1021. A legend said that the mlecca armies were subdued by the force of mantras, so the Shambhala prophecy predicting the mlecca invasion and its subsequent defeat could be a legendary reference to the actual events in Kashmir.[6]

The Buddhists did not enjoy their success for long. Another and more powerful tide of Allah's warriors dislodged the followers of Buddha from northern India and forced them to escape northward to the safety of the Himalayas and farther to Tibet. From there, Buddhism was later reintroduced into India.[7] It is highly likely that these runaway Buddhist communities searching for sanctuary in the north created the legend about the mysterious oasis of the true faith, bliss, and plenty shielded from the outside world by high, snowcapped mountain peaks. Unable to stop the advancing Muslims, these escapees might have also found spiritual consolation in the prophecy that a legendary redeemer would reappear and inflict a horrible revenge on the enemies of Buddha's teaching. Whatever events contributed to the rise of the Shambhala myth, it is obvious that the prophecy was directed against Islam. The old texts containing the Shambhala legend repeatedly mentioned "the barbarian deity Rahmana," a reference to al-Rahman (the Merciful in Arabic). One of the texts directly pointed out that the lord of the barbarians was "Muhamman, the incarnation of al-Rahman, the teacher of the barbarian Dharma, the guru and swami of the barbarian Tajiks."[8]

Those who shaped the Shambhala prophecy were clearly preoccupied not only with the spiritual resistance against the "barbarian Dharma" but also with military logistics of the coming battle. Besides the millions of wild and mad elephants and thousands of warriors and horses that Rudra Chakrin would gather for his final battle, the legend mentioned the variety of weapons to be used against the "people of Mecca." There were not only chariots, spears, and other conventional hardware of ancient combat, but also sophisticated wheel-shaped machines of mass destruction. There would also be a special flying wind machine for use against mountain forts. According to the Shambhala prophecy, this prototype of a modern-day napalm bomber would spill burning oil on the enemies. Moreover, the protectors of the faith would use a harpoon machine, an analogy of a modern-day machine gun, designed to simultaneously shoot many arrows that would easily pierce the bodies of armored elephants. The defeat of the mlecca barbarians would launch the Age of Perfection (*Kritayuga*), when the true faith would triumph and the Shambhala kingdom would expand over the entire world. People would stop doing evil and manifest only virtuous behavior. At the same time, they would enjoy their riches, freely indulge in sensual pleasures, and live long lives, up to nine hundred years. Cereals in the fields and fruit trees would grow on their own, bringing plentiful crops and fruits. At this new age, not only a selected few, but everyone would be able to reach spiritual enlightenment.[9]

Modern seekers, including practitioners of Tibetan Buddhism, either downplay the militaristic aspects of the Shambhala myth or do not talk about them at all. Instead, they focus on the spiritual inner aspects of the prophecy. Whenever they mention the Shambhala war, current books on Tibetan Buddhism usually explain it as a metaphor for the battle against internal demons that create obstacles for spiritual seekers on their path and that the victory of Rudra Chakrin over his enemies means spiritual enlightenment. The deans of modern Tibetan Buddhism remind us that elimination of the enemies of Shambhala does not mean actual annihilation of the infidels but overcoming one's own ignorance and sins. Even particular details of the Shambhala war have been reinterpreted according to modern religious ethics. One of Rudra Chakrin's major generals, usually depicted riding nearby and holding a banner, became a symbol of deep awareness. The four divisions of the Shambhala king's army now stand for four major feelings: love, compassion, joy, and equality. In the modern version of Shambhala, even Muhammad, the actual prophet of Islam, evolved into a metaphor of destructive behavior.[10]

I do not mean to downgrade the current interpretation of the Shambhala legend as an inward path to spiritual enlightenment. Nor am I saying that this Shambhala does not fully match traditional and indigenous versions of the legend. If all versions of the Shambhala legend, past and present, were put into a time context, they would all appear as sound and valid. After all, religions do not stay frozen in time and space. People constantly shape and reshape them according to their contemporary social and spiritual needs, and Tibetan Buddhism is certainly not an exception. In fact, such modern-day revisions of aspects of this faith should be commended as an attempt to bring Tibetan Buddhism closer to modern humanistic values. Hopefully, these efforts will set a good example for present-day mlecca people, some of whom are still frozen in the medieval time tunnel and do not want to part with aggressive notions.

Kalachakra Tantra: Shortcut to Spiritual Perfection

The legend about the Shambhala kingdom and its subsequent war against Muslim intruders did not exist as a separate story. From the very beginning, the myth was an inseparable part of the Kalachakra teaching—a set of meditative and astrological techniques (tantras) first written down in Sanskrit in the 800s and then translated into Tibetan in the 1200s. Kalachakra (*Dus'khor* in Tibetan), translated from Sanskrit as "the Wheel of Time," describes esoteric techniques (meditations, mantras, and visualization of deities) that help the faithful achieve enlightenment in their lifetimes. These techniques sprang up in northern India around the 600s as a challenge to Hinduism, which expected people to undergo a chain of reincarnations before reaching enlightenment. As always happens with alternative movements, a few centuries later this Buddhist counterculture itself evolved into canonized practices taught by lamas, "experts" in Kalachakra who knew the "correct" path.

In Buddhism, there are three ways of doing tantras. In "father" tantra, by reciting appropriate mantras, adepts think themselves intensely into merging with a particular deity and absorbing its spiritual power. In "mother" tantra, adepts seek to create a state of emptiness and bliss by controlling and transforming sexual desire—the gateway to birth and rebirth. This is the reason some tantras are so focused on sexuality. Finally, in "dual" tantras, an adept combines both father and mother techniques. As a result, the adept appears as a powerful deity and simultaneously reaches eternal bliss through mastering bodily fluids. Kalachakra belongs to this third type of tantras.

Original Kalachakra texts did not survive. What is available now are their renditions called *Sri Kalacakra* and *Vimalaprabha*, translated from Sanskrit into Tibetan by the famous writer Bu-ston in the mid 1300s.[11] These texts reveal that the glorious Gautama Buddha introduced Kalachakra to Suchandra, the first king of Shambhala, who began to teach these sacred techniques to the people of his kingdom. The Kalachakra teaching is divided into "outer," "inner," and "other" segments. The first part deals with the outside world and describes the universe, astrology, geography, and various prophecies. For example, here astrological formulas can be found explaining how natural rhythms affect an individual's existence. The Shambhala legend, including the description of the glorious kingdom and its war against the mlecca, is a part of this outer section, which was open to everyone.

The other two segments are reserved only for the initiated. The inner Kalachakra deals with the anatomy of the mystic body; adepts of Kalachakra and other tantras believe the body is a collection of energy centers linked through channels. Various bodily fluids (the most important being semen and menstrual blood) flow through these channels. The task of adepts is to empower themselves by "controlling" these fluids. The third, or "other," Kalachakra details how to spread, balance, and

9

manipulate these energy flows and how to attune them to the movement of the sun, planets, and stars; Tibetan Buddhism views a human body and the outside world as intertwined projections of each other. The same section contains a list of hundreds of deities and mandalas and explains how to practice chanting and how to visualize and merge with various deities.[12]

Like a great deal of original Tibetan Buddhism, Kalachakra was a male-oriented teaching designated to empower male adepts through seventeen initiations. Lower-level initiations, known as the "stage of production," were available to all males. In fact, people could partake of this basic Kalachakra on a mass scale, visiting public initiations conducted by the Dalai Lama, the Panchen Lama, and other qualified masters. During these gatherings, adepts usually swore to follow the path of enlightenment, repent, and avoid misdeeds. They were also expected to suppress their egos and offer their minds, spirits, and bodies to the Kalachakra master performing the initiation. The goal of this technique was to turn adepts into empty vessels that the master was to fill with the spiritual power of a particular deity. Incidentally, the suppression of personal ego is not only a Kalachakra requirement, but also an essential attribute of all of Tibetan Buddhism. In other words, during these lower-level initiations, adepts ritually "destroyed" themselves as human beings and were "reborn" as deities.

Initiations of the highest level, the "stage of perfection," were accessible only to a few chosen lamas and were conducted in absolute secrecy. There was surely something to hide from laymen, for many of these rituals were designated to teach an adept to control his sexual drive and channel it into spiritual bliss. These types of initiations required the presence of *karma mudra*, young women whose ages ranged from ten to twenty years; in modern times, actual females have frequently been replaced with ritual objects symbolizing women. At the same time, old Kalachakra texts inform us that an adept could not reach enlightenment without the presence of the *karma mudra*. During these initiations an initiate was sexually aroused in the presence of a naked woman and was challenged to restrain himself from ejaculation. For instance, one of the old texts prescribed that a master show an undressed girl to an adept and ask him to stroke her breasts.[13] Like other tantras, Kalachakra is focused on preservation and return of semen, which is viewed as precious energy of creation and the key to spiritual enlightenment: "The yogin needs to avoid with every effort passion for emission, by which avoiding it will attain the motionless bliss, liberating himself from the bonds of transmigration," and "All yogins attain Buddhahood through the interruption of the moment of ejaculation."[14] The man who could not hold on was called an animal, whereas the one capable of restraining himself from ejaculation was considered a hero with divine attributes.

Top initiations included even more challenges for an adept. In one of them, a master was to have intercourse with a *karma mudra* by allowing his semen to flow into her vagina in order to create "red-white fluid." Then this mix of the male (white) and female (red) fluids was collected and fed to an initiate with the words, "This is your sacrament, dear one, as taught by all Buddhas." Another high initiation required an adept to have intercourse with a female participant, but again without ejaculating. Moreover, in the seventeenth, the last initiation, a student was to copulate with several women, dipping his *vajra* in their vaginas to get female fluid without spilling his seed. These ritual manipulations were directed to empowering an adept through "sucking" the female power of creation and merging it with the male one, which would turn the initiate into a superhuman transgender being—quite a misogynistic technique from a present viewpoint.

To hide these esoteric techniques from laypeople, old texts used various metaphors to make it hard to grasp the content of the rituals. For example, the vagina was routinely referred to as "lotus," sperm was called "enlightenment consciousness," menstrual blood was labeled "the sun," and breasts were the "vase that holds white." Although until recently, Kalachakra masters did not reach an agreement about whether the presence of the second sex should be actual or symbolic, it is obvious that in the past, Kalachakra practices did involve ritual use of

11

sexuality. The best evidence for this is the images of Tibetan Buddhist gods, who were frequently portrayed brandishing various morbid objects such as skulls and weapons while simultaneously having sex with their divine female consorts.

As important as it might be, channeling sexual fluids into spiritual energy was not the only technique used at the stage of "perfection." In the highest initiations, an adept was to ingest various substances forbidden in Tibetan Buddhism, such as menstrual blood, flesh, urine, pieces of skin, liver, and anal excrements. It was assumed that by exposing himself without fear to these disgusting substances, an adept was capable of going beyond good and evil toward spiritual bliss. In other words, to reach enlightenment, an initiate had to bravely stare the Devil in his eye. Or, as an old tantric wisdom said, "Those things by which evil men conduct are bound, others turn into means and gain thereby release from the bonds of existence."[15] The same logic might explain why Tibetan-Mongol culture became so fascinated with the morbid. Buddhist art widely depicts images of skulls, severed heads, corpses, and scenes of murders. Monks were encouraged to meditate upon corpses in various stages of decay. It was also recommended that the highest Kalachakra initiations be performed at crematoria, charnel fields, graves, and murder sites.[16]

God Protectors and Defenders of the Buddhist Faith

What immediately strikes one who looks at the images of Tibetan Buddhist deities is that many of them do not appear to be friendly beings. One definitely will not find here any weeping Holy Marys or suffering Christs. Instead, there are plenty of menacing and angry faces, sickles, daggers, and necklaces and cups made of human skulls, along with corpses trampled by divine feet. The greater part of the text of *The Handbook of Tibetan Buddhist Symbols*, the most complete description of Tibetan Buddhist iconography, deals with weapons, weapon-related artifacts, severed limbs and heads, human skulls, and bones.[17]

Tibetan Buddhism has two special groups of deities that are invoked during a time of trouble to combat internal demons or enemies of the faith. The first are god-protectors (*yi-dam*—Hevajra, Sang-dui, Mahamaya, Samvara, and Kalachakra)[18] who shield lamas from demonic forces. The second are eight terrible ones (*dharmapalas*), protectors of the faith (Begtse, Tsangs-pa, Kuvera, Palden Lhamo, Yama, Yamantaka, Hayagriva, and Mahakala), who wage war without mercy against all enemies of Buddhism.[19] Depicted on sacred scrolls or cast in bronze, these deities have wrathful features, and their body postures manifest anger and aggression as if saying, "Beware, demons and enemies of the faith."

Figure 1.2. Black Mahakala, one of the wrathful deities in Tibetan Buddhism. Bronze sculpture.

The avenging terrible ones are usually portrayed as short, muscular beings who wave various weapons (hatchets, battle axes, and swords) and crush human and supernatural enemies of Buddhism. Some of them wear crowns made of skulls with flaming pearls, ornaments of human bones, and necklaces of freshly severed human heads. One of the most important attributes of both god-protectors and the terrible ones are the skull cups (*kapala*) filled with the blood of enemies. Moreover, many of these deities are frequently depicted having intercourse with their divine female companions—a reference to tantric practices.

The most ferocious defender of the Buddhist faith is Palden Lhamo, the personal goddess-protector of the Dalai Lama and the holy city of Lhasa. On painted sacred scrolls, Palden Lhamo is frequently portrayed

Figure 1.3. Palden Lhamo, a wrathful deity, protector of the Dalai Lama and the city of Lhasa. Bronze sculpture.

as a black, bony, four-armed lady with barred teeth, riding a horse. In her upper right hand she holds a chopper, and her second right arm holds a large red scull cup. The upper left hand brandishes a diamond-shaped dagger. The body of the goddess is covered with snakes, wreaths made of human skulls, and necklaces of severed heads. Her own head is topped with a crown of flowers. The upper part of her body is covered with elephant skin and her hips with skin of an ox. Sometimes she is also pictured as standing amid a cemetery.

A gory legend, which one will never find in current coffee-table books about Tibetan Buddhism, recounts how this goddess turned into such a ferocious being. Palden Lhamo was married to the king of Ceylon, who did not care about Buddhism, and that drove her crazy. As a die-hard true believer, Palden Lhamo took a horrible oath: if she failed to convert her husband to the true faith, she would destroy all her children in order to interrupt the royal lineage so hostile to Buddha's creed. No matter how hard she tried, the goddess could not convert her infidel husband, and, eventually, while the king was away, she had to fulfill her terrible oath by murdering their only son. Not only did the queen kill the little one, but she also skinned him, ate his flesh, and drank his blood from a skull cup. Having completed this ferocious act, Palden Lhamo saddled her horse, using the son's skin as a saddle, and galloped northward. Furious, the devastated father shot at her with a poisonous arrow and hit her horse. The runaway queen pulled out the arrow and uttered magic words: "May the wound of my horse become an eye large enough to overtake the twenty-four regions, and may I myself extirpate the race of these malignant kings of Ceylon!" Sadly, the legend does not have a happy ending. Unpunished, the sadistic mother continued her journey through India, Tibet, and Mongolia, eventually settling in southern Siberia.[20] One does not need to guess twice to figure out the brutal moral of the story: loyalty to one's faith is supreme.

Modern-day literature about Tibetan Buddhism, which has been adjusted to Western ideas of human rights and universal peace, does not mention these facts from the past lives of the terrible ones, which is perfectly fine: people who do not wish to be stuck in a medieval time tunnel usually change their religion and move on. For example, *Celestial Gallery*, an oversized coffee-table book composed by current adherents of Tibetan Buddhism in the West, asks us not to fear Palden Lhamo's garlands of skulls because she is simply "the wrathful mother who tramples on the enemies of complacency and self-deception" and challenges us to step on the path of spiritual evolution. The same book also reveals that her demonic forms symbolize our own dark forces we have to deal with.[21]

The worship of wrathful *dharmapalas* was, and still is, very popular in the Tibetan Buddhist world. Common folk believe that prayers to the terrible ones are more effective than those addressed to benevolent gods, who are good anyway. In the past, to appease the ears of Palden Lhamo, Mahakala, Begtse, and other angry gods, lamas usually played thighbone trumpets made from human or tiger thighbones. Equally pleasing for these deities were sounds produced by skull drums made of human skins stretched over two human craniums. People could solicit the help of these gods through various offerings. The most effective one, at least in the past, was blood, preferably from humans. The best blood was to be taken from a corpse or extracted from people suffering from a contagious disease, for example leprosy. Menstrual blood of widows and prostitutes was also considered very effective. Another type of good blood could come from the blade of a sword or from a young healthy man killed during battle.[22] The text of a 1903 sacrificial prayer addressed to Genghis Khan (who had been turned into a protective deity) to ward off enemies of the faith, robbers, and lawbreakers prescribed, "Mix the following in brandy in equal parts: the blood of a man who has been killed, swarf from an iron bar by which a man has been killed, and offer this with flour, butter, milk and black tea. When this kind of sacrifice is offered, without any omission, then one will certainly be able to master anything, be it acts of war, enemies, robbers, brigands, the curses of hated opponents, or any adversity."[23]

As soon as Maitreya is born, he will walk seven steps forward, and where he puts down his feet a jewel or a lotus will spring up. He will raise his eyes to the ten directions, and will speak these words: "This is my last birth. There will be no more rebirth after this one. Never will I come back here, but, all pure, I shall win Nirvana!"

—Prophecy of Buddha Maitreya

Two

Power for the Powerless: The Mongol-Tibetan World and Its Prophecies

In modern times, the people of Mecca were no longer a threat to Tibetan Buddhism. In fact, now the mlecca were on the defensive, trying to shield themselves from the advances of Western civilization. Beginning around the 1500s, Muslim encroachments on the followers of Buddha subsided, replaced by assertive advances by the Chinese, later joined by the Russians and, at the very end of the nineteenth century, by the English. These new "barbarians" did not care about converting the Mongols and Tibetans to their religions. Their major interests were power and land for the Chinese and Russians and trade for the English. In the 1600s and 1700s, the Manchu Dynasty that ruled China secured control over Mongolia, Tuva, and Tibet. In the meantime, the Russian Empire rolled into southern Siberia and the Far East, taking over the Altai and Trans-Baikal area, clashing with China over spheres of influence. Finally, in the 1890s, Britain, firmly established in India, began banging on the gates of Tibet, demanding that the "Forbidden Kingdom" open itself to international trade. When it refused, in 1904, like a bolt of lightning, the English thrust into the heart of Tibet, crushing Buddha's warriors armed with swords and antiquated muskets. China and Russia did not like such aggressive advances in their backyard, and soon the three powers became involved in the Great Game over who would control Inner Asia.

Rulers of China and Russia subdued the princes in Mongol-Tibetan countries and turned them into their vassals, leaving Buddhist clergy alone. Frequently, Buddhist monks were pitted against secular princes, who were treated as potential rebels. In the 1600s and 1700s, Tibetan Buddhism began to flourish, and lamas were free to conduct missionary work. As a result, by the end of the eighteenth century the "yellow faith" had spread all over Mongolia and made successful inroads in southern Siberia. The privileged status of the Buddhist teaching, which eventually crippled secular power, might explain why later monasteries and monks usually headed social and political movements in the Tibetan-Mongol world. It also explains why, in modern times, at first Tibet and then Mongolia became theocracies (states headed by clergy).

Tibet was ruled by the Dalai Lama ("Ocean of Wisdom" in Tibetan), the chief religious leader and administrator. Yet he did not enjoy total power. The Panchen Lama, abbot of the Tashilumpho monastery, traditionally exercised control over the eastern part of the country. Panchen Lamas, whom many viewed as the spiritual leaders of Tibet, did not pay taxes and even had small armies. This special status originated from the seventeenth century, when Lobzang Gyaltsen, abbot of the Tashilumpho monastery, spiritually guided the fifth Dalai Lama (1617–82), the great reformer who built up Tibet. As a gesture of deep gratitude to his spiritual teacher, the Lhasa ruler endowed the abbot with the title of Panchen Lama, "Great Scholar," and granted Tashilumpho a special tax-exempt status. In modern times, this privileged status of the Panchen Lamas became a liability, undermining and chipping away Tibetan unity and sovereignty, to the joy of its close neighbors, some of whom did not miss any chance to pit the Ocean of Wisdom against the Great Scholar.

Theologically speaking, Panchens stood even higher than Dalai Lamas. Tashilumpho abbots were considered the reincarnation of Buddha Amitabha (one of the five top Buddhas, in addition to Gautama), whereas Dalais were only reincarnations of Avalokitesvara, who was only a bodhisattva and the manifestation of Buddha Amitabha.[1] Besides, the faithful linked Panchens to the Shambhala prophecy; at the end of the eighteenth century one of the Tashilumpho abbots composed a guidebook to this great northern land of spiritual bliss and plenty,[2] and many monks came to believe that in the future the Great Scholar would be reborn as a Shambhala king to deliver people from existing miseries. Despite such impeccable religious credentials, real power in Tibet belonged to the Dalai Lama.

In Mongolia, traditionally much power was concentrated in the hands of the Bogdo-gegen (Great Holy One). This third most prominent man in the Tibetan Buddhist hierarchy, after the Dalai and the Panchen, was considered the reincarnation of the famous Tibetan scholar Taranatha, who had lived in the 1500s. At first, Bogdo reincarnations were found among Mongol princely families, but, haunted by the specter of Mongol separatism, the Manchu emperors curtailed this practice and ordered that all new Bogdo come only from Tibet.[3] After the country freed itself from the Chinese in 1912, the Great Holy One was elevated to the head of the state and, just like Tibet, Mongolia became a theocracy.

Tibetan Buddhist countries were mostly populated by nomads who raised horses and sheep. About 30 percent of the entire male population were lamas. Tibet was the only country that, besides the nomads, had large groups of peasants and craftsmen. As parts of the Chinese Empire, Mongolia, Tibet, and Tuva, as well as the Kalmyk, Buryat, and Altaians within the Russian Empire enjoyed considerable self-rule. As long as they recognized themselves as subjects of their empires and agreed to perform a few services (usually protecting the frontiers and paying tribute), they were left alone. Moreover, in China, the Manchu Dynasty, following the old tactics of divide and rule, went further, segregating Tibetan Buddhist people from the rest of the populations. Mongols and Tibetans were not allowed to mingle with the Chinese, wear their clothing, or learn their language. At the same time, Chinese peasants were forbidden to settle in Tibet and Mongolia.

At the end of the nineteenth century everything changed. Famine and population pressure in China put an end to no-settlement policies. While mountainous Tibet was of little interest, the pasturelands of the Mongols looked very appealing, and the Manchu began to squeeze them from their native habitats and curtail their traditional law. By the beginning of the twentieth century, southern (Inner) Mongolia was flooded with Chinese, and in all major cities of the northern (Outer) part of the country, Mongol officials were replaced with Chinese mandarins. Simultaneously, between the 1880s and 1910s, after serfdom in Russia was terminated, hundreds of thousands of settlers flocked to southern Siberia in search of good pasture and plow lands. Although Siberia was large enough to absorb many of these newcomers, in the Altai and the Trans-Baikal, the most lucrative settlement areas, Russian newcomers began to clash with local nomads over land. Between 1896 and 1916, to speed up colonization and link the eastern borderlands to the rest of the country, the Russian government built the Trans-Siberian railroad. To the dismay of indigenous folk, the Russian Empire, like its Manchu counterpart, cracked down on their traditional self-rule and law. Jealous of Russian advances and fearful that the Russians would roll southward into Mongolia and on to the Far East, the Chinese doubled their colonization moves, expanding to Manchuria and further into Inner Mongolia, where the number of Mongols soon shrank to 33 percent. Replicating Russian steps in Siberia, in 1906 the Chinese government built a railroad to Inner Mongolia, drawing this borderland area closer to Beijing. The centuries-old policy of noninterference was shredded. From then on there would be no peace between the Mongols and the Chinese. As one historian of the period wrote, the entire Mongol history in the first half of the twentieth century became saturated with anti-Chinese sentiments.[4]

Although the rugged terrain of Tibet did not attract the hordes of settlers and it was fortunate to avoid the fate of Mongolia, the Forbidden Kingdom was not immune to anti-Chinese sentiments. Tibetans equally distrusted the Manchu Empire, which wrecked their sovereignty in 1908 by bringing a detachment of troops to Lhasa, stripping the Dalai Lama of his power, and giving decision-making authority to two governmental inspectors (*ambans*) sent from Beijing. Besides, in eastern Tibet, the Manchus kicked out all local administrators and replaced them with Chinese bureaucrats. Although these measures were a response to the 1904 military strike at Tibet by the English, the Forbidden Kingdom recognized them as an attack on its sovereignty.

Anti-Chinese Prophecies in Tibet and Mongolia

Resorting to prophecies such as Shambhala was one way for Tibetans and Mongols to empower themselves to deal with the Chinese advances. As early as the 1840s the French missionary Abbé Huc, who visited the Tashilumpho monastery, described how this particular myth served as a spiritual resistance against China's infringement on Tibetan sovereignty. The version of the prophecy that he heard said that when the Buddhist faith declined, the Chinese would take over the Forbidden Kingdom. The only place where the true faith would survive would be the Kalon (Kalachakra?) fellowship, a sacred brotherhood of the Panchen Lama's devoted followers, who would find refuge in the north somewhere between the Altai and Tuva. In this mysterious faraway northern country, a new reincarnation of the Panchen Lama would be found.

In the meantime, the subjugated people would rise up against the invaders in a spontaneous rebellion: "The Thibetans will take up arms, and will massacre in one day all the Chinese, young and old, and not one of them shall trespass the frontiers." After this, the infuriated Manchu emperor would gather a huge army and storm into Tibet, slashing and burning: "Blood will flow in torrents, the streams will be red with gore, and the Chinese will gain possession of Thibet." That was when the reincarnated Panchen Lama, the "saint of all saints," would step in to free the faithful from the infidels. The spiritual leader of Tibet would assemble the members of his sacred society, both alive and dead, into a powerful army equipped with arrows and fusils. Headed

23

by the Panchen, the holy army would march southward and cut the Chinese into pieces. Not only would he wipe out the enemies of the faith, but he would also take over Tibet, Mongolia, all of China, and even the faraway great state of Oros (Russia). The Panchen Lama would eventually be proclaimed the universal ruler, and the Tibetan Buddhist faith would triumph all over the world: "Superb Lamaseries would rise everywhere and the whole world will recognize an infinite power of Buddhic prayers."[5]

The world of Inner Asian nomads was saturated with epic legends, myths, fairy tales, and stories, which common folk, mostly illiterate shepherds, shared with one another or received from storytellers and oracles. Prophecies were an important part of this oral culture, helping the populace deal with the uncertainties of life and mentally digest dramatic changes in times of troubles.[6] Spreading like wildfire over plains and deserts, prophecies comforted people, mobilized them against enemies, and guided them to the correct path. Not infrequently, learned lamas put these messages down on paper and passed them around as chain letters to other monasteries.

In the Mongol-Tibetan world people took these prophecies very seriously. For example, Abbé Huc was stunned by how passionately Tibetans believed in the reality of the Shambhala prophecy, taking for granted not only its general message but also its particular details of what was about to happen: "Everyone speaks of them as of things certain and infallible." Although loaded with Christian biases, the perceptive missionary also noted the explosive power of this lingering prophecy: "These absurd and extravagant ideas have made their way with the masses, and particularly with those who belong to the society of the Kalons, that they are very likely, at some future day, to cause a revolution in Thibet."[7] As if anticipating actual events that would take place in Inner Asia in the early twentieth century, the holy father correctly predicted that it would take only one smart and strong-willed individual to come from the north and proclaim himself the Panchen Lama in order to ride these popular sentiments.

Besides Shambhala, people of the Mongol-Tibetan world shared other tools of spiritual resistance. One of them was turning epic heroes and actual historical characters into sacred beings. For example, the famous Genghis Khan became a god-protector of Mongol Buddhism. Another popular deity was Geser Khan, a legendary hero immortalized in epic tales widespread among the Buryat, eastern Mongols, and Tibetans. Sent by the god Hormusta to free people from evil, Geser

Figure 2.1. Geser the Lion, an epic hero-liberator in Mongol-Tibetan folklore.

Figure 2.2. A shrine devoted to Maitreya, the Buddha of the new era, Mongolia, 1913.

won back his kingdom through a horse race, defeated demons in Tibet, and crushed barbarians who preyed on Mongolia, even chasing them down in faraway Persia. Indigenous bards who recounted his glorious deeds added their own details to the plot. Some storytellers merged the character of Geser with the image of the Shambhala king who was expected to resurface from the north and deliver people from the demonic forces.[8]

The most ancient prophecy, predating Shambhala and Geser, was about Maitreya (called Maidari by Mongols), the Buddha of compassion and of a new age, who was commemorated in numerous statues and temples. Maitreya is the most worshipped Buddha besides Gautama, the Buddha proper and founder of the faith.[9] Maitreya, who would be the fifth and the last Buddha, was expected to come in thirty thousand years after the faith deteriorated and the world underwent a terrible war, natural calamities, and epidemics. Buddhists believed that after this era of darkness Maitreya would descend upon the earth and bring about the golden age of prosperity and spiritual bliss.

Many minor individual prophecies were issued by the Dalai Lama, the Panchen Lama, the Bogdo-gegen, and monastery oracles. At the turn of the 1900s, these public messages were increasingly filled with anti-Chinese sentiments. Addressing his fellow Mongols, the Bogdo-gegen predicted, "There will be an unimaginable amount of suffering. Black-headed Chinese become many; they do not love the religion of Buddha and they have reached the extremes of disorder, so that it is impossible to accept the well-established law of predecessors as an example and to follow the order of Heaven." He also instructed the faithful not to socialize with the Chinese infidels or use their products and clothing and even openly called the Mongols to revolt.[10]

Oirot/Amursana Prophecy in the Altai and Western Mongolia

Simultaneously, spiritual resistance was brewing in the Altai and western Mongolia where nomads shared the popular Oirot/Amursana prophecy, no less powerful and no less explosive than Shambhala. Around the 1890s, people began to spread word from camp to camp about the miraculous resurrection of a glorious prince who had finally come to redeem them from oppression. The Mongols and some Altaians called him Amursana. At the same time, many nomads in the Altai argued that his real name was Oirot and that Amursana was his chief lieutenant. Whatever his name, this redeemer was said to have returned after hiding in a northern country for 120 years, and now, in charge of a mighty army, he would take revenge on enemies and bring together his Oirot people. Who were the enemies? In the Altai, they were the floods of Russian settlers who squeezed native shepherds from their alpine pastures; in western Mongolia, they were the Chinese merchants and bureaucrats who came to control the lives of nomads.

Both Oirot and Amursana were personifications of the glorious Oirot confederation (named after the ruling Oirot clan), which in the 1600s united Turkic- and Mongol-speaking nomads of western China, western Mongolia, and the Altai. Assertive Oirot princes embraced Tibetan Buddhism and frequently acted as patrons of Dalai Lamas; they also constantly challenged the Chinese Empire. Eventually the Manchu Dynasty became fed up with these warlike nomads and unleashed genocidal warfare against them, slaughtering all Oirot men, women, and children. The few who survived scattered, hiding in the mountains, deserts, and taiga forests, and later giving rise to the Altaians, Kalmyk, Tuvans, and western Mongols. The nomadic empire was gone, but its glory became imprinted in folk memory in the form of legends about Amursana and Oirot, who were expected to resurrect and save the nomads from alien domination. In fact, these legends became so popular that one of the refugee groups that escaped to the Altai Mountains, in literature usually called the Altaians, began to refer to themselves as the people of Oirot or simply the Oirot.

The real Prince Amursana (1722–57) was the last Oirot prince and in fact was very arrogant and opportunistic. At one point, he served the Chinese but then fell out of favor and turned against them. Folk memory chose this second "noble" part of his life for celebration and glorification. Fighting a losing battle against his former masters, Amursana escaped to Russia, where he soon caught a plague and died in Siberia. This sudden disappearance of the prince in the faraway northern country later sparked legends about his subsequent return to his former subjects to deliver them from the Chinese and the Russians. Eventually, lamas declared the popular hero a manifestation of the menacing Mahakala, protector of the Buddhist faith. The lingering prophecy agitated nomads to such an extent that in the 1890s they asked a Russian geographer-explorer visiting in western Mongolia if he was a vanguard of the Amursana army they expected to ascend from a northern country to liberate them from the Chinese.[11]

There were many versions of the Oirot/Amursana legend. One of them was recorded by the musicologist Andrei Anokhin in 1919: Many years ago, Prince Oirot ruled the Altai. Oirot defended everybody, and there were neither poor nor discontented people in his domain. Then the Oirot people became surrounded by enemies who destroyed this idyllic life (a clear reference to the genocide of the Oirot confederation by the Chinese). Unable to protect his own people, Oirot retreated to Russia and married a maiden princess—an allusion to the Russian empress Elizabeth who accepted several runaway Oirot clans under her wing as her subjects. Before his departure, Oirot did two things: he cut his horse's tail to the root, and he also cut a larch tree down to the level of his stirrups. Then the prince declared that he would come back to the Altai only when his horse's tail grew again and the larch tree grew so big that it would cover a whole army with its leaves. Another important element of this tale was Oirot's statement that the news about his return would be announced by a twelve-year-old girl and marked by the shifting of a glacier on the highest Altai mountain. Similar legends, only about Amursana, circulated in western Mongolia.

In the Altai, the news that Oirot was finally coming was revealed in 1904 by Chet Chelpan, a humble shepherd who frequented Mongolia, and Chugul Sorokova, his twelve-year-old adopted daughter. Both claimed to have seen the messenger of the legendary prince, who confided to them that Oirot would soon drive all Russians from the Altai and restore the old way of life. Chet Chelpan also prophesied that Oirot would be sent by Burkhan (the image of Buddha), which Chet considered the Spirit of Altai and the Oirot nation. In the meantime, as the good shepherd instructed his flock, the Oirot people were to reject all contacts with the Russians, destroy Russian money, and stop using Russian tools. This was the birth of the Ak-Jang (white or pure faith), an Altaian version of Tibetan Buddhism that drew on bits and pieces of Buddha's teaching, indigenous shamanism, epic tales, and memories of the Oirot confederation. Behind Chet and his daughter stood a group of indigenous activists headed by Tery Akemchi (White Healer), who had apprenticed in Buddhist monasteries in Mongolia where they picked up elements of Buddhism and brought them to the Altai.

The Oirot/Amursana prophecy was further bolstered in 1911 when Ja-Lama (1860–1923), a Russian Kalmyk immortalized in Ferdinand Ossendowski's esoteric bestseller *Beasts, Men and Gods*,[12] showed up in western Mongolia, declared himself the reincarnation of Amursana, and led a local liberation movement against the Chinese. When news about the reincarnated Amursana reached the Altai, the prophecy was already adjusted to local needs and acquired an anti-Russian spin. The Altai nomads expected Amursana to arrive accompanied by seventeen reincarnated lamas, seven hundred dogs, and seven thousand mighty warriors who would crush the Russians.

The legends about Oirot/Amursana, which were familiar to all people of the Altai and western Mongolia, helped override clan and territorial differences and merge the nomads into nationalities. The good shepherd Chet Chelpan asked his flock to forget all quarrels and live "like children of one father" and "like the herd headed by one stallion." Ja-Lama was even more explicit, telling his nomadic warriors that they were fighting and dying for Mongolia. Later, in eastern Mongolia, the Shambhala prophecy served the same purpose: to unite the Mongols against the Chinese. In their song about northern Shambhala, Red Mongol soldiers sang that they would be happy to die fighting against the Chinese infidels and to be reborn in the Shambhala kingdom.

Tibet was a more complicated case. By the early twentieth century, the Forbidden Kingdom was already a united country ruled by the thirteenth Dalai Lama (1875–1933), who was working hard to make his

Figure 2.3. The thirteenth Dalai Lama, supreme leader of Tibet, 1920s.

domain into a sovereign nation. So here, instead of bringing the Tibetans together, the Shambhala prophecy and the Panchen Lama, who stood in its shadow and challenged Lhasa, disrupted nation building.

When Empires Collapse:
Mongolia, Altai, Tibet, and the Panchen Lama

In 1911, the Chinese Empire collapsed. Six years later, the same fate befell the Russian Empire. The chaos, civil wars, violence, and banditry that followed the demise of these two giants activated Mongol-Tibetan prophecies that helped people get through tough times. Common shepherds, princes, lamas, warlords, and even several European adventurers were all eager to tap into such redeeming legends as Shambhala, Maitreya, Amursana, and Oirot. Much of this prophetic baggage served the goals of nationalism. Amid the anarchy and chaos that reigned over northern Eurasia in the 1920s, the Kalmyk, Buryat, Oirot, Mongols, Tuvans, and Tibetans began to take power into their own hands and shape themselves into nationalities and nations. Moreover, driven by nationalist dreams, a few assertive leaders promoted grand political schemes that went beyond the existing cultural and geographical boundaries. Brought into the spotlight by a whirlwind of revolutionary changes, some of these "redeemers" peddled projects that would bring all Turkic-speaking nomads together into one large state. Others toyed with the idea of reviving the seventeenth-century Oirot confederation. Some dreamers wanted to build up a pan-Mongol state that would unite people of the "Mongol stock" in Siberia, Mongolia, and Manchuria. Finally, several prophets worked to gather all Tibetan Buddhist people into a large pan-Buddhist theocracy.

In 1912, a year after the Chinese revolution put an end to the Manchu Empire, the people of northern (Outer) Mongolia, backed up by Russia, drove the Chinese out of the country and made the Bogdo-gegen (head of Mongol Buddhists) the supreme ruler of their new independent theocracy. In 1918, when the Russian Empire was gone and amid the raging Civil War, the Cossack platoon leader Grigory Semenov, the Buryat intellectual Elbek-Dorji Rinchino, and a dozen of his friends educated at Russian universities, gathered in the Siberian town of Chita and announced they had created a great pan-Mongol nation. To the dismay of Mongol leaders who did not want to be part of this, the adventurous gang of dreamers was all set to travel to the Paris peace conference to seek recognition from the great powers as an independent nation. The whole scheme suddenly collapsed when Japan, which originally backed the project, abruptly changed its mind. With no support from below, the rascals who peddled the "great Mongol nation" scattered; half of them were murdered by a Chinese warlord in Manchuria who lured them to an "official banquet" and then executed them for separatism.

The same year in the Altai, the indigenous landscape painter and folklore collector Grigory Gurkin, along with his friend Russian anthropologist Vasilii Anuchin, launched the Karakorum state (a reference to the legendary capital of the Genghis Khan's empire). Riding the popular Oirot prophecy, they declared an autonomy of the Mountain Altai and began to contemplate a "Republic of the Oirot," which was to revive the seventeenth-century Oirot confederation by uniting Turkic- and Mongol-speaking nomads of the Altai, Tuva, and western Mongolia. Anuchin, who suffered from delusions of grandeur, pushed his indigenous comrades to charge ahead "fearing nothing" and to "shape history in a revolutionary manner." Speaking in front of the "children of Oirot," the agitated scholar argued that the populations of these areas were one tribe and one kinship family: "Formerly they represented one great nation—Oirot. To bring them together again into one family and into one state is crucial because all these tribes craving for unification are now neglected by everybody. These tribes will give rise to a great Asian republic that will occupy an area exceeding Germany and France together."[13]

In 1911, taking advantage of the collapse of the Chinese Empire, the Tibetans revolted against the Chinese, kicking out their inspectors and troops. Still, in the northeastern part of the country, the warriors of the Forbidden Kingdom had to fight repeatedly against the Chinese from 1913 to 1919 before they finally secured the Tibetan borders and sovereignty. In the meantime, the Dalai Lama returned from exile in India and began to move his theocracy toward full-fledged nationhood. To empower his emerging nation, the Lhasa ruler made a few modest steps to modernize. He had a telegraph line built between northern India and Tibet and a small electric power station erected. Yet his major goal was raising an army equipped with modern weapons, requiring additional taxes. Now everybody, including monasteries, which previously enjoyed tax-exempt status, had to contribute to this defense project. The clergy were not enthusiastic about this project at all and were equally upset

Figure 2.4. The Panchen Lama, spiritual leader of Tibet, standing in front of a Mongol dwelling after his escape during one of his tours of Inner Mongolia, 1930.

about the power station, telegraph, and English military instructors the Dalai Lama invited to drill Tibetan soldiers.

Conservative monks, fearful that these innovations would corrupt Tibetan Buddhist tradition, began to look to the Panchen Lama for support. The abbot of the Tashilumpho monastery, who was simultaneously a powerful lord in eastern Tibet, did not like the infringement on his privileges and refused to pay taxes. In 1921, his followers erected a large statue of the Buddha Maitreya, and he invited the Dalai Lama

Figure 2.5. The Tashilumpho monastery, headquarters of the Panchen Lama, 1910s.

to consecrate the project. The Lhasa ruler was infuriated and severely rebuked the abbot for wasting so much money at a time when Tibet needed a modern army to defend itself. There was so much bad blood between them that the Panchen Lama became paranoid about his safety, and in 1923 he fled from Tibet to Chinese Mongolia and never came back.[14] He became popular with the Mongols, who accepted him as their spiritual leader after their Bogdo-gegen died in 1924. The runaway abbot liked to visit their nomadic camps, performing public Kalachakra initiations for thousands.

Ja-Lama: Amursana-Mahakala and a Budding Dictator

In the meantime, in western Mongolia another spiritual celebrity rose in power and captivated the minds of local nomads. It was the aforementioned notorious Ja-Lama, who in 1911 declared himself the reincarnation of Amursana, rallying the disgruntled Mongols, who wanted to free themselves from the Chinese and were ready to accept the legendary redeemer.[15] He showed up at the right place and right time. The nomads of the Altai and western Mongolia were already scanning the horizon for someone with marks of Amursana and Oirot, who would come from the north and rescue them. The Russian folklore scholar Boris Vladimirtsov, who visited western Mongolia in 1913, stressed that the loss of land and Chinese domination stimulated the Mongols to search for signs of the legendary redeemer.[16]

Ja-Lama grew up in the lower Volga River area, where his fellow Kalmyk, the runaway splinters of the Oirot confederation, had resided since the 1600s. His family eventually moved back to Mongolia, where the boy was put in a monastery for education. Ja-Lama proved to be a smart student and was sent to continue his training in Tibet. Yet the youth had a wild temper and allegedly killed a fellow monk during a heated argument. To take the life of a fellow Buddhist was a very serious crime, and the youth had to escape to Beijing, where for a few years he earned his living by printing Buddhist calendars. His first attempt to plug himself into the Amursana prophecy took place as early as the 1890s, when he wandered into western Mongolia and declared himself the grandson of the prince. Although many nomads followed him, the situation was not yet right. At that time, Chinese authorities quickly apprehended the rascal, and the "royal offspring" had to flee southward to Tibet.

After the 1911 Chinese revolution, when the Mongols rose up against the "yellow peril," the timing was perfect. The spiritual trickster resurfaced in western Mongolia, where local nomads welcomed him. At one point, to enhance his legendary northern origin Ja-Lama donned a Russian officer's military uniform with chevrons; according to the prophecy, Amursana escaped to the land of the "maiden tsarina" (Elizabeth of Russia) and became one of her generals before coming back to save his people.

Professor Ossendowski portrayed Ja-Lama as a desert magician who suddenly popped out of nowhere with a Colt revolver under his sash.

Figure 2.6. The notorious Ja-Lama, a Kalmyk expatriate who declared himself the manifestation of Mahakala and took charge of western Mongols, c. 1912–13.

After an intellectually stimulating dialogue, the reincarnated one impressed the professor with his supernatural power by slashing the abdomen of a comrade and then quickly repairing it without leaving any scars. Unlike authors of other accounts of "Amursana," Ossendowski was a very perceptive observer who did not restrict himself to simply listing the miraculous deeds of the notorious Kalmyk. The writer correctly described Ja-Lama as an ardent nationalist who worked to bring the various tribes of western Mongolia together into one nation. Taking full advantage of the Mongols' dislike of the Chinese, Ja-Lama invoked "blood and soil" sentiments among his followers. His major military coup was the successful seizure of Kobdo, the only major battle during the Mongols' liberation movement in 1911–13. Before storming the town, Ja-Lama blessed his nomadic warriors with words that appealed not only to their religious feelings but also to their nationalistic sentiments: "You must not fear death and must not retreat. You are fighting and dying for Mongolia, for which the gods have appointed a great destiny. See what the fate of Mongolia will be!"[17]

Figure 2.7. Mongol warriors during the liberation war against the Chinese, 1911–13.

To boost his spiritual power in the eyes of followers, from time to time Ja-Lama visualized and merged with the powerful god Mahakala, one of the "eight terrible ones," defenders of the Buddhist faith. He was also prone to literal interpretations of Tibetan Buddhist mythology and iconography. After the victory over the Chinese at Kobdo, Ja-Lama performed a public tantra session for his warriors. It was scripted according to ancient Kalachakra texts and involved a sickle, skull cups, blood, and hearts ripped out from the chests of the enemies. During this ceremony, Ja-Lama, in a trance, turned into wrathful Mahakala, using the blood and hearts of prisoners to fill his skull cup the way Mahakala was portrayed doing on sacred scrolls. When a representative of the Bogdo-gegen rode into the crowd and confronted Ja-Lama with orders from the Bogdo-gegen to stop the ritual, he was killed in the ensuing melee. By morning, mixed with blood and soil, the sparks of civic notions lay dead, sacrificed to the altar of faith and race.[18]

Figure 2.8. A Mongol commander during the liberation war against the Chinese. Battle banners smeared with the blood of enemies are in the background.

Ja-Lama awed nomads of western Mongolia with his power and embarked on building his own fiefdom, where he began to rule as a modern dictator. About two thousand people recognized him as their ruler. Order and discipline were his obsessions. Near the monastery of Munjok-kurel, he erected a tent town populated by lamas and regular shepherds. Felt yurts were pitched in strict geometrical lines in straight rows rather than chaotically as the Mongols normally did. "Amursana" demanded complete obedience and enforced a strict religious discipline, humiliating and punishing lamas who dared to drink or smoke, which was against traditional Tibetan Buddhism. Those who broke the code of faith were forced to get married and were turned into soldiers. Ja-Lama announced that in his new-era state, there would be "few lamas, but only good ones." The rest of the clergy had to become productive laborers. In his tent town all people, clergy and laypeople, were subjected to regular physical labor, kept busy building a dam and digging an artificial lake to provide a permanent water supply. Nobody was allowed to just hang around as in the past.

This budding dictator was definitely up to something serious. On one hand, he preached the return to original teachings of Tibetan Buddhism. On the other, he wanted to make his people modern. He planned to build schools, import machinery from Russia, and teach the Mongols the art of agriculture. Besides order and discipline, another obsession was hygiene, which he relentlessly promoted, in stark contrast to the filth of the surrounding nomadic encampments. All of his town was neat and clean, unusual for contemporary Mongols, who dumped their garbage near their dwellings. In fact, when Ja-Lama saw people throwing trash around or drinking liquor, he severely punished the culprits. Those who continued to disobey were simply beheaded.[19]

Like his colleagues from the Altai, the reincarnated Amursana with a zeal for modernization nourished a great plan to unite all nomads of western Mongolia and western China into a large state—another attempt to revive the great Oirot confederation in its seventeenth-century borders. These ambitions seriously disturbed the Bogdo-gegen and his court, who were afraid that the reincarnated redeemer might widen traditional differences between eastern (Khalkha) and western (Oirot) Mongols and eventually split the country in two. In 1914, following up on these fears and using Ja-Lama's brutalities as an excuse, the Bogdo-gegen solicited the assistance of a Russian consul to apprehend "Amursana," who formally remained a Russian subject. Ambushed and arrested by a platoon of Cossacks, Ja-Lama had to spend several years in exile in northeastern Siberia, the coldest place on earth. Yet this was not the end of the lama with a gun. After the 1917 Russian Revolution, Ja-Lama would spread his wings once again.

Whoever wishes to go to Shambhala must enter the right path and practice meditation. He must have faith and an irresistible urge to attain enlightenment for the benefit of all human beings.

—Taranatha

■ Three

Alexander Barchenko: Budding Red Merlin and His Ancient Science

On December 1924 in Moscow's Lubyanka Square, Gleb Bokii, chief of the Special Section, the most guarded unit of the OGPU Soviet secret police, was sitting in his office, expecting three visitors.[1] The first two men he knew quite well: Konstantin Vladimirov and Feodor Leismaier-Schwarz were his former colleagues from the Petrograd (St. Petersburg) branch of the secret police. Bokii himself had begun his career in Petrograd, cradle of the Communist Revolution. In fact, as one of Lenin's oldest comrades-in-arms, he had not only helped unleash the revolution but actively participated in the Bolshevik military takeover in 1917.[2] A few months after that, Bokii had been among the few comrades who founded the Bolshevik secret services.

Yet, the coming meeting was not merely a reunion of old friends. The former comrades were to introduce a third man, with whom the chief of the Special Section had become indirectly familiar after leafing through his police file. He was Alexander Barchenko, a medical school dropout and popular mystery writer before the revolution who considered himself a scientist and did research on the human brain, telepathy, shamanism, and collective hysteria. Bokii knew that although Barchenko did not have any degrees he liked to be called Doctor and to deliver public lectures to various audiences, including Baltic Red sailors. He

43

also noted that the "doctor" constantly talked about the mysterious land of Shambhala and wanted to bring its spiritual wisdom and psychological techniques to Red Russia. Somehow, Bokii had become intrigued with this man.

Figure 3.1. "Red Merlin" Alexander Barchenko, head of the United Labor Brotherhood and seeker of Shambhala wisdom. Prison photo, Moscow, 1937.

There were reasons for this fascination, and it was not because the chief of the Special Section was himself a college dropout and shared with Barchenko the same Ukrainian origin. Recently, dark thoughts had begun to visit Bokii. He had started thinking about the fate of the whole Communist project and his role in it. Something had gone terribly wrong. A highly intelligent man and offspring of a noble lineage whose roots went back to the time of Ivan the Terrible, Bokii had intentionally sacrificed his comfortable life to fight for the liberation of the oppressed masses of the Russian Empire and had spilled other people's blood on the altar of the revolution. At the same time, he was appalled by what happened after the revolution. Blood, blood, so much blood! All enemies were already subdued, but there was no change for the better. He noticed that after the death of Lenin, the charismatic chief of the

Bolshevik revolution, the new elite, many of them his closest comrades, had immediately become caught in a mortal struggle for power, slandering and dumping each other, while others helped themselves from the state's coffers.

Bokii, who was not good in intrigues, had become disgusted with this behavior and had withdrawn from political life, observing silently what was going on around him.[3] Instead of the envisioned working people's paradise where all people would feel like brothers and sisters, the revolution had turned ugly. It unleashed bestial instincts of the crowd, which in its rage attacked everything and everyone that seemed "bourgeoisie." How to tame this crowd and attach a human face to the Communist project, how to "breed" a better race of people who would be well rounded, intelligent, and caring about one another? It would be interesting to hear what this Barchenko, whom his friends described as a talented researcher, had to say about all this. Could his claim be true that somewhere in Inner Asia lived enlightened masters who had the key to shaping and reshaping human minds? Like all good Bolsheviks, Bokii believed in the unlimited possibilities of science and was convinced that it could resolve all kinds of problems. And imagine the possibility for intelligence work when you could read human minds at a distance. That is what Barchenko claimed to know.

Barchenko was equally excited about the coming introductory meeting. It was not his first contact with the mighty spying machine that was striving to entangle all of Russia in its surveillance web. The first meeting had taken place five years before and at first had given him chills. Barchenko vividly remembered that winter day at the end of 1919. A freezing wind blew through the streets of hungry Petrograd. People were using their furniture as firewood to keep themselves warm inside their homes. The great city lay paralyzed in a gray ice-cold mist. Few dared to venture outside, especially without necessity. People were afraid of being caught in the Red Terror, the campaign of intimidation and mass executions Bolsheviks had unleashed against their opponents. After millions died during the Great War and the subsequent Civil War, human life did not have any worth. Streets of the city were ruled by violent mobs of soldiers, workers, and peasants. Gangs of criminals, frequently posing as revolutionaries, and revolutionaries doing criminal business on the side were eagerly "confiscating" the riches of the bourgeoisie and looking for "exploiters" to liquidate.[4]

Barchenko was petrified by the anarchy reigning in the country. He was especially stunned by the hatred the populace demonstrated toward anyone who appeared to be a well-rounded person. For masses of peasants and the urban underclass, a person who did not wear working class, peasant, or soldier's garb, or whose talk was too bookish or who happened to wear glasses could easily become a target to be humiliated or simply shot.[5] It seemed that Barchenko had nothing to fear. He was always poor as a church mouse, and he even observed the new "folk" dress code, wearing the old long felt soldier coat he had brought with him from the front when coming home to recuperate from his war wounds. Still, many times, when he ran across the most flamboyant representatives of the populace, their talk and behavior made him want to be as unobtrusive as possible. Barchenko felt defenseless before this victorious ignorance that now ran the show. Besides, despite his masquerade, because of his poor eyesight he had to wear glasses, which exposed him as a man of intelligence. As such, he easily could be taken by a revolutionary mob as a bourgeoisie and a potential enemy. Like well-trained dogs, members of the street populace could immediately sense that he did not belong to their pack.

Barchenko had a wife and a child to feed and was struggling to survive. An offer in 1919 to lecture to the Red Baltic sailors had come as a blessing. At least, it guaranteed him an in-kind payment in the form of a loaf of black bread—money had been abolished by the new regime. This offer had also provided an excellent chance for him to spell out his spiritual ideas about the salvation of the bleeding world. After the Bolshevik coup, Barchenko had thought a lot about how to convince the revolutionary masses and the Bolshevik elite, which rode the violent sentiments of the crowd, to be more humane and compassionate to each other. He had felt the lectures could be a good start. Through the Red sailors, the foot soldiers of the Bolshevik revolution, he could eventually reach out to the top Bolshevik leaders and explain to them the value of spiritual life and ancient knowledge, without which the country would go down. Thus, during the winter of 1919–20, Barchenko had begun lecturing to the sailors in Petrograd.[6] Eventually, Barchenko and two sailors who knew how to read and write, I. Grinev and S. S. Belash, sat down together to compose a petition to Georgy Chicherin, Bolshevik Commissar for Foreign Affairs, soliciting support for the project and permission for the Red sailors to accompany the scientist on an expedition to search for Shambhala. Barchenko was on cloud nine, happy to have such associates.[7]

Unfortunately, instead of support, the petition had brought Barchenko a lot of troubles. The fleet commanders, who found out that the odd "professor" was trying to pollute the pure revolutionary minds of the sailors with false knowledge, had quickly alerted the Bolshevik secret police. The latter had already received detailed information about Barchenko through its informers: Red Russia was gradually turning into a state where people were strongly encouraged to keep an eye on one another. Yet, instead of being arrested, Barchenko had simply been invited to the secret police headquarters for a talk. Still, one can imagine what horrific pictures Barchenko had probably drawn for himself thinking about the coming "talk." In the atmosphere of the Red Terror and Civil War, he was well aware that the Bolshevik secret police officers did not look for evidence. The major factor that decided a person's fate was what class he or she belonged to. Unfortunately, as the child of a notary clerk, Barchenko did not have the politically correct background to be spared if in trouble: he was neither a worker nor a peasant.

However, his fears had been false. To his amazement, among his interrogators had been Konstantin Vladimirov, a playboy bohemian who had visited one of his lectures. Vladimirov had been all politeness. As it turned out, the playboy, an intelligent Jew, worked as a secret police officer in a unit that combated counterrevolution. The other two,

Estonians Eduard Otto and Alexander Ricks, had proved no less intelligent and polite. They had informed Barchenko about the complaint but immediately added that they did not believe all the lies spread about him and did not consider his lectures counterrevolutionary. Moreover, the three officers then shocked the "doctor" by asking permission to learn more about Shambhala wisdom. Barchenko was thrilled, and eventually, all three became good friends. And Vladimirov would lead Barchenko to Bokii.

Mastering Brain Rays

Barchenko was born in the town of Elets in Orel District into the family of a court notary and received a good education, completing grammar school. In 1904, he entered the medical school at Kazan University. The next year, Barchenko transferred to Tartu University in Estonia, at that time part of the Russian Empire. There he met Alexander Krivtsov, a professor of Roman jurisprudence who liked to treat his students as friends and was very interested in esoteric teachings. There was nothing strange about this. In the early twentieth century through the First World War, many educated people all over Europe, including Russia, were involved in the world of the occult. In Russia this period, known as the Silver Age (1880s–1918), saw the rise of interest in spiritism, Theosophy, Tibetan Buddhism, and Freemasonry. For Barchenko, the meeting with Krivtsov was a landmark, an intellectual initiation into the world of the occult and esoteric that shaped his future spiritual quest.

The professor especially fascinated the mind of the youth with his stories about a French esoteric writer named Marquis Alexandre Saint-Yves d'Alveydre (1842–1909), who wrote about the mysterious land of Agartha that was hidden somewhere in the mountains of Inner Asia and possessed science and spiritual wisdom far superior to what was known in Europe: "The story of Krivtsov gave me the first push that moved my mind toward the quest that filled all my life. Assuming that remnants of this prehistoric science might have somehow in some form survived to the present day, I began to study ancient history and gradually immersed myself in the realm of the mysterious."[8]

Soon, hoping to make more money to provide for his wife and a small son, Barchenko moved to St. Petersburg and turned to writing fiction, plugging into the popular fascination with the occult. On the eve of World War I, he was already a successful author, producing adventure mystery stories and novels that sampled cutting-edge paranormal discoveries and Oriental magic. His two major novels, *Doctor Chernii* (Doctor Black, 1913) and *Iz mraka* (Out of Darkness, 1914), are set in Russia, India, and Tibet and describe the mysterious adventures of Dr. Alexander Chernii, a professor of medicine, Theosophist, junior mahatma, and member of a secret order with headquarters in the foothills of Tibet. The plots revolve around the professor's attempts to put secret knowledge possessed by the order to public benefit and the efforts of his mahatma comrades to keep it secret.

In 1911, in addition to fiction writing, Barchenko toyed with contemporary popular science and even conducted a series of "scientific" experiments. His major interests were thought transfer and energy, topics popular with the educated Western public in the early twentieth century, especially after the discovery of X-rays, radiation, and the theory of relativity. Many scientists and spiritual seekers became involved in what one can call "positivist occultism," a scientific explanation for spiritual and paranormal phenomena. Scientists involved in this research argued that paranormal effects were possible because invisible brain rays produced sound waves, which conveyed thoughts at a distance and even moved objects.

Barchenko, familiar with this research, jumped on the bandwagon of this scientific fad and performed his own experiments on thought transfer. His technique was very simple. Two volunteers with completely shaved heads put on aluminum helmets specially designed by the writer for this occasion. The helmets were linked by a long piece of copper wire. Barchenko placed oval screens in front of both participants and asked them to stare at the screens. One volunteer was a receiver, while the other, the transmitter, was to think hard of a word or an image and mentally beam it to the recipient. Barchenko claimed that beaming images was no problem, whereas with words, as he admitted, there were many mistakes.

Subterranean Blues: Agartha and Synarchy

Plugging himself into thought-transfer research and reading popular literature about hypnosis and magnetism, Barchenko could not get rid of the compulsive questions that had haunted him since the time he learned about d'Alveydre and his Agartha. What if all knowledge that modern science bragged so much about had already been known to the ancients and then had been wiped out by barbarian hordes? What if Agartha, the mysterious subterranean country d'Alveydre wrote about, indeed still harbored remnants of this superior knowledge? What if the French occultist was also right in suggesting that traces of the advanced ancient science could be found scattered in great religious texts such as the Bible, Koran, Kabala, Rig Veda, and others, as well as in ancient symbols, rock art, and folk legends? Barchenko took the message of the French esotericist very seriously. In his *Mission of India in Europe* (1886), d'Alveydre appealed to a French president, a Roman pope, and a Russian emperor, asking them to learn from the wisdom of Agartha. In a similar manner, a desire to penetrate the mysterious subterranean country and retrieve its wisdom in order to enlighten the Russian elite about the correct political and spiritual path eventually became a life-long obsession for Barchenko.

Besides Agartha, Barchenko became drawn to Synarchy, a social theory propagated by d'Alveydre. The French writer noted there were two types of human organization: Synarchy (the total and benevolent state) and anarchy (total lack of state, political and social chaos). D'Alveydre viewed all of history as a tug of war between these two opposing systems. Examples of anarchy were revolutions, class war, secularization, unemployment, decline of tradition, prostitution, alcoholism, poverty, slums, and other vices of modern society.

According to d'Alveydre, for the past five thousand years, people had been living in a state of anarchy. Yet, it had not always been like that all the time. At the dawn of history, humans lived in a synarchical social state based on tradition, security, and hierarchy. The synarchical government was a pyramid composed of three layers. The top leadership was a group of priests who controlled advanced science and technology. The second layer consisted of the initiated ones and the third of the common people. In modern time, this well-ordered society, strongly reminiscent of Plato's totalitarian republic, had become almost extinct except in mysterious Agartha. Here, the synarchical priests were able to preserve high wisdom immune to anarchy with its modern vices. The task was clear: the wisdom of Agartha was to be retrieved and the ancient synarchical form of government restored in order to overcome anarchy and to bring back social and spiritual stability.

According to D'Alveydre, the subterranean kingdom not only represented the best form of government but also possessed the wonders of technology: "They explored everything around them, above and underneath, including the role of magnetic currents flowing from one pole to the other. They examined everything in the air, even invisible beings that exist there, even electricity transformed in an echo after being formed in the heart of the earth. Air fleets of zeppelins have allowed them to observe what is still for us out of reach. Electric railroads, made not from iron but from highly durable glass, crisscrossed this kingdom. Chemistry and physics had advanced to the highest degree, unimaginable to the modern reader."[9] Large chunks of his writings read like the science fiction of his famous contemporary and compatriot Jules Verne, who similarly described in his novels technological wonders in space, air, and underwater. In fact, d'Alveydre's Agartha strongly resembled parts of *Twenty Thousand Leagues Under the Sea* (1870), *Journey to the Center of the Earth* (1864), and *The Mysterious Island* (1874). Like Jules Verne's Captain Nemo, a sad romantic hero who, fearful that the populace might misuse his laser beams and other technological miracles, went underwater with his submarine, residents of Agartha, plagued by similar fears, went underground, taking along their own advanced knowledge. In both cases the message was obvious: superior technology and the best political system would be open only to highly spiritual and morally perfect people.

Synarchy and Agartha were clearly an esoteric response to the insecurities of the emerging modern society with its chaotic industrial development, city slums, urban worker revolts, and expansion of popular democracy. Like d'Alveydre, many contemporaries viewed these developments as anarchy and chaos. In the early 1900s, the ideas of people like d'Alveydre gradually mutated into a conservative intellectual movement called *traditionalism*. Traditionalists insisted that modern society could be redeemed through an ancient order based on tradition, hierarchy, and a universal ideology that would unite people instead of splintering them into competing groups and classes.

D'Alveydre located his conservative utopia in Inner Asia, feeding on the European romantic Orientalist tradition, which claimed that the source of European civilization was the classical Orient, especially Aryan India. In fact, a desire to look for answers in the "Himalaya" became a staple for several generations of scholars and writers in the eighteenth and nineteenth centuries. Commenting on this cultural fad of his romantic contemporaries, Adolph Erman, a German explorer of northern Asia, ironically called it an attempt to establish a mysterious depot for everything that was elsewhere undiscoverable.[10]

The same "out of Asia" romantic Orientalism became one of the sources of Helena Blavatsky's Theosophy—the fountainhead of modern Western esotericism. When d'Alveydre was developing his Agartha political utopia, Blavatsky was shaping her own version of the Inner Asian paradise she labeled Shambhala, the habitat of the so-called Great White Brotherhood. Unlike d'Alveydre's underground utopia, which was based on the heavily refurbished Nordic myth of Asgard, she drew on Tibetan Buddhist tradition and anchored her mysterious Asian kingdom high in the Himalayas. Blavatsky's dreamland was a hub of high spiritual wisdom devoid of Agartha's political and technological traits offensive to present-day spiritual sensibilities. This might explain why her Shambhala became more popular with current seekers than d'Alveydre's subterranean country. As for Barchenko, in his talks he frequently merged these two "ancient centers of knowledge" into Shambhala-Agartha, indicating that he was feeding on both sources.

War, Revolution, and Brothers from Bolshevik Secret Police

Carnage and chaos caused by World War I, revolutions, and the bloody Civil War petrified Barchenko. He became convinced more than ever that the wisdom of Shambhala-Agartha should be retrieved to save the country. In fact, the occultist himself had suffered the horrors of war and revolutions. Drafted into the army at the very beginning of the war, Barchenko was seriously wounded and, as he stressed, suffered from "epileptic fits" caused by "organic damage to the brain."[11]

Like many educated Russians, Barchenko was appalled with the magnitude of popular violence unleashed by the 1917 Bolshevik revolution. Although he shared the deeply rooted belief of the old Russian intelligentsia that individualism and private property were evil and collectivism was inherently good, the Communist takeover with its dictatorship, despise of intellectuals, and terrorism against the rich and the middle class appeared to him as mass insanity. So did the mob rule, which disgusted him: "I received the October Revolution in a hostile manner, taking into consideration what lay on the surface—the sentiments of the crowd. I linked the proletariat to the dregs of society. In my view, workers, sailors, and Red guards behaved like beasts. This attitude planted in my soul a desire to hide away and to shelter myself from the revolution."[12] Yet soon the first shock from the Bolshevik revolt passed away. He saw that the new regime had seriously entrenched itself and that the "dictatorship of proletariat" was not a short-lived project. Like many middle-class people who did not join the two million Russians who left the country for Europe and the United States, Barchenko had to reconcile himself to the Bolsheviks.

A few years later, the original desire to hide away from the revolution gave way to the wish to reach out somehow to the Bolshevik elite, which spoke the crude language of violence well understandable to urban and village underclass people impoverished by war and upset about modernization. Barchenko began contemplating how to ennoble the Communist project by using the ancient science hidden in Inner Asia: "The contact with Shambhala is capable of pulling humankind out of the bloody deadlock of insanity—the violent struggle, in which people hopelessly drowned themselves."[13] Revisiting d'Alveydre's conservative utopia through the prism of the Bolshevik revolution, he started talking about the ancient "Great Federation of World People" built on communist principles and eventually came to advocate a Communist theocracy controlled by peaceful and spiritually charged high priests of Marxism.

Lecturing for Red Baltic sailors was Barchenko's first outreach. Soon his seductive Shambhala-Agartha talks reached the ears of the Bolshevik secret police, leading to his invitation to the headquarters of the Petrograd secret police on Gorokhovaia Street in 1920 and his eventual friendship with Otto, Ricks, and Vladimirov, the security officers who interviewed him. Soon, a fourth officer named Feodor Karlovich Leismaier-Schwarz joined them. Among these four, Vladimirov and especially Leismaier-Schwarz became close to Barchenko's family. The writer and his wife lovingly referred to this soft and spineless man (God knows how he became a secret police officer) as "Little Karl."

Vladimirov (1883–1928), an outgoing type interested in the humanities and all things esoteric, constantly hung around Barchenko. In fact, Barchenko and this Russian Jew from the Estonian town of Pairnu had much in common. Vladimirov had similarly enrolled in a medical school and then dropped out. Both suffered from delusions of grandeur and always tried to cling to the political elite. Yet, in contrast to Barchenko, who called himself a "Communist without a membership card," Vladimirov did become a member of the Bolshevik Party as early as 1900. The future secret police officer had also tried his hand at writing poetry and painting, but it had not worked out. His real passion was graphology—the penetration of people's souls and minds through analysis of their handwriting. This hobby, in which he excelled, made him valuable to the Bolshevik secret police. Vladimirov not only tried to read psychological profiles of individuals through their handwriting but also attempted to predict their future behavior.

His interests also included tarot, Rosicrucianism, yoga, Hermetism, and telepathy, and his reading list included such prominent esoteric authors as Vivekananda, Annie Besant, and Eliphas Levi. Although he was an intellectual playboy with wide contacts in esoteric and bohemian circles of St. Petersburg, he somehow joined the Bolshevik secret police in 1918 as an investigator in a counterrevolutionary unit. Such a strange metamorphosis could have happened for purely material reasons—he had a wife and four children to feed, and working for the secret police guaranteed good food rations. Given the shortage of educated people in all Bolshevik institutions, as a member of the party with a prerevolutionary tenure, formally he was more than qualified for this position. Yet only a year later, in 1919, he was expelled from his job. Then in September of the same year, Vladimirov was reinstalled; then a year later he was fired again.

A bookish man with a lack of self-discipline and a big mouth, yet not devoid of human compassion, Vladimirov simply did not fit such a serious and brutal organization as the Bolshevik secret police. It is known that in September of 1918 he was involved as an investigator in the case of a former lady-in-waiting of the tsarina, Anna Vyrobova, who was blamed for plotting against the revolution. The woman remembered that at first Vladimirov threatened her but then began to apologize—very uncharacteristic behavior for a Red secret police officer.[14]

In addition to graphology, esotericism, and socializing with people of arts and letters, Vladimirov had another passion, which proved fatal. Despite his marriage, he enjoyed the company of several attractive young ladies, impressing them with his eloquent poetry, art, and occult talk. In 1919, when he was investigating an Englishman who was mistakenly arrested as a spy and died in prison, the prisoner's beautiful Estonian wife, Frida Lesmann, came to ask Vladimirov to intervene on her husband's behalf. Vladimirov could not bypass such a wonderful opportunity and for several months had an affair with her. In 1926, when Soviet Russia and Britain clashed and were about to break diplomatic relations, his former colleagues somehow dug up information about this affair and turned Vladimirov into a handy scapegoat. To his amazement, he learned he was an undercover agent for the English spy Frida Lesmann. Although Vladimirov begged desperately to be spared, pointing out that he had no other interests except carnal pleasure, all was in vain. The bohemian Bolshevik was shot as a spy anyway.

A "vegetarian" by revolutionary standards, along with his comrades Bokii, Otto, and Ricks, Vladimirov nevertheless took part in the Red Terror, a campaign unleashed by Bolsheviks to intimidate "alien" non-laboring classes and rival socialist parties into total submission. Everything started with the murder of Moses Uritsky, head of the Bolshevik secret police in Petrograd. Leonid Kanegisser, a young officer of Jewish origin whose family received a nobility title from the Russian tsar, was devastated when the Bolsheviks executed one of his friends. On August 30, 1918, the youth walked into the headquarters of the Bolshevik secret police and shot the "Red Moses." Caught on the spot, the perpetrator explained that the murder was not only an act of revenge but also an attempt to cleanse the name of Abraham's descendants of the Communist stigma. Coupled with the murder of another Red Moses, Moses Goldstein (Volodarsky), who was in charge of Bolshevik media and propaganda, and attempts on the lives of top revolutionary chiefs Vladimir Lenin and Grigory Zinoviev, Kanegisser's action produced a brutal backlash in the form of summary arrests and executions of "counterrevolutionaries." The Petrograd secret police, now headed by Gleb Bokii, Uritsky's deputy, became a merciless tool of the Red Terror. In an act of revenge, the new head ordered the execution of several hundred enemies of the revolution.

Mysteries of Arctic Hysteria and Glavnauka

In 1920, amid cold, hunger, and anarchy, Barchenko finally saw light at the end of the tunnel. The world-famous psychologist Vladimir Bekhterev invited him to join his Institute of Brain Studies and Psychic Activities, or Institute of the Brain for short. Bekhterev, a scientist with a long prerevolutionary career, was one of the first in Russia to research hypnosis and suggestion. Among other things, Bekhterev and his colleagues were interested in psychological infection, when excitement spread from person to person and manifested itself in various mass movements, religious hysterias, collective hallucinations, and demonic possessions.[15] Although he interpreted the Bolshevik revolution as a clear case of mass hysteria, Bekhterev, being a good opportunist, found it useful to cooperate with the new regime and soon began to enjoy the Bolsheviks' financial support. Soviet leaders assumed that Bekhterev and his institute could uncover useful psychological techniques that could be used in Communist propaganda and education.

Sponsored by the Bolshevik government, Bekhterev organized the Committee for the Study of Mental Suggestion. Several of his colleagues accepted the popular concept of brain rays and openly conducted parapsychological research. Tuning into the Communist utopia, which aspired to engineer new human beings free of old bourgeois prejudices, Bekhterev argued that people could change society by concentrating and directing positive thoughts to one another. Eventually, through conscious self-control and self-improvement, people would create an environment that would "breed" people of a better caliber. Later, in the 1930s, Maxim Gorky, the supreme dean of Soviet writers, elevated Bekhterev's research to the status of ideology, putting it into the foundation of Socialist Realism. This Soviet dogma required people who worked in arts and letters to drag common folk into a bright future by presenting positive images of an ideal futuristic Communist society, depicting life not as it was but as it should be. The expectation was that Socialist Realism would speed up human evolution toward a bright Communist future.[16]

CHAPTER THREE

At Bekhterev's suggestion, in 1921 Barchenko went on a field trip to explore arctic hysteria in the Saami land near the Finnish border. Travelers, anthropologists, and psychologists who visited Siberia and the Russian north wrote about a mass craze that infected entire communities of natives, especially in winter and spring.[17] They described how, for no apparent reason, some natives dropped on the ground, arched their backs, and began singing or imitating the behavior of others. For example, not infrequently explorers observed a woman who, like a zombie, would sit on the ground moving her body back and forth for several hours while murmuring a song. Accomplished hysterics usually followed any orders and commands they received from people who happened to be nearby. If ordered, they would easily jump from a roof, breaking their feet, and they would also expose themselves in public, masturbate, or attack somebody with a knife. What a wonderful applied research field for a scientist in a state interested in engineering a new type of people for the Communist future!) 101

Satisfied with Barchenko's fieldwork, Glavnauka, a special umbrella structure created by the Bolsheviks to promote science, endorsed and hailed his research: "Having examined the findings of biologist A. V. Barchenko in the field of ancient Eastern natural philosophy (*natuphilosophie*), the committee recognizes their outcomes as serious and valuable, both from scientific and political points of view."[18] Moreover, it recommended "to immediately provide him with funds to organize a biophysical laboratory." On top of this, Glavnauka appointed Barchenko as a permanent research fellow. Several months later, the spiritual seeker became head of a new biophysical laboratory set up in the building of the Petrograd Polytechnic Museum. Backed by Glavnauka, the happy Barchenko began thinking about an expedition to Inner Asia to retrieve the ancient wisdom of Shambhala.

Along with powerful friends came powerful enemies. One of the most influential ones, who eventually ruined Barchenko and squeezed him out of Glavnauka, was the famous Buddhist scholar Sergei Oldenburg (1863–1934). Although a bourgeois intellectual inherited by Soviet

58

academia from the old regime, Oldenburg became an influential Bolshevik fellow traveler. From 1904 to 1929, he occupied the powerful position of Secretary of the Russian/Soviet Academy of Sciences. This status allowed him to exercise much control over the humanities and sciences in the country.

Oldenburg, the leading academic authority on Tibetan Buddhism, was one of the first with whom Barchenko shared his idea of the Shambhala-Agartha expedition. Yet this contact proved not only frustrating but also harmful for his project. The skeptical Oldenburg made fun of the entire idea. Moreover, in his talks with colleagues the scholar-bureaucrat began openly to call Barchenko a charlatan. Even after 1925, when the secret police formally took Barchenko under its wing, Oldenburg continued to assail the "ancient scientist" as a con artist. In all fairness, it was obvious that Barchenko, who had only a superficial knowledge of Tibetan Buddhism, was a dwarf compared to Oldenburg who, as one of the deans in this field, was well versed in the Buddhist tradition and the languages of the area. In 1923, attacked by his powerful opponent, Barchenko dropped out of the research community and left Glavnauka.

His salvation came from the astronomer Alexander Kondiain and his wife, Eleanor Mesmacher, participants in his arctic expedition and fellow occultists, who sheltered Barchenko and his former and new wives in their large apartment on Red Dawn Street in downtown Petrograd. Barchenko was also pleased to find out that this Russianized Greek was also ready to accept him as a spiritual teacher. Besides, the new friend was blessed with a phenomenal memory and could read several Eastern languages, including Sanskrit. For Barchenko, who was determined to penetrate the hub of ancient wisdom in Inner Asia but did not know the languages of the area, Kondiain became not only a savior but also a great asset.

United Labor Brotherhood on Red Dawn Street

In 1923, after his troubles with Oldenburg and Glavnauka, Barchenko wanted to rejuvenate himself spiritually. He was inspired by a small Buddhist/Communist commune that he set up at Kondiain's apartment on Red Dawn Street. Women were mastering the art of sewing, and men were practicing carpentry. In the evening, together they read and discussed spiritual and occult literature. In the 1920s in Soviet Russia, before the totalitarian dictatorship spread its tentacles, people were involved in various social experiments. Alternative communes and informal clubs, usually with a progressive and avant-garde spin, populated the cultural landscape. While monitoring them, the secret police did not yet harass these groups too much, as long as they loosely fit socialism.

Besides Kondiain and Mesmacher, Barchenko's commune included Natalia and Olga, his old and new wives, and children from both families. Mesmacher remembered: "We lived as one family in a commune. We shared everything and took turns doing chores. At our meetings we frequently scrutinized the behavior of one member or another in the commune, pointing to his or her mistakes."[19]

Barchenko developed guidelines for his commune, which he named United Labor Brotherhood (ULB). His friends Otto, Ricks, Leismaier-Schwarz, and Vladimirov, the former Cheka/OGPU officers, or "checkers" as Mesmacher jokingly dubbed them, were also part of this project. Although kicked out of the secret police, Vladimirov continued on his own to report diligently to his former service on all his friends. To his credit, in these secret updates, full of gossip, he never slandered Barchenko.

The goal of ULB was to foster a community of people who, through studying mysticism and philosophy as well as working on traditional crafts as a team, would spiritually upgrade themselves. The blueprint for ULB was G. I. Gurdjieff's United Labor Commonwealth, which Barchenko learned of from his close friend Peter Shandarovsky, a former member of Gurdjieff's circle who chose to remain in Russia. Barchenko's brotherhood had two ranks: students and brothers. In order to reach the brothers' level one had to exercise rigorous spiritual discipline and live by the highest moral standards. The first step in this direction was renouncing property, which was not a controversial issue—in Red Russia private property was scorned as evil anyway. Despite being a leader, Barchenko modestly stated that he was still a student. A good esoteric commune had to have its own symbols, and ULB was no exception. The symbol of a brother was a red rose with a white lily petal and a cross, symbols of full harmony. The rose and the cross were borrowed from the Rosicrucian tradition; the lily came from *Musurgia Universalis* by Athanasius Kircher (1602–80), a German Jesuit esoteric scholar. A black-and-white hexagon was the symbol of a student, meaning that students still had to work hard to tune their lives to universal rhythm and harmony.[20]

Barchenko was well familiar with several major texts of the Western esoteric tradition. At the same time, for a person who craved to penetrate the hub of ancient knowledge in Inner Asia, he lacked any deep knowledge of Tibetan Buddhism. Barchenko simply felt inadequate in front of such giants as Oldenburg who were well read in this area, knew Tibetan and Sanskrit, and had hands-on experience with local cultures. The Shambhala-Agartha seeker was well aware that a question would always arise of how he, with no expertise in Tibetan Buddhism, could be qualified to lead an expedition to the area.

In an attempt to eliminate this drawback and to ground himself in Tibetan Buddhism, Barchenko moved for several months onto the premises of the Buddhist Kalachakra temple in Petrograd. In fact, he did so right after his fatal conflict with Oldenburg, before setting up his little commune on Red Dawn Street. This unique Buddhist complex, which included a temple and a dormitory, was erected with the personal blessing of Emperor Nicholas II a year before the Bolshevik revolution. Its formal goal was to accommodate the spiritual needs of visiting Buddhists. The project was initiated by Agvan Dorzhiev (1858–1938), a Buryat lama from Siberia who for many years served as a chief tutor of the thirteenth Dalai Lama and then, after 1900, as Tibetan envoy to Russia. Dorzhiev nourished an ambitious idea: to bring all Tibetan Buddhists under the wing of the Russian emperor, whom he advertized to his brethren as the reincarnation of the legendary Shambhala king. The temple also served as a gathering place for spiritually charged elite and middle-class Russian bohemians who craved Oriental spirituality. One of them was the painter Nicholas Roerich, who heavily contributed to the project by designing stained glass for the second floor of the temple.

So in the summer of 1923, Barchenko moved into the Buddhist dormitory and was introduced to a variety of interesting characters, including Bolshevik fellow travelers from Tibetan Buddhist lands, some of whom came to Petrograd to establish contacts with the new regime and find out about its liberation prophecy. Barchenko engaged these people in conversations, trying to learn from them. First of all, he got in touch with Dorzhiev, whom the Bolsheviks inherited from the old regime. After 1917, this activist lama befriended the new masters and began to promote Red Russia as the new Shambhala. But most important for Barchenko were his talks with a Mongol, Khaian Khirva, and a Tibetan, Naga Naven. The former was head of State Internal Protection (GVO), the secret police of revolutionary Mongolia, a sister spy structure sponsored and built up by Red Russia. Khirva was a shady character, and not much is known about him except that, before embracing Communism and becoming one of the top leaders of Red Mongolia, he was a young lama who preached poverty as a lifestyle.[21] Khirva was the first to reach out to Barchenko by knocking on the door of his apartment. He was definitely Barchenko's kindred spirit. The lama-turned-secret-police-chief wanted to promote Communism in Inner Asia by explaining to his nomadic brethren that the ethics and teachings of Tibetan Buddhism and Communism were similar. Moreover, he nourished a desire to educate Communist leaders of Russia about the wisdom of

Kalachakra tantra and Buddhism in general—the same idea that so captivated the mind of Barchenko.

Naga Naven was the governor of Western Tibet who quit on the Dalai Lama and threw his lot with the Panchen Lama, the spiritual leader of Tibet, who in 1923 escaped to Mongolia and challenged the Lhasa ruler from there. Naven came to Soviet Russia to solicit Bolshevik support for the Panchen Lama, but in the early 1920s the Bolsheviks still gambled on the Dalai Lama and refused to listen to Naven. The Tibetan introduced Barchenko to Kalachakra tantra and told him more about the Shambhala prophecy as it existed in its indigenous hub—Tibet.

After his brief stay with the Tibetan Buddhists, Barchenko referred to his spiritual pursuits by the word *Dunkhor*, derived from *Dus'khor*, a Tibetan word for Kalachakra tantra. Yet, there was certainly no way for a European like Barchenko, who did not speak and read Tibetan, to learn in a few months the wisdom that Tibetan monks usually explored for four years at special monastery schools. It is obvious that Barchenko "mastered" Kalachakra through the prism of Western esotericism, mostly Synarchy and Hermeticism.[22] As a result of the talks with Naven and Khirva, Barchenko's desire to become the "Red Merlin" for the Bolshevik regime grew stronger. He recovered from his spiritual crisis and returned to the world. More than ever he became determined to enlighten the Soviet government by retrieving the Shambhala wisdom that would benefit and ennoble the Communist cause.

The first and foremost goal was to inform the Bolshevik elite about the powerful scientific knowledge that Barchenko was convinced was hidden in Shambhala-Agartha, waiting to be unlocked. The crown jewel of this Eastern wisdom was Kalachakra tantra, which provided necessary spiritual tools. The brightest and smartest of the Bolsheviks were to master psychological techniques that would help shape people's minds in the right direction and allow them to control and determine the future.

Simultaneously, Barchenko would unfold for commissars his political plan that would stop social conflicts. Instead of pitting urban and

idealist

village underclass people against the bourgeoisie and middle class, he wanted the Bolsheviks to cultivate professional associations that would help stop the vicious circle of class warfare between the haves and the have-nots. In order to build up a perfectly harmonious society, the new Red masters, like high priests in d'Alveydre's Agartha, were to cultivate a commonwealth of professional guilds, consisting of productive and hardworking members. Strikingly similar projects captivated the minds of Barchenko's contemporaries in Europe and beyond, and one of them, Italian dictator Benito Mussolini, a former socialist, was already putting them into practice, setting up fascist professional corporations as the backbone of the new classless society. In 1927, in a letter to a native Buryat scholar, the exited Barchenko wrote, "Anyone, who is initiated into the mysteries of Dunkhor-Kalachakra, must admit that only the classes based on professional affiliations can mutually aid each other. Only these types of classes will eventually become healthy living limbs of the state body and humankind in general. Only this type of social division will be capable of turning people on our planet into a healthy reflection of Buddha, whose limbs serve and strengthen each other instead of fighting one another and ruining the whole body, as happens nowadays in our society."[23]

Barchenko came to view the 1917 Communist Revolution as the beginning of the global cultural showdown between the rotten Western civilization, based on die-hard individualism, and the Orient, benevolent cradle of collectivism and high spiritual wisdom—a recurrent notion from the early nineteenth-century German Romantics to present-day avatars of multiculturalism. According to Barchenko, the first step for the Bolshevik elite was to strengthen their ties to Eastern countries and learn from Oriental wisdom. Barchenko might have begun to view himself as a social therapist or some sort of Red Merlin who would reveal high Buddhist wisdom to the Bolshevik leadership: "After deeply immersing myself in Dunkhor-Kalachakra, I began to aspire to introduce the most powerful and selfless leaders of Russia into this mystery and to inform them about the correct view and the true value of the ancient and modern culture of the East."[24]

At the end of 1923, the budding prophet returned to his work at Glavnauka. Now confident of his knowledge of Tibetan Buddhism, Barchenko revived his idea of an expedition to Shambhala to retrieve the hidden wisdom. Yet again the same stumbling block stood in his way: scholar-administrator Oldenburg. Barchenko's project was discussed at a closed session of Glavnauka, and Oldenburg immediately suggested that the whole scheme be thrown out. His objection sealed the fate of the project. But Barchenko was stubborn and did not want to give up. Cornered by the powerful scholarly opponent and desperate to find a way out of the situation, he turned to his "checker" comrades, Vladimirov, Otto, Ricks, and Leismaier-Schwarz, asking them to introduce him to somebody high up who might appreciate his grand plan.

A desire to retrieve the sacred Inner Asian wisdom and enlighten the Soviet elite about its power became an obsession: "Until Soviet Russia's leaders realize what high positive values the East has secretly been harboring since ancient times, they are constantly doomed to repeat steps that are harmful and destructive both for the Orient and for Russia, even though these are driven by the best and purest aspirations." Soon everybody in the esoteric circles of Moscow and Petrograd knew about his compulsive politico-spiritual utopia. Some seekers began to treat him with caution as a tool of the Soviet government. Others simply called him a kook. Barchenko brushed aside these slurs: "To be honest, if one approaches my idea as paranoia and 'impractical fantasy,' I have to admit that my 'insanity' is 'incurable.'"[25]

Although the "checkers" no longer worked for OGPU, they responded to Barchenko's plea and activated old contacts. Remembering this episode, Barchenko stated, "The comrades told me that my work is so important that I should report about it to the government, and especially to Dzerzhinsky, the head of the All Union Economic Council. On their advice, I wrote to Dzerzhinsky about my work."[26] Reaching Felix

Dzerzhinsky was not easy. The only person of power accessible to them was their former boss Gleb Bokii, head of the Petrograd secret police in 1918. Vladimirov took the trouble to go to Moscow at the end of 1924 to deliver Barchenko's letter about ancient science personally. The letter at first landed on the desk of Jacob Agranov, one of Bokii's colleagues. Agranov became intrigued and several days later went to Leningrad (the new name for Petrograd) to meet the "occult doctor" at an OGPU safe house. Barchenko remembered, "In this talk with Agranov, I informed him in detail of my theory about the existence of a hidden scientific collective in central Asia and revealed my plan to establish contacts with the owners of its secrets. Agranov was very positive about my report."

To speed up the process, Vladimirov convinced Barchenko to write another letter addressed directly to the OGPU collegium, the council of top officers who ran the Bolshevik secret police. Vladimirov, who always liked to be in the spotlight, again volunteered to deliver the letter. A few days later, he returned with happy news: the "powerful ones" expected the Shambhala-Agartha seeker to come to Moscow and brief them about ancient science. Barchenko could not dream about having better luck. Now he and Vladimirov, along with Leismaier-Schwarz, who also joined the exciting venture, hurried to Moscow, where they again met Agranov: "During this meeting, Agranov told me that my report about a hidden ancient scientific community was included in the OGPU collegium meeting agenda. He also added that my proposal about establishing contacts with the carriers of the Shambhala secrets in the East had a chance to be approved, and that in the future I should stay in touch with Bokii, a member of the collegium, about this."[27]

In a short time Agranov stepped aside, and Barchenko had his fateful meeting with Bokii. The chief Bolshevik cryptographer, sensing in the Shambhala-Agartha seeker a kindred spirit, took Barchenko under his wing and tuned his ear to Barchenko's "scientific prophecy." Formal contacts quickly evolved into friendship.

He's the learned one, the bearer of great illusion,
The fulfiller of aims with great illusion,
The delighter with delight through great illusion,
The conjuror of an Indra's net of great illusion.
 —Verse on the Great Mandala of the Vajra Sphere,
Kalachakra Tantra

Four

Engineer of Human Souls: Bolshevik Cryptographer Gleb Bokii

Gleb Bokii, chief cryptographer of the Soviet Union and Barchenko's patron, was one of those idealists who took the liberation of the "wretched of the earth" close to their hearts. He came from a Ukrainian noble lineage that traced its roots to the time of Ivan the Terrible. His father was a professor of chemistry and the author of a textbook popular in Russian schools and universities. Raised as a well-rounded person on good literature and good music, young Bokii enrolled in the St. Petersburg Mining College. Quite possibly he would have followed the same career route as his father had it not been for one incident. In 1894, his brother Boris invited him to take part in a student demonstration against the authorities. There was a brief fight with police, and both of them, along with other demonstrators, were arrested. On top of this, Bokii was beaten. Although the siblings were immediately released after their father filed a petition (the tsarist regime was far more liberal than the totalitarian state Bokii and his comrades would later build in Russia), the incident upset their father, who soon died from a heart attack.

The two brothers drew different conclusions from this incident. Blaming himself for the death of their father, Boris quit playing a revolutionary and devoted all his time to science. Gleb, on the contrary, blamed the regime and decided to fight it to the very end, eventually becoming a professional revolutionary and joining the Marxist underground. Although he was still interested in science, the desire to change the world and the romantic lure of underground life overrode all other pursuits. After four years of college, young Bokii eventually dropped out, devoting all his time to the cause. It is possible that his mother also inadvertently contributed to Gleb's drift toward Marxism—the "religion" of science and reason. After her first infant son contracted scarlet fever during communion and died, she denounced God, stopped going to church, and became militantly antireligious.[1]

Like all contemporary Marxists, young Bokii and his comrades viewed themselves as the spearheads of history who had mastered the laws of human evolution and found the key to the liberation of humankind in the "scientific" prophecy of Karl Marx. The founding father of Marxism insisted on the coming revolutionary Armageddon that would climax in the fight of industrial workers (forces of goodness) against capitalists (forces of darkness), which would eventually lead to a communist paradise, a society in which people would live happily as brothers and sisters without money, private property, or greed. The people who would lead the laboring masses into this final battle were to be a vanguard communist party, a small group of revolutionaries who knew what to do and would educate the populace, navigating it in the "right" direction.

Young Bokii's formal initiation into organized Marxism took place in 1900 when he joined Vladimir Lenin's Union for the Liberation of Labor, a clandestine organization that, after several splits and mutations, evolved into what became known as the Bolsheviks, proponents of a violent communist revolution. The next step was learning the underground craft. After he was given a secret password, the young man's first assignment was to go to an apartment occupied by a certain Helena Stasova, famous for her knowledge of clandestine work, and help her. Knocking on the door, Bokii uttered the code phrase, "I want to see the thief." The woman responded, "I am the thief."[2] From that moment Bokii's life dramatically changed. He had joined the revolutionary elect, a tightly controlled underground Marxist organization with numerous branches all over the Russian Empire.

To wake the lethargic masses for active rebellion against the regime, much work had to be done: printing flyers and newspapers, conducting secret inspirational talks with factory workers, and organizing strikes. Young Bokii turned out to be a quick learner and soon excelled in this craft. During one of his arrests, police confiscated ordinary school blue books filled with mathematical formulas. In reality, these were ciphered records of his revolutionary cell. This particular cipher was a personal invention of Bokii, and he was the only one who knew the key. The best cryptographers of the tsarist secret police racked their brains trying to figure out these formulas, but they could not crack this tough nut. An investigator kept pressing the young Marxist, "Admit this is some kind of a cipher." Yet Bokii stubbornly replied, "If this is a cipher, go ahead and decipher it." So the officer had to return the blue books.[3]

Between 1900 and 1917, Bokii's life was filled with propaganda activities, arrests, and long prison sentences. Overall, the revolutionary enthusiast was arrested twelve times and twice was exiled to Siberia. In 1907–08, he spent almost a year in solitary confinement. The result of all the time in prison and exile was tuberculosis. Although Bokii received treatment after being released, he did not complete it, and the illness turned into a chronic ailment. Later, after the Bolshevik revolution, when he was doing counterintelligence work in Central Asia against Muslim insurgents in 1920, Bokii had a recurrence. Hearing from someone that dog meat helped cure tuberculosis, he tried it, which certainly appalled the followers of Allah. His secret police colleagues, who disliked Bokii for his independent mind and aristocratic origin, made up a story, picturing this skinny intellectual as some Russian equivalent of Dracula who got his power by drinking human blood and munching on dog meat.[4]

In 1917, after the demise of the tsarist regime, Bokii returned to Petrograd from exile and promptly joined the Military-Revolutionary Committee set up by the Bolsheviks to speed up a communist revolution. This mob of mostly self-appointed radical intellectuals, workers, and soldiers headed by Lenin and his right-hand man, Leon Trotsky, was the group that scripted and executed the famous 1917 Bolshevik revolution. Their immediate plan was to get rid of the so-called Provisional Government. This impotent structure established by liberal bourgeoisie and moderate socialists was unpopular among the grass roots anyway: it did not pull the country out of the bloody Great War and talked such nonsense as democracy, elections, and republic, which sounded Greek to most of the populace. Bokii vigorously contributed to the demise of this government by organizing workers into paramilitary units and simultaneously overseeing Lenin's bodyguards.

Agent of Red Terror

In October 1917, amid the anarchy and chaos caused by the collapse of the Russian Empire and the crumbling Provisional Government, Lenin and his comrades quickly gained power. They abolished money, outlawed private property, and introduced an iron-fisted dictatorship. A grand experiment of building an ideal and perfect society was on the way. With his rich experience of clandestine work and interest in secret codes, ciphers, and symbols, Bokii was a natural choice to become one of the leaders of Cheka/OGPU—the revolutionary secret police created to combat crime and weed out opponents of the new regime. Although Bokii was not thrilled about this assignment, he accepted it in earnest: the revolution needed to defend itself. When the poet-terrorist Leonid Kanegisser killed his boss Moses Uritsky and someone made an attempt on Lenin's life, an infuriated Bokii took over as the head of the Petrograd Cheka and was ready for revenge. He became one of the chief agents of the infamous Red Terror, trying to intimidate into submission all bourgeoisie and colleagues from friendly socialist parties.

In October 1918, Bokii proudly reported that under his guidance the secret police shot eight hundred counterrevolutionaries and imprisoned 6,229.[5] Although many of those liquidated were innocent and did not work against the Bolshevik revolution, it hardly mattered; they belonged to the bourgeois class anyway. In the Marxist scheme of social evolution, this was a vanishing class of exploiters that would have no place in the future Communist society. After all, a great cause demanded great sacrifices, and if some people suffered on the way to the bright future it was unavoidable collateral damage. That was how many leading Bolsheviks rationalized their violence. In a snowball effect, the Red Terror unleashed by the Bolsheviks expanded from Petrograd and Moscow all over Russia and provoked an equally fierce and savage resistance from the supporters of the old regime. The clashes quickly escalated into the bloody Civil War (1918–22) between the Bolshevik "Reds" and the "Whites," supporters of the old regime.

Although Bokii consecrated himself with blood, to some of his more militant comrades he appeared not sufficiently tough. Several Bolshevik chiefs wanted to escalate the revolutionary terror by lynching and executing all "enemies of revolution" on the spot without any arrest or even a slight investigation. Bokii had some doubts about this tactic and might have started asking himself uncomfortable questions. Eventually he began to argue that instead of executing actual and potential enemies, it would be better to round them up and ship them to concentration camps. There, through the miracles of redemptive labor, they would be hammered into good Communist citizens. The Bolshevik government officially announced the creation of concentration camps for "class enemies" on September 5, 1918. This ad hoc project later gave rise to the notorious Gulag, a monstrous system of penal labor camps that was widened and perfected under Stalin. Although Bokii did not create this system, he definitely was one of its chief intellectual sparks.[6]

Amid the Red Terror, this "liberalism" expressed by Bokii outraged Zinoviev, the Bolshevik dictator of Petrograd and himself the target of an unsuccessful murder attempt. In September 1918, Zinoviev ordered that the terror be escalated: "To subdue enemies, we need our own socialist militarism. From the population of one hundred million people we now have in Soviet Russia we must save for us ninety million. As for the rest, we have nothing to offer them. They should be exterminated."[7]

Moreover, Zinoviev ordered Bokii to arm workers and give them the right to identify and execute all enemies of the revolution without any arrest. Asked how would they be able to spot the enemies, Zinoviev answered that "class instinct" of the workers would easily allow them to detect who were bourgeoisie and who were people of labor. When Bokii inquired if Zinoviev was sure that some zealous worker guided by class instinct would not shoot him by mistake, Zinoviev was furious and used all his influence to remove Bokii as head of the Petrograd secret police, a post Bokii had occupied for barely a month. Zinoviev was not the only one to express such a bloodthirsty attitude. In fact, during the Red Terror, it was the prevailing sentiment among Bolsheviks. In the same year, the Latvian Martin Latsis, one of the top secret police officers, stressed, "Cheka does not judge the enemy, it strikes him. It shows no mercy. We, like the children of Israel, have to build the kingdom of the future under constant fear of enemy attack."[8]

Bokii might have eventually been stunned with the magnitude of the terror and brutality he had helped unleash. It is known for sure that his revolutionary idealism cracked somewhat in 1921 when Red Baltic sailors in the Kronstadt fortress, the major spearheads of the 1917 Red takeover, revolted against the Bolshevik dictatorship and terror. Eighteen years later Bokii admitted, "The Kronstadt events produced an indelible impression on me. I could not reconcile myself to the idea that the very sailors who took part in the October revolution revolted against our party and power."[9] The second blow to his faith was the death of Lenin, the charismatic chief of the Bolsheviks, in 1924. Bokii, totally devastated, treated the death of his revolutionary guru as the decline of Communism. Leon Trotsky, an outstanding Bolshevik intellectual and head of the Red Army, crossed swords with Joseph Stalin in a fight for leadership. Stalin was a unique combination of a street thug, an intellectual, and a master of bureaucratic games. When Trotsky tried to outsmart him by talking ideas and ideology, Stalin, for whom ideology was secondary, turned to his favorite Byzantine techniques: backstabbing, surveillance, and smearing his opponents with dirt. This vicious struggle for succession, which resulted in Stalin's enthronement, depressed Bokii. He could not stomach Stalin as the chief of the party. Eventually, this attitude cost Bokii and other old Bolsheviks their lives. In 1937–38, Stalin mowed down all of Lenin's comrades and brought his own people to power.

Sometime in the mid-1920s, Bokii detached himself from active political life and began to avoid Bolshevik Party cell meetings, which appalled his romantic soul with their drudgery and boredom. Instead, he retreated into his immediate intelligence work. In 1921 the top Bolshevik elite appointed him chief cryptographer responsible for diplomatic and spy codes and electronic surveillance in Red Russia. At the same time, Bokii began to pose disturbing questions for himself. Is it possible to construct the perfect society devoid of social and economic problems and make people selfless and noble? What is absolute truth? What represents an absolute evil and an absolute good? These questions gradually led him to a different realm. Bokii summarized his quest thusly: "I did not see any prospects for our revolution and became involved in mysticism."[10]

Contemporary accounts stress that this originally die-hard Marxist revolutionary, one of the top spy chiefs of the early Soviet Union, stuck out among his secret police colleagues. In his memoirs, celebrity singer Fyodor Chaliapin, who later immigrated to the West, remembered that Bokii was the only Bolshevik leader who produced a pleasant impression on him. The singer met him in 1918 during the time of the Red Terror:

> Once I found in my dressing room a basket filled with wine and fruit. Then the one who sent me this kind gift appeared himself. I saw in front of me a dark-haired skinny man with a sunken chest, dressed in a black blouse. The color of his face was something between dark, pale, and earthly green. His olive-shaped eyes were clearly inflamed. I realized right away that my visitor suffered from tuberculosis. The man spoke in a pleasant and soft voice. All his gestures and body movements manifested

trust and good nature. He held by hand a small girl, his daughter. The man introduced himself. This was Bokii, the famous chief of the Petrograd Cheka, whose appearance and manners totally contradicted what I had heard about him. I have to state honestly—Bokii produced the best impression on me. I was especially touched by his fatherly kindness to his daughter.[11]

Apparently, the revolution appeared to Bokii in his idealistic dreams as a noble enterprise that would establish a commonwealth of well-rounded people who would live in harmony, perfecting their minds and bodies. Reality turned out to be brutal and ugly. Instead of a peaceable kingdom he saw a nightmare—the rivers of blood he himself helped to spill. Bokii might have felt that against his will the tide of events had carried him away from the noble goals of the project and that there was no way to stop it. He was especially perturbed that the Communist Revolution did not better the minds of people as he and his idealistic comrades expected. The Bolshevik elite did not think twice about taking advantage of material perks that came along with their new position as the ruling class. Better than anybody, the chief Bolshevik cryptographer saw the greed and corruption of many of those who should have been role

Figure 4.1. Gleb Bokii, master of codes and chief cryptographer of the Bolshevik regime. Moscow, 1922.

models of the first working-class state where wealth was expected to be spread around evenly. Still, like some of his Bolshevik brethren, he never blamed the "noble cause" he served. It was always "bad people" who grossly spoiled it.

Bokii was one of those idealistic Bolsheviks who hated to use the special privileges the Communist elite promptly reserved for itself after seizing power. He lived with his second wife and one of the daughters from his first marriage in a small apartment.[12] His relatives and friends never dared to use his official Packard convertible for personal needs—a practice widespread among other Bolshevik bosses. In winter and summer, he wore the same raincoat and crumpled military cap. Bokii also had an odd habit—he never shook hands with anybody, a practice perhaps acceptable in Western countries but impossible to imagine in Russia. So this aristocrat-turned-revolutionary was a strange man, a "white crow" among his secret police comrades, who instinctively felt he was not one of them. His habit of issuing categorical judgments about other people did not help either, and soon he antagonized many of his colleagues. At the same time, Bokii was far from an ascetic. He was a passionate womanizer and also liked to sit with a glass of good wine in the company of friends, sharing intellectual conversation, but he never dominated a conversation.[13]

The Special Section: Code Making and Wonders of Science

In hindsight, it was clear that, like his idealistic comrades of the same caliber, Bokii was doomed. What shielded him for a long time was the nature of his work and the peculiar status he and his Special Section enjoyed within the OGPU secret police. Although Bokii was one of the heads of OGPU, his section was not subordinated to but only affiliated with the secret police. The Special Section was created on January 21, 1921, by a special decision of the Soviet government as the cryptographic service reporting directly to the top leadership of the Bolshevik Party. As the head of this autonomous unit, Bokii provided information directly to Lenin, Trotsky, Stalin, and other top communist bosses, bypassing the OGPU leadership.

Besides regular secret police funding, the section had an independent source of income from manufacturing and selling safe boxes to various Soviet departments inside and outside the country. Bokii could personally dispose of these funds. Treated as the most secret unit of Soviet intelligence, the Special Section resembled the American National Security Agency. Lev Razgon, who worked for this unit for two years and later became Bokii's son-in-law, remembered, "In the entire complex and vast Soviet intelligence and police apparatus, this department and its director were, perhaps, the most inaccessible of all."[14] People who worked for the section were even forbidden to reveal not only the location but the very existence of the place to their relatives.

Figure 4.2. Former building of the Commissariat for Foreign Affairs. The two upper floors were occupied by Gleb Bokii's Special Section, which specialized in cryptography and occult experiments.

The greater part of the section's services was housed not at the OGPU major premises on Lubyanka Street but on two upper floors of the Commissariat for Foreign Affairs building on the corner of the Kuznetsky Street Bridge and Lubyanka Square. Unlike the rest of the secret police, Bokii's unit did not arrest and interrogate anybody. Its chief tasks were deciphering foreign cables and codes, developing reliable ciphers for Soviet embassies and spies, and conducting electronic surveillance, an emerging hot spy craft that promised wide opportunities. Bokii and his people were able to decipher and read all British, Austrian, German, and Italian diplomatic traffic and to partially access Japanese, American, and French cables. His code breakers were far more successful than those of any similar services in the West.[15] The chief Bolshevik cryptographer gradually expanded the range of his work, adding to his formal duties the exploration of paranormal and esoteric phenomena that might be useful in intelligence work. By the end of the 1920s, the activities and research projects of the Special Section ranged from perfecting electronic spy devices and developing remotely controlled explosives to exploring things mysterious and anomalous. From time to time, Bokii's researchers brought in shamans, mediums, and hypnotists, who were scrutinized to detect the source of their extraordinary abilities.

Because of the nature of their work, people hired for the Special Section usually were highly educated and intelligent folk: cryptographers, linguists, translators, and scientists. Many, like the graphologist Konstantin Vladimirov, possessed unique expertise in exotic fields. There were also academic scholars and scientists like Professor Pavel Shungsky, a student of Japanese culture and language and later a military intelligence officer, or the young chemist Evgenii Gopius, who experimented with remotely controlled explosives. Several experts employed by the section were individuals with "politically incorrect" backgrounds: barons and counts inherited from the old regime.[16] Georgy Chicherin, Commissar for Foreign Affairs, who clashed with OGPU from time to time, once confided to a colleague: "The experts who decode foreign dispatches are absolutely unrivalled. Bokii, the head of this section, has enlisted some old professionals from the time of the tsars. He pays them highly, and gives them apartments more sumptuous than the ones they occupied before the revolution. They work for fifteen or sixteen hours a day."[17]

Like many other Bolsheviks, the head of the Special Section believed in the wondrous powers of science and sought to explain everything from a materialistic viewpoint, including paranormal phenomena. Bokii was very interested in thought transfer—the scientific fad that captivated popular imagination both in Russia and in the West in the beginning of the twentieth century. He assumed that, like radio signals, thoughts could be sent back and forth. Nikolai Badmaev, a Siberian native and expert in Tibetan medicine who cured several of the Soviet elite, remembered that during one of their meetings Bokii wondered how Tibetan doctors applied hypnosis and why mantras should be recited only in Sanskrit. Shrewdly tuning his curative philosophy to politically correct materialist and scientific sentiments, Badmaev suggested that, once uttered, the words of a mantra produced sound waves that had a healing effect on human minds and bodies. Bokii, who was convinced that the surrounding world represented an interconnected information system, was pleased to hear such an explanation.[18] As an intelligence officer, he certainly contemplated the wide opportunities that might arise from using mantras and reading the thoughts of an opponent at a distance.

It was natural that his secret police colleagues were jealous of the autonomous status of Bokii and his Special Section. Indeed, it was unfair. The chief cryptographer knew everything that was going on in OGPU, while OGPU leaders did not know what he was up to in his elite unit. The fact that members of the section were frequently cited for emulation did not help either. Unfortunately, Bokii himself added to this animosity. Proud of his clan of experts, he scorned other OGPU departments as "loafers" and did not miss a chance to play flamboyant pranks on his colleagues within and outside of the secret police.

One of his wireless stations that monitored all suspicious radio communications once intercepted a transmission ciphered in an unfamiliar code. Bokii's people quickly deciphered the message, which was sent from a moving object and said, "Send me one case of vodka." The message came from Genrikh Yagoda, the future head of OGPU, who was having fun on a motorboat in the company of two girls. Bokii decided to play a practical joke and sent the information about the "suspicious object" to Yagoda's own unit. Soon, Yagoda's people were trying to break into the OGPU food supply base that was preparing to deliver vodka to the motorboat, narrowly avoiding a shoot-out. In another case, Bokii bet Maxim Litvinov, Chicherin's deputy, a bottle of French cognac that his people could steal classified documents from the safe in Litvinov's guarded office. Special Section people somehow managed to sneak into the office and steal the papers, which Bokii then returned to Litvinov. The top bureaucrat was so upset that instead of keeping his end of the deal, he complained directly to Lenin about Bokii's mischief.[19]

In the fall of 1924, two months before Barchenko came to Moscow to report to the OGPU bosses about his ancient science, Bokii returned from a depressing inspection trip to the Solovki concentration camp, his pet project to hammer alien classes into good Soviet citizens. On December 19, 1923, five political prisoners in that camp had been shot for violating curfew. Somehow the news leaked to the West, and Bokii was included in a commission to investigate the incident.[20] Although each time during his ceremonial visits to the camp he was treated as a high dignitary who was to see a Potemkin village, he could not help noticing that the place looked like a real hell: prisoners lived in cramped barracks and were hungry, cold, and subject to various abuses. It is difficult to say if Bokii continued to believe in the redemptive nature of this labor-camp project. Yet it would be natural for a person capable of pondering questions of absolute evil and absolute good to have at least some doubt on seeing his own idea turned into such a brutal material force.

Soviet Secret Police Master Ancient Wisdom

Amid his frustrations and doubts, the chief Bolshevik cryptographer met Barchenko and learned about his ancient science: "I became acquainted with Barchenko through Leismaier-Schwarz and Vladimirov, former officers of the Leningrad Cheka. They came to visit me at the OGPU Special Section accompanied by Barchenko and recommended him to me as a talented researcher who had made a discovery of extraordinary political significance. They also asked me to get him in touch with OGPU leadership in order to put his idea into practice."[21]

After several meetings with Barchenko, Bokii finally invited him to report on Kalachakra and Shambhala to the collegium of OGPU top bosses in Moscow on the evening of December 31, 1924. Records of the meeting are not available, yet one can suggest that Barchenko expanded on the applied nature of his ancient science. He most certainly tried to convince them there were people in the East who for hundreds of years had read people's thoughts and by the power of their minds could receive and send information over long distances. Barchenko certainly would not fail to stress that he and others had already "scientifically" proven the actuality of thought transfer. After a brief deliberation, the collegium, headed by OGPU chief Felix Dzerzhinsky, entrusted Bokii to look into this matter and take practical steps if needed. Barchenko remembered, "The meeting of the collegium took place late at night. Everybody was tired and they listened to me inattentively. They hurried to be done with this and other issues. Yet, with the support of Bokii and Agranov, we were able to secure a favorable decision. Bokii was assigned to familiarize himself with the details of my project, and if it could be useful, to fulfill it."[22]

In the beginning of 1925, at Bokii's suggestion, Barchenko moved to Moscow, where the chief of the Special Section secured an apartment for him and employed him as a consultant. The circumstances of the occultist miraculously changed. Despite his earlier contempt for material possessions, Barchenko was now happy not only to improve

Figure 4.3. Twelve chiefs of the Bolshevik secret police cluster around their boss, Felix Dzerzhinsky, in the middle. Gleb Bokii, seated, with his head leaning on his hand, is second to Dzerzhinsky's left. Moscow, 1921.

his living conditions, but also to receive the abundant funds Bokii began providing to him. It appeared that finally Barchenko was nearing his dream of becoming the Red Merlin for the Bolshevik government. In a secret neuropsychology lab created by Bokii, he could also perfect his ideas about thought transfer, psychology, and parapsychology, experimenting with various mediums, hypnotizers, and shamans. Earlier in Glavnauka, Barchenko's ancient science had always been open to the academic scrutiny of such qualified peers as Oldenburg. Now, surrounded by an aura of secrecy, the Red Merlin was guaranteed that nobody would interfere with his research. Later, in 1934, the lab moved to the newly created All Union Institute of Experimental Medicine (Vsesoiuznii intitut eksperimental'noi meditsiny, VIEM) and was renamed as a neuroenergy laboratory. VIEM was a research institute established by Soviet authorities in 1932 to conduct applied studies on the human brain, hypnosis, toxic poisons, and drugs.[23]

Figure 4.4. Projected main building of the Institute for Experimental Medicine (VIEM). This clandestine "new age" Stalinist research center, which was involved in engineering a new type of human being, prolonging life, and simultaneously perfecting lethal substances, was launched in 1934 but never completed because of the war.

In the 1920s, when the Bolshevik utopia firmly entrenched itself in power, there was no shortage of quacks who besieged the Soviet government and the secret police, advertising their miraculous remedies and technologies designated to advance the country toward a bright future. It was little wonder that early Bolshevism saw a variety of grand social and cultural projects promoted by various eccentric individuals. The entire political and cultural climate during this decade encouraged people like Barchenko to come out of the closet. The sudden collapse of the Russian Empire and the drastic changes in the life of the country created an impression that everything was possible. Many of those who came to associate themselves with the new regime were ready to "storm the skies."

Many of these adventurous characters insisted that what they were doing was hard science based on experiments. Scientific knowledge was a sacred cow in the eyes of the Bolsheviks. They believed science could work miracles and linked it to the Marxist theory of progress. Like his comrades, Bokii was convinced that scientists were capable of reshaping nature, society, and the minds of people in the "right direction." Many Bolsheviks hoped that social and physical knowledge would help them engineer a harmonious social order free from any vestiges of the old world and social dissent. A new Communist landscape appeared to them as a perfect, symmetrically designed garden populated by people liberated from outdated spiritual and cultural values. The prospect of retrieving scientific knowledge that, according to Barchenko, was hidden in the caves of Shambhala and could be used to advance the Communist cause might have looked appealing to the chief cryptographer. Bokii might have originally become captivated with Barchenko's ideas promising awesome practical results for intelligence work: thought transfer and reading people's minds at a distance, using altered states, Oriental psychological techniques, solar energy, and so forth. Consciously or unconsciously, Barchenko plugged well into the Bolsheviks' scientific faith.

Bokii might gradually have become interested not only in Barchenko's "science" but also in his "ancient science." After all, the Bolshevik cryptographer was already posing bigger philosophical questions by the time he met the budding Red Merlin. Eventually, Barchenko exposed his secret police patron to various esoteric theories, and Bokii silently let Barchenko enter his life. When the chief of the Special Section began pondering on the fate of the Bolshevik revolution and on what constituted absolute good and absolute evil, Barchenko already had an answer:

> As the revolution was moving forward, all human values were demolished and many people were brutally exterminated. I asked myself the following questions: why and how had the oppressed toilers turned into a herd of roaring animals who on a mass scale exterminated intellectuals, the spearheads of human ideals? I also wondered what should be done to change the sharp animosity between the populace and people of thought. How can one resolve this contradiction? Recognition of the dictatorship of the proletariat did not fit my worldview. Gradually, I became

convinced that all bloody sacrifices to the altar of the revolution were in vain and that the future might bring new revolutions and more blood, which would further degenerate humankind. The key to the solution of the problems was in Shambhala-Agartha, the oasis of secret Eastern wisdom, which maintains the remnants of ancient knowledge and stands higher in its social and economic development than modern humankind. This means that one needs to find a path to Shambhala and establish connections with this country. This task is not for everyone but only for the people of a high moral caliber. These seekers should be selfless, free of material possessions and property, and have no aspirations for personal enrichment. We also need to develop a middle ground among people of different worldviews who are capable of raising themselves above temporary social rivalries in order to understand and resolve more pressing issues.[24]

At some point, Barchenko might have shared with Bokii his vision of the future, which did not exactly coincide with the Soviet project focused on uncompromising class warfare. It is possible that Bokii, exposed to the Bolshevik dirty linen and plagued by frustrations, tuned his ear to the "doctor's" prophecy and thought seriously that scientific knowledge of Shambhala could help the Communist cause. That Bokii totally bought Barchenko's stories about the Himalayan country possessing some high spiritual wisdom seems unlikely. Yet it is quite probable that the chief of the Special Section came to share a scientific belief that in Inner Asia there were spiritual practitioners of Tibetan Buddhist and Sufi origin who had mastered superior psychological techniques that could ennoble and empower the Communist project. Listening to Barchenko's talk, Bokii might have assumed that these practitioners kept their secrets well guarded. Such reasoning perfectly fit the mindset of the cryptographer, who had spent the first half of his life in a revolutionary underground filled with clandestine activities. The second part of his life, after the 1917 revolution, was covered with a similar aura of secrecy: electronic surveillance, code making and code breaking. The well-guarded clandestine world of symbols, codes, and behind-the-scenes activities eventually became an intimate part of Bokii's character. His office door had a peephole with a one-way glass through which he routinely examined his visitors.[25] Living in a bubble of secrecy, members of an intelligence community are usually susceptible to things esoteric and mysterious, and Bokii was no exception.

At the end of 1925, he encouraged Barchenko to begin classes about Kalachakra tantra and Western occult wisdom for members of the Special Section. However, to Bokii's frustration, six colleagues who at first volunteered for these meetings soon became bored: "The students were not prepared to absorb the mysteries of ancient science."[26] As a result, the occultist and his secret police friend moved their classes to private apartments, inviting close friends who were interested in esotericism, Tibetan medicine, and the paranormal. They frequently met in downtown Moscow at a large apartment occupied by Ivan Moskvin, a member of the Central Committee of the Communist (Bolshevik) Party, and Sofia Doller, Bokii's former wife. Moskvin was one of the driving forces behind the VIEM project. Among those who frequented Barchenko's talks about Oriental wisdom were former college mates of Bokii, the engineers Mikhail Kostrikin and Alexander Mironov, as well as Bolshevik luminaries such as Boris Stomniakov and Semen Dimanshtein. The former worked at the Commissariat for Foreign Affairs as one of Chicherin's deputies, while the latter was a member of the Communist Party Central Committee responsible for nationalities policies. Even the notorious Yagoda, who, after Dzerzhinsky's death in 1926 became the de facto head of the OGPU secret police, dropped by out of curiosity. Barchenko was surely thrilled with all these visitors: his dream to enlighten the Soviet elite about the wisdom of Shambhala was gradually turning into a reality. A few more steps, and he might reach people at the very top of the pyramid of power.

The content of Barchenko's classes was a smorgasbord of Western esotericism and bits and pieces of Tibetan Buddhism he had learned from his Mongol and Tibetan contacts while staying in the Leningrad

Kalachakra temple. In 1937, when arrested and pressured by Stalin's henchmen to give them the gist of these classes, Bokii remembered:

> According to Barchenko, in ancient times there existed a culturally advanced society that later perished as a result of a geological catastrophe. This was a communist society, and it existed in a more advanced social (communist) and materially technical form than ours. The remnants of this society, as Barchenko told us, still exist in remote mountain areas at the intersection of India, Tibet, Kashgar, and Afghanistan. This ancient science accumulated all scientific and technical knowledge, representing a synthesis of all branches of science. The existence of the ancient science and the survival of that society is a secret carefully guarded by its members. Barchenko called himself a follower of this ancient society, stressing that he was initiated into it by messengers of its religio-political center.[27]

Tantra for the Commissar

It was not only at the Moskvin apartment where Bokii and his comrades conjured an ideal society and perfect human minds and bodies. In deep secrecy, the chief Bolshevik cryptographer maintained another meeting place, a fenced summer cottage (dacha) in the Kuchino area of the Moscow suburbs. Here, away from curious eyes, he could temporarily forget his troubling thoughts about the fate of the revolution and allow his imagination to run wild and free. In this retreat, Bokii and a few trusted men and women from his Special Section indulged in naturism, wining, and dining. On weekends when weather allowed, Bokii and these selected few, naked or partially naked, worked in the garden of the summer cottage, raking and gathering fruits and vegetables. The chief cryptographer added an esoteric spin to these retreats, calling them "the cult of unity with nature" and composing a special charter for his "summer cottage commune," as it became known in his inner circle. The charter prescribed nude sunbathing as well as collective bathing for men and women. The collective work in the nude was usually followed by communal meals, accompanied by generous drinking and group sex. [28]

It is likely that in order to justify these group-sex practices the Bolshevik cryptographer might have resorted to Kalachakra tantra rituals, which he might have learned from either Barchenko or Badmaev, the doctor of Tibetan medicine, although there is no evidence that these two were part of the nature commune. Given the general social environment of Red Russia in the 1920s, these peculiar nature retreats did not look odd. In early Bolshevik Russia, very much like in Western countries in the 1960s, free love, contempt for so-called traditional family values, and various projects of collective living ran amok. In fact, several Left-leaning theoreticians elevated sexual promiscuity to the level of the new Bolshevik morality. From time to time, pedestrians on the streets of Moscow and Leningrad and passengers in trams bumped the naked bodies of nudists, who viewed their public exposure as a revolutionary act.

Although the existence of this commune is corroborated by documents, its particular details are obscure. Later, in 1937, Bokii's former colleagues from the Special Section, arrested and pressured by secret police, portrayed the dacha commune as a chain of drinking sprees and sexual orgies. Although it is hard to accept all these testimonies at face value, there might be some truth in them. According to a certain N. Klimenkov, who took part in these retreats, the "nature people" from his Special Section not only practiced collective gardening and sex, but also played crude pranks on one another. The favorite ones were mock church services and religious funerals. Dressed in Russian Orthodox Church garb confiscated from clergy, some of the commune's members acted as priests, while others played the role of corpses to be buried. Once an agent named Fillipov, while drunk, nearly suffocated when buried in the ground during one mock service. Some mornings the "nature people" would awaken to find their vaginas and penises smeared with paint or mustard. To maintain these regular retreats, the participants set aside 10 percent of their monthly salaries. Eventually, with the advent of Stalin's conservatism and puritanism in the early 1930s, rumors of the dacha commune reached the ears of OGPU leadership, and a Communist Party cell reprimanded Bokii, forcing the cryptographer to shut down his clandestine experiment in alternative living.

Besides the unity-with-nature fad, these retreats might have had something to do with Bokii's sexual life. Besides his great concern about how to perfect the Communist cause and human nature, libido was an issue that clearly disturbed the frustrated commissar, now in his forties. In 1920 he divorced his wife, and before remarrying he went on a quest for a new partner. To be on good terms with their boss, several women from his Special Section were ready to please him. To the rest, both married and unmarried, Bokii's advances became a big headache for a while. Several female agents and secretaries tried to dress and look as ugly as possible at work. For some time, Bokii shared a bed with the wife of Maiorov, one of Special Section's workers, and then with the wife of another colleague named Barinov. Unable to withstand such moral pressure, both men committed suicide. One jumped under the wheels of a train, and the other shot himself. Slowly but surely, Bokii was becoming like those secret police monsters who worked around him.

The cryptographer was clearly seeking to increase his sexual potency, and this quest also took an esoteric turn. From somewhere he acquired a morbid collection of mummified penises, which he kept in his apartment.[29] It is known that in several branches of the Kalachakra tantra school, mummified limbs (hands, arms, penises, and skulls), especially those that belonged to deceased lamas, were used for empowerment. Most likely, Bokii received this strange collection from Badmaev, who frequented the Moskvin apartment and at one point cured Bokii. The cryptographer might have viewed these dried organs as a healing aid from the arsenal of Tibetan medicine.

The Abortive Shambhala Expedition

Besides nature retreats and empowering himself with mummified penises, the priority on Bokii's agenda was organizing an expedition to Inner Asia to establish contact with Shambhala. Everything seemed to have gone smoothly in this direction. The chief cryptographer was ready to invest enormous funds in this project. Encouraged by the enthusiasm of his powerful patron, Barchenko widened his exploratory goals by adding Afghanistan to the Tibetan itinerary of the future expedition. There the Red Merlin hoped to uncover secrets of ancient Sufi brotherhoods—clearly a result of his intensive reading of d'Alveydre, who placed this Central Asian country in the center of his subterranean Agartha kingdom.

To prepare themselves for the coming Asian mission, Barchenko and his close friends, including Vladimirov, immersed themselves in learning Mongol and Tibetan languages, reading anthropological literature, and mastering riding horses. Although the proposed expedition was defined as scientific and was not classified, Bokii did not want to advertise it too much because of the involvement of his Special Section. But Vladimirov, as always boastful and flamboyant, spilled the beans, and word about the exotic Oriental venture spread in the esoteric circles of Leningrad. One of his acquaintances, a struggling Leningrad sculptor with occult interests, begged Vladimirov to take him and two of his girlfriends. Soon Barchenko found himself besieged by acquaintances and acquaintances of acquaintances asking to join the expedition. Eventually, Bokii kicked out Vladimirov, who ironically was to serve as political commissar for the expedition, an ideological watchdog to make sure its participants would not deviate from the Bolshevik line—an odd role for Vladimirov, who had to be watched himself.

Such a large enterprise involving travel to foreign countries needed approval from Georgy Chicherin, Commissar for Foreign Affairs, a close friend of Lenin and a career diplomat with prerevolutionary tenure. In July 1925, accompanied by two OGPU officers, Barchenko visited Chicherin. At first, the commissar sounded very supportive. In fact, Chicherin was already working to orient Soviet foreign policy more toward Asia and away from the West, which he did not like anyway. Yet, the next day the chief Bolshevik diplomat completely changed his mind. It could be that the personality of the Red Merlin and his grand dreams aroused suspicion. For Chicherin, an experienced diplomat, it was relatively easy to figure out such characters as Barchenko. A rivalry between OGPU and the Commissariat for Foreign Affairs surely played its role as well.

An aristocrat from an impoverished noble family, Chicherin had been raised as a well-rounded intellectual in a home bubble surrounded by his protective mother, aunt, and nanny. Like Bokii, he was a high-class revolutionary idealist who joined the Red cause far before 1917 in order to liberate the "wretched of the earth." As a young adult, Chicherin studied history and law at St. Petersburg University, with a brief detour into the mists of German philosophy: Kant, Hegel, and the like. At one point he realized that all this knowledge was just intellectual masturbation. He craved a noble cause and real action that would change the world and found it by bumping into Lenin and Trotsky, who gave the intellectual an activist agenda. The new convert to Marxism quit his job as a minor diplomatic clerk and moved to Western Europe, where he frequented émigré salons while preparing for the revolution.

Now the commissar lived the life of a committed bachelor, enjoying playing Mozart at night in the company of his cat. He was seriously disturbed that some snooping folk from OGPU had passed around word he was a homosexual and hinted about his intimate relations with his chief of protocol. There was always bad blood between him and the secret police. Those bastards, Chicherin complained to a junior colleague, not only gossiped behind his back but spied on all the top Bolsheviks, installing microphones everywhere, including his own office—and Bokii was in charge of all those techs.[30] That skinny cryptographer with penetrating eyes, enormous sexual drive, and equally enormous power thought he could do whatever he wanted. He even took several floors of Chicherin's commissariat building for his Special Section. Now, through this quack Barchenko, Bokii had the nerve to casually inform him that all passport paperwork for their Shambhala expedition was already going through rank-and-file clerks in Chicherin's own commissariat without his knowing about it! The Commissar for Foreign Affairs would have none of it. Chicherin was ripe for a good intrigue and a small revenge.

So after he sent out his original memo in which he endorsed the Barchenko-Bokii project, the commissar decided to call OGPU bosses to check if the expedition had their approval. The first person he called was Meer Trilisser, chief of the Foreign Espionage Department. Technically, Bokii, as the head of the autonomous Special Section, was not obligated to report about his plans to him or to any other OGPU boss. Yet, during this phone conversation, Trilisser was angry or acted angry. He told Chicherin that Bokii had never informed him about the project, adding that Bokii's initiative was flawed and that there were other ways to penetrate Inner Asia.

Soon, the intrigue against Bokii sparked by Chicherin involved the powerful Genrikh Yagoda, second in command in the Soviet secret police. This "brutal, uncultivated, and gross individual" and "past-master of intrigue," as a former coworker described him,[31] also played ignorant and spoke against Bokii's project. Although both Trilisser and Yagoda were members of the OGPU collegium that had heard Barchenko's report and agreed to assign Bokii to work out practical recommendations, now, a few months later, they played against it. Both men resented Bokii's privileged status within OGPU and would not miss a chance to make life harder for the arrogant aristocrat. So the intrigue against Bokii within OGPU gave Chicherin an excellent chance to kill a project from the rival commissariat whom he despised anyway.

The next day, in his follow-up memo, Chicherin did not denounce outright the whole project but cast strong doubt on selected routes and especially on the person in charge of the expedition:

For nineteen years, a certain Barchenko has been searching for the remnants of some prehistoric culture. He has a theory that in prehistoric time humankind had developed an extremely advanced civilization that far surpassed the present historical period. He also believes that in Central Asian centers of spiritual culture, particularly in Lhasa and in some secret brotherhoods in Afghanistan, one can find surviving scientific knowledge left by this advanced prehistoric civilization. Comrade Barchenko approached Comrade Bokii, who became extremely interested in his theory and decided to use the manpower and resources of his Special Section to locate the remnants of this prehistoric culture. The OGPU collegium that heard Barchenko's report similarly became interested in this project and decided to use some funds they probably have at their disposal. Two comrades from OGPU and Barchenko have visited me to secure my support.

I told them that they should exclude Afghanistan from their agenda outright. Not only will Afghan authorities not let our chekists [secret police officers] search for any secret brotherhoods, but also the very fact of their presence in that country will produce repercussions in English mass media, which will not miss an opportunity to portray this expedition in a totally different light. As a result, we will create trouble for ourselves. I repeat again that our chekists will not be allowed to contact any secret brotherhoods. However, my attitude to the trip to Lhasa was totally different. If the sponsors who support Barchenko have enough money to organize the expedition to Lhasa, I would welcome this as another step to establish links with Tibet. Yet there is one condition. First of all, we need to gather more definitive information about the personality of Barchenko. Second, he needs to be accompanied by experienced controllers from the ranks of serious Communist Party comrades. Third, he needs to promise not to talk politics in Tibet and especially to avoid talking about relations between Tibet and other Eastern countries. This expedition demands large funds, which our commissariat does not have. Finally, I am totally convinced that there had been no advanced civilization in prehistoric times in this area. Yet, I assume that an extra trip to

Lhasa will not harm but help strengthen the connections we are now establishing with Tibet.[32]

Chicherin's ambiguous memo and the intrigues of Bokii's colleagues eventually buried the Shambhala project. In all fairness, it would have been hard for Bokii and Barchenko to succeed anyway. The whole idea of searching for remnants of an ancient civilization using OGPU money sounded naive. Even under the most favorable circumstances, the secret police would hardly have rushed to approve the "scientific" expedition in search of a mythological Shambhala. Chicherin and Bokii's rivals within OGPU had better and more reliable plans or, as Trilisser put it, other ways to penetrate Inner Asia. Besides his personal dislike of OGPU, Chicherin's reason for not endorsing the secret police venture might have been simply that he did not want it to interfere with his own Tibetan scheme, already underway.

The expedition organized by Chicherin was headed by a seasoned revolutionary, Sergei Borisov, an educated indigenous Oirot from the Altai, who worked as a consultant in his Eastern Department. Borisov, who helped win over Mongolia for Red Russia, was a trusted man. As a native, he was expected to mingle well with Inner Asians. When Bokii and Barchenko approached Chicherin in 1925, Borisov was already on his way to Lhasa with a group of Bolshevik fellow travelers disguised as lama pilgrims. Borisov was not interested in retrieving ancient Shambhala wisdom. His goal was to probe anticolonial and anti-English sentiments in Tibet and to use, if possible, ancient prophecies to stir revolts in the Forbidden Kingdom.

During the same year Chicherin was pleasantly surprised to discover another Tibet expert. In December 1924, the Russian émigré painter Nicholas Roerich, then living in New York and also striving to reach Shambhala, contacted the Soviet embassy in Berlin. Roerich had already made several trips to the Tibetan-Indian border. In exchange for Soviet support of his new expedition, the painter offered to monitor British activities in the area and to trumpet the

Bolshevik agenda by highlighting similarities between Buddhism and Communism.

Last but not least, Chicherin already had at his disposal one more Tibet expert, Agvan Dorzhiev, the former Dalai Lama tutor, now a Bolshevik fellow traveler. Cast against Borisov, Dorzhiev, and Roerich, Barchenko and Bokii appeared as naive amateurs and dreamers. For Chicherin and for his colleagues from Comintern and the secret police, Shambhala, and similar prophecies were the realm of geopolitics rather than inward psycho-techniques that could perfect human minds. Clearly Chicherin dismissed as gibberish Barchenko and Bokii's plan to go to Inner Asia and retrieve ancient wisdom that that might benefit the Communist cause.

White Water Land, Rabbi Schneersohn, and Beyond

Having failed to penetrate Inner Asia, the core of legendary Shambhala and Agartha, the chief cryptographer and his friend did not give up. Changing the geography of their quests, the seekers of high wisdom had to focus on domestic manifestations of that legend. Using Special Section funds, Bokii, on his own, began financing Barchenko's trips to various corners of the Soviet Union to gather information on esoteric teachings and groups: Tibetan Buddhists, shamanists, Sufis, Russian Orthodox sectarians, Hasids, and others. All these activities made perfect sense because Barchenko and his patron believed that all contemporary esoteric teachings were surviving splinters of the universal ancient science.

Barchenko made trips to southern Russia to contact Sufis in the Crimean peninsula. Later, he brought their leader, Saidi-Eddini-Dzhibavi to Moscow and introduced him to Bokii. In 1925, he also made a long trip to the Altai, a mountain area in southern Siberia on the Mongolian, Russian, Kazakhstan, and Chinese borders, to explore, among other things, shamanic drumming. He tried to find out why and how the sound of drumming plunged people into altered states. Using his status as an elite scholar, Barchenko confiscated several shaman drums from a local museum and brought them to Moscow for his experiments.

In the Altai and also during another trip to Kostroma in central Russia, he met so-called Old Believers, Russian Orthodox sectarians who resisted attempts to modernize the Orthodox Church and subject it to state control. One of the Old Believers' tenets was hiding from the world in the wilderness and seeking a utopian dreamland called Belovodie (White Water). To the seekers, this folk utopia, which Barchenko certainly treated as a Russian version of Agartha and Shambhala, was a safe place with fertile ground and abundant crops and especially a safe haven where people could worship freely and experience spiritual bliss. In the Altai, Barchenko also investigated the legend about "subterranean folk" called the Chud—a possible link to Agartha. In some undefined ancient times, as the legend goes, the mysterious Chud, who faced constant oppression and harassment from authorities in this world, hid away underground by cutting wooden beams to support the roofs of their subterranean dwellings. From then on, the Chud lived an invisible life, resurfacing only when the world faced a calamity.

Generously funded by Bokii, the Red Merlin traveled all over the Soviet Union, shopping around for esoteric wisdom. The goal of his ventures was not only to collect splinters of the universal ancient science: Barchenko and his patron nourished an ambitious idea to convene sometime in 1927–28 in Moscow a congress of all esoteric groups and use them to advance the Communist agenda.[33] In hindsight, this plan perfectly fit the religious reform movement sponsored in the 1920s by the Soviet government and its secret police. The goal of the Bolsheviks was to identify and bring together religious leaders who were ready to work closely with them to promote Communism and to weed out those who insisted the government should keep its hands off religion and spirituality.

Not much is known about the work of Barchenko for the Special Section between 1925 and the early 1930s. However, there is intriguing ancillary evidence from an independent source that shows how he contacted people from esoteric and religious groups. This source is Rabbi Joseph Schneersohn (1880–1950), the head of the Chabad Lubavitch Hasidic movement. This prominent leader of traditional Jews, who resided in Leningrad in the early 1920s, defied the religious reform movement and stubbornly refused to put his community under the control of the Bolshevik secret police. Schneersohn remembered how on October 1, 1925, Barchenko asked him to provide all available information about Kabala and the Star of David. The Red Merlin was convinced that "mastery of this knowledge could be a source of great power."[34] Barchenko most likely viewed Kabala as a manifestation of the universal ancient science. As a jack-of-all-spiritual-trades, he was not aware that he had picked the wrong man and the wrong tradition, unless the Kabala business was just an excuse on the part of his secret police patron to get access to the stubborn rabbi. It is clear that traditional and conservative Hasidic teaching, which was alien to any universalism, could not provide any feedback to Barchenko's "mystical international."

Trying to win Schneersohn's trust, Barchenko flashed reference letters from several Moscow scholars and confided to the rabbi that he "dealt with the occult (which was also based on mathematics) to reveal mysteries and predict the future." He also disclosed that "he had already organized a group in Moscow to pursue this study, for which they received a governmental permit. They were joined with keen interest by many leading scholars."[35] Barchenko claimed that he wanted to learn from the rabbi the "great truth" that would help create and destroy social worlds—a spiritual technique for social engineering. Having been repeatedly harassed by Bolsheviks, the rabbi was very cautious, assuming that Barchenko was either insane or a secret police provocateur. The latter assumption was not totally unfounded.

Barchenko's exciting tales about prospects of influencing and engineering the future through ancient science sounded to the rabbi like pure heresy. However Schneersohn did not want to antagonize a person with high connections, so he acted as if he was interested in working together and even assigned his young assistant Menachem Mendel to translate excerpts from Hasidic literature to educate Barchenko about Kabala. As a gesture of gratitude, the Red Merlin sent Schneersohn several hundred golden rubles, a large amount of money.[36] But the wise rabbi returned the money, saying that the translation work was free—a smart decision. In 1927, when the rabbi was arrested by OGPU, interrogators tried to incriminate him for receiving payments for illegal religious activities.

Barchenko's persistent efforts to engage the rabbi in occult work and his no-less-persistent attempts to convince him to accept money make one wonder if the Red Merlin was driven only by spiritual curiosity. Could it also be that Barchenko was simultaneously acting as an OGPU agent provocateur, trying to set up a rabbi who refused to place himself under the "protection" of the secret police? Barchenko never tried to hide his links to the government, and he never mentioned OGPU—the name scared people away. However, directly and indirectly, he always stressed that he enjoyed official support. And all his ventures required a lot of money. Overall, from 1925 to the early 1930s, Barchenko received about 100,000 rubles from Bokii[37]—a huge amount of money, roughly the equivalent of $200,000 at that time!

The perfect age will dawn anew, better than anything that has happened before.

—Shambhala Prophecy, early Middle Ages

The cause has been launched and will not die. I know the roads this cause will travel. The tribes of Jenghiz Khan's successors are awakened. Nobody shall extinguish the fire in the heart of the Mongols! In Asia there will be a great State from the Pacific and Indian Oceans to the shore of the Volga. The wise religion of Buddha shall run to the north and to the west. It will be the victory of the spirit.

—Baron Roman von Ungern-Sternberg (1921)

Five

Prophecies Draped in Red: Blood and Soil in the Heart of Asia

I n late 1920, at the northern section of the Chinese-Tibetan Border, a group of Russian officers led by Professor Ferdinand Ossendows-ki, former minister of finances in the White Siberian government, were fleeing for their lives from the terror of Red Russians, who were quickly gaining control over northern Eurasia. His party planned to make a daring flight southward through Tuva, Mongolia, and Tibet to the safety of British-owned India. Traveling mostly at night to avoid Bolshevik patrols and wandering bandits, the professor and his friends covered almost two thousand miles, crossing snowy plains, mountains, and deserts, subsisting primarily on raw frozen meat. Before entering Tibet, the party decided to rest at the place called Koko Nor. Just as the exhausted Whites, thinking that they were finally safe, decided to rest, they were suddenly showered with a spray of bullets from local nomad-ic brigands. Two officers dropped dead. Hoping to escape from the trap, the Whites tried to parley with the attackers. To arouse the sympathy of the bandits, Ossendowski confided that his party was escaping from the wrath of the Bolsheviks in Red Russia. To his amazement, one of the bandits informed him that they "knew the Bolsheviki and considered them the liberators of the people of Asia from the yoke of the white race."[1] The political "debate" continued in earnest the next day after the "progressive" bandits prepared one more trap, silently surrounding the camp of the "reactionaries" during the night and awakening them at dawn with another spray of bullets.

Ossendowski, armed with a Mauser pistol, and his officer friends were excellent marksmen and hardened fighters, but now they realized that proceeding farther to India might be dangerous. Paranoid about the possibility of meeting another band of politically indoctrinated bandits, the Whites decided to ride back to Mongolia. After losing six more men, the small party was finally able to get rid of its pursuers.

This meeting between indoctrinated Tibetan bandits and the Ossendowski party is both symbolic and revealing. It clearly shows that the anticolonial liberation gospel of the early Bolsheviks did reach distant corners of Asia and stirred ethnic, national, and even racial feelings of indigenous people.

The professor's story serves as a good parable to what I propose in this chapter: Shambhala and sister prophecies, on the rise in Inner Asia between the 1890s and 1930s, served nationalist and separatist causes by invoking "blood and soil" sentiments in the world of Tibetan Buddhism. I also want to show how the Bolsheviks tried to latch onto these prophecies. After the collapse of the Russian and Chinese empires, the Mongols, Tibetans, Oirot, Tuvans, Buryat, and Kalmyk were suddenly on their own, getting a taste of independence. Like other nationalists the world over, their leaders turned to easily understandable indigenous tales, legends, and prophecies to bring the mostly illiterate people together as nationalities and nations. Better than anybody else the Bolsheviks understood the power of nationalism and set forth to ride indigenous lore and prophecies to win the masses of Inner Asia to their side.

Communism as a Secular Prophecy

We left Bokii and Barchenko when their ambitious project of an expedition to Tibet had been successfully buried by the combined efforts of Georgy Chicherin, Commissar for Foreign Affairs, and Meer Trilisser, chief of the OGPU foreign intelligence branch. Grounded in the world of real politics, Chicherin and Trilisser sensed that the plan to uncover in Inner Asia some ancient wisdom that would help control minds and engineer new types of human beings was flaky. Their desire to see real action rather than listen to vague stories about powerful spiritual techniques hidden by Himalayan masters was the chief reason Barchenko and Bokii failed to win support for their Shambhala project.

After the 1917 revolution, Chicherin, Trilisser, and other Bolsheviks quickly embraced anti-Western sentiments because, to their dismay, industrial workers in Europe and North America somehow did not rush to embrace the message of worldwide Communist revolution that the Bolsheviks so persistently sent out all over the globe. The Bolsheviks came to regard their Western brethren as corrupted and pampered by bourgeois perks. Asian folk were a different breed. These were truly the wretched of the earth; poor and hungry, they lived under the colonial oppression of the West. Unlike their spoiled counterparts in Europe and America, Asians were ready to go to the barricades. The Bolsheviks hoped they could reach out to these impoverished masses, stir them with their liberation gospel, and lead them in a revolt against their oppressors, especially England, the chief colonial culprit.

What eased the plans of the Bolsheviks was that their own prophecy, Marxism, contained a strong religious element that could be easily customized to fit the prophecies and needs of preliterate people facing the advance of modern Western society and looking for social and economic miracles to help them deal with this advance. Indeed, the philosophy of Marxism, and the communist movement it stirred, played the role of a surrogate religion. Like any religion, it claimed absolute truth and provided a universal explanation of the past and the future. Marxism also prophesized that all evil would eventually be phased out once and for all in the course of the coming worldwide revolutionary Armageddon, which would sweep away capitalism and oppression. This final battle for the liberation of human beings would open the gates to the new age of goodness when all people would live as brothers and sisters in total harmony and equality.[2] By replacing divine power with the secular prophecy, Marxism established a convenient link between the traditional religious expectations of people and emerging modern life. After all, the communist movement sprang up as a Romantic answer to the tensions caused by the industrial revolution in the nineteenth century.

After the 1917 revolution, Communism in Russia acquired features of a secular prophecy that resembled religious revitalization in tribal societies facing rapid modernization. The anthropologist Anthony Wallace, who studied such prophetic movements, was among the first to note this striking similarity:

> Communist movements are commonly asserted to have the quality of religious movements, despite their failure to appeal to a supernatural community, and such things as the development of a Marxist gospel with elaborate exegesis, the embalming of Lenin, and the concern with conversion, confession, and moral purity (as defined by the movement) have the earmarks of religion. The Communist Revolution of 1917 in Russia was almost typical in structure of religious revitalization movements: there was a very sick society, prophets appealed to a revered authority (Marx), apocalyptic and Utopian fantasies were preached, and missionary fervor animated the leaders.[3]

Thus, the portraits of living and deceased Bolshevik leaders such as Lenin, Trotsky, and then Stalin replaced old Russian Orthodox Church icons, and new revolutionary monuments and palaces substituted for Christian churches. The pyramid of power was headed by the Bolshevik (Communist) Party, which Stalin (a graduate of a Greek Orthodox theological seminary) once referred to as a sacred order.

After they took power, Lenin, Trotsky, and their comrades expected that soon the tide of Communism would roll on all over the globe and other nations would follow Red Russia to form the world federation of Soviet republics. In 1919, in their zeal to speed up this second coming, the Bolsheviks launched Communist International (Comintern), a Moscow-based organization with branches in various countries.

One aspect of Marxism gave the Bolsheviks many headaches. Karl Marx, the founding father of the prophecy, predicted that the communist revolution would triumph first in economically advanced states of Europe and North America rather than in such underdeveloped countries as Russia, China, and Mongolia. He reasoned that only highly developed nations with an industrial working class were ripe for communism. Marx prophesized that without this class redemption, which was to be guided by a revolutionary party, there was no way to liberate humankind from the bondage of capitalism and make the leap into the golden age of communism. Yet, contrary to Marx's prophecy, a communist revolution took place in the backward Russian Empire, a vast Eurasian country with a predominantly peasant population still living in a premodern age.

Red Russia Turns to the East

Sometime in late 1920, desperately trying to keep the revolutionary fire aflame, the Bolsheviks turned to the East, hoping to woo Muslim, Hindu, and Tibetan Buddhist societies wanting to rid themselves of national and colonial oppression. Lenin and his followers hoped that, under proper guidance, it would be easy to navigate the anticolonial sentiments toward Communism, so the immediate goal of Red Russia in Asia was to bond with the Eastern colonial periphery against the imperialist West. The most enthusiastic Bolsheviks even came up with the heretical idea that all Oriental people were oppressed by the capitalist West and automatically qualified as a surrogate working class ripe for Communist revolution.[4]

What might have also eased the Bolsheviks' flirt with the East was the fact that after the revolutionary holocaust of the Civil War (1918–22) Russia appeared more Asian than European. The 1917 Communist Revolution, which took the form of a bloody crusade of peasants and the urban underclass against all things bourgeois, literally washed away the spirit of Western civilization along with its representatives—educated aristocrats and middle-class intellectuals. That is how the Bolsheviks, a small sect of revolutionary intellectual-idealists, suddenly found themselves in charge of a populace ranging from illiterate Russian and Muslim peasants to the Stone Age hunters and gatherers of Siberia.[5] To railroad Marxism and Communism into this "heart of darkness," the Bolsheviks not only relied on force but also had to customize their ideas to peasant and tribal cultures.

To woo the Asians living on the eastern periphery of the former Russian Empire and beyond, Comintern set up a special Eastern Division in 1919. A year later in Siberia, driven by the same goal, a seasoned and talented Bolshevik organizer, Boris Shumatsky, established a parallel structure, the Eastern Secretariat, to spearhead the Communist gospel in northern and Inner Asia. The Moscow and Siberian organizations soon merged.

Figure 5.1. Boris Shumatsky (standing, seventh from left), a polyglot Bolshevik organizer, with his indigenous fellow travelers who railroaded the Communist prophecy in Mongolia. Standing, third from left, is Elbek-Dorji Rinchino, the first Red dictator of Mongolia; c. 1921.

Shumatsky was the ideal man for this task. First of all, his revolutionary credentials were impeccable. Unlike many revolutionary leaders such as Lenin, Trotsky, Chicherin, and Bokii, who had middle-class and

bourgeois backgrounds, Shumatsky was a self-taught worker intellectual—a poster proletarian of Marxist propaganda. A railroad mechanic
by profession, he had inherited from his Jewish parents a love for books
and learning. He also spent many years in the Marxist underground,
printing revolutionary flyers, leading workers' strikes, and of course doing time in prison. His languages were his most important asset. Growing up in Siberia and rubbing shoulders with indigenous children in the
Trans-Baikal area, he learned to speak fluent Buryat in addition to his
home-spoken Yiddish and Russian. This frontier Bolshevik could easily
mingle with the Buryat and the closely related Mongols.

The first major attempt to rally Bolshevik sympathizers from the
Eastern periphery was made in 1921, when more than a thousand nationalist activists from Muslim and Buddhist areas were brought to Russia to listen to the gospel of revolution. Grigory Zinoviev, a demagogue
with a love for superlatives, worked up this crowd by calling for a holy
war against the British imperialism (which some of his listeners took
literally). Karl Radek, a Polish Jewish intellectual and Comintern leader,
invoked the spirit of Genghis Khan, inciting the Asian fellow travelers to storm into Europe and help cleanse it from capitalist mold. The
Comintern bosses excited their listeners to such an extent that many
of them began to shout, "We swear!" simultaneously brandishing their
sabers and revolvers.[6]

A brief romance of Red Russia with Tibetan Buddhism in the 1920s
was part of these efforts to woo Eastern masses to the Bolshevik side.
Historian Emanuel Sarkisyanz explored in detail how Bolsheviks linked
their prophecy to messianic expectations of the Eastern populace. He
was the first to note that, to anchor themselves in Tibetan Buddhist
areas, Red Russia and her indigenous allies plugged into such popular
local prophecies as Shambhala, Geser, Oirot, and Amursana. In fact, as
early as the 1920s, Alexandra David-Neel, the first Western woman to
go native Tibetan Buddhist, noted with amazement that bits and pieces of the faraway Bolshevik gospel had somehow trickled down into
Tibetan oral culture. Moreover, several lamas she talked to identified

Shambhala with Red Russia. They also argued that Geser Khan, an epic hero-redeemer from Tibetan, Mongolian, and Buryat folklore, was already reborn in Russia and ready for action.[7]

While persecuting Russian Orthodox Christianity, the major ideological enemy of the Bolsheviks, Lenin and his comrades did not at first assault Tibetan Buddhism, which was treated as a religion of formerly oppressed people. In August 1919, the Bolsheviks even sponsored an exhibition of Buddhist art, a revolutionary act that simultaneously attacked Christianity and reached out to Buddhists. Introducing the exhibit, Sergei Oldenburg, the chief administrator of Russian/Soviet humanities at that time, linked Tibetan Buddhism to Communism by saying that Buddha's teaching had promoted the brotherhood of nations and would certainly help advance the Communist cause in Asia.[8]

The chief spearhead of the dialogue between the Bolsheviks and Tibetan Buddhism was the Buryat monk Agvan Dorzhiev (1858–1938). At the very end of the nineteenth century, this prominent Buddhist served as the chief tutor of the thirteenth Dalai Lama, then a young adult. In the early 1900s, Dorzhiev became His Holiness's ambassador to the court of the Russian tsar. An ardent advocate of the unity of all Tibetan Buddhist people, Dorzhiev concluded that faraway Russia did not represent a threat to Tibet and could be easily manipulated against China and England to protect the sovereignty of the Forbidden Kingdom.

The Buryat lama began to spread word among his fellow believers and in the St. Petersburg court that the Russian Empire was destined to become the legendary northern Shambhala and that the Russia tsar was in fact the reincarnate Shambhala king who would come and save Tibetan Buddhists from advances by the Chinese and English. In his dreams, Dorzhiev began to picture a vast pan-Buddhist state under the protection of the tsar and stretching from Siberia to the Himalayas. Russian monarchs were certainly flattered by these divine references, but they were not too eager to extend their patronage so far southward in fear of antagonizing the English. When in the 1890s Emperor Alexander III read about the project of expanding Russian influence into

Figure 5.2. Agvan Dorzhiev in his Buddhist Kalachakra temple in St. Petersburg.

Inner Asia by using the Shambhala prophecy, he remarked in the margins, "All this is so new, so unusual and fantastic, that it is difficult to believe in its success."**9**

Moscow's Liberation Theology: Political Flirtation With Tibetan Buddhism

Unlike the tsars, the early Bolsheviks, who lived by the maxim "We are born to make a fairy tale into reality," never thought it was too fantastic to use popular lore to promote their agenda. So they eagerly plugged themselves into existing Buddhist prophecies, eventually benefiting from some of them. Red Russia inherited Dorzhiev from the old regime as the Tibetan ambassador and was glad to use him to reach out to the Tibetan Buddhist masses. Dorzhiev was at first equally enthusiastic about working with the Communists. Although later he became frustrated with them, for a short while in the early 1920s he tied his geopolitical dreams to the advancement of Red Russia's interests in Mongolia and Tibet.

This Buryat lama did not approve of the luxurious lifestyle and elitism of some of his fellow Buddhists and also hoped to use the advent of Communism to humble the rich and privileged in monastic communities. Driven by this noble goal, Dorzhiev launched a religious reform among the Buddhist clergy in Siberia, advertising it as a return to the original teaching of Buddha and as a way to maintain a dialogue with the Bolsheviks. In fact, he went quite far, trying to remodel Tibetan Buddhism in Russia according to Communist principles. The Buddhist congresses he organized to promote his reform split the faithful into progressives and conservatives. In progressive monasteries that accepted Dorzhiev's norms, all private possessions were confiscated and turned into collective assets. Clergy ranks were also eliminated, and all monks were obligated to perform productive labor. Instead of silk (a symbol of luxury), monks' robes were to be manufactured from simple fabric— an effort designed to draw the clergy closer to the masses. Moreover, to eradicate elitism followers of Dorzhiev dropped the veneration of monks who were considered reincarnations.[10] The chief goal, as Dorzhiev spelled out, was "to cleanse monasteries of all lazy bums and freeloaders, who have nothing to do with Buddha's teaching."[11]

Bolshevik authorities, particularly the secret police, welcomed these efforts, which in fact replicated the official reform movement the Bolsheviks themselves pursued in the 1920s in their relations with all denominations. Their long-term goal was to split Christians, Judaists, Muslims, and Buddhists into rival groups and gradually phase them out.[12] A lingering problem for the Bolsheviks working in Tibetan Buddhist areas was a chronic lack of literate people who they could use to do propaganda work and promote the Communist cause. Laboring folk—common nomads and shepherds—were certainly comrades through and through, but they were all too illiterate to be used as an intellectual resource. That was how the Bolsheviks and their fellow travelers decided to gamble on low-ranking monks, many of whom had at least an elementary education. Viewed by the Bolsheviks as oppressed by the elite of Buddhist monasteries, junior monks could be well incorporated into the Marxist scheme as wretched of the earth with a good revolutionary potential.

Given that the number of monks in the world of Tibetan Buddhism reached 30 percent of the male population, they were not a small force. One of Chicherin's diplomats, a future Soviet ambassador to Mongolia, once remarked, "This is a formidable force, and it is so formidable that even monks themselves do not quite realize it."[13] In all fairness, the Bolshevik strategy to woo low-ranking lamas to their side was not totally flawed. In Tibetan Buddhist monasteries people were not equal, and there was a large class of disgruntled monks whose discontent could grow if properly stimulated. There were rich monks who owned vast estates and cattle and lived in private cells, receiving better food. At the same time, most of the clergy remained humble temple servants throughout their lives, apprenticing with and serving the privileged ones.[14] If circumstances were right, the grudge some of these people might have harbored against their well-to-do brethren could be converted into a rebellion. In the 1920s, Bolsheviks successfully instigated such class warfare in Mongolia, where many low-ranking lamas empowered themselves by joining the ranks of revolutionary bureaucracy and then harassing the ones who stayed loyal to their monastic communities.

The Communist advance in Inner Asia was spearheaded by Bolshevik indigenous fellow travelers from the Buryat and Kalmyk, two Tibetan Buddhist groups residing within the former Russian Empire. The Buryat, an offshoot of the Mongols, lived in southern Siberia on the Russian-Mongolian border. The Kalmyk, splinters of the glorious Oirot nomadic confederation who escaped from Chinese genocide to Russia in the 1600s, settled northeast of the Caspian Sea in the area where Asia meets Europe. Many Buryat and Kalmyk lamas routinely apprenticed in Mongol and Tibetan monasteries and frequented Lhasa on religious pilgrimages. Since the 1700s, tsars incorporated many males from these two borderland groups into the ranks of the Cossacks. This paramilitary class was specially formed from former runaway Russian serfs and non-Russian nationalities residing on southern and eastern borders to protect the frontiers of the empire. Since most Kalmyk and Buryat spoke at least basic Russian, they served as convenient middlemen, building cultural bridges between Russia and the Buddhist populace of Inner Asia. In the early 1900s, several dozens of these indigenous folk were able to graduate from Russian universities, where they were injected with popular ideas of socialism, anarchism, Marxism, and Siberian autonomy.

Figure 5.3. Buryat pilgrims en route from Siberia to Mongolia. The Buryat, Tibetan Buddhist people from Siberia, were used by the Bolsheviks as middlemen to propagate the Communist liberation prophecy in Inner Asia.

In 1919, writer Anton Amur-Sanan and teacher Arashi Chapchaev, two Kalmyk intellectuals who joined the Bolshevik cause, wrote directly to Lenin suggesting their kinfolk be used to advance Communism among the "Mongol-Buddhist tribes." Particularly, they came up with an attractive project to send to the Tibetan-Indian border an armed Red Army cavalry unit staffed with Kalmyk disguised as Buddhist pilgrims. The goal was to raise havoc in the very backyard of British imperialism. Lenin was very enthusiastic about this idea but had to put it on hold because the unfolding Civil War temporarily cut European Russia off from Siberia and Inner Asia.[15] This cavalier scheme reflected well the revolutionary idealism of the early Bolsheviks, who aspired to liberate the whole earth and lived in expectation of global revolutionary Armageddon that would cleanse the world from the rich oppressors and transport the poor into an earthly paradise. In fact, the same year, Red Army commander-in-chief Trotsky suggested that a Red Army cavalry corps be formed in the Ural Mountains and thrown into India and Afghanistan against Britain. In the Bolsheviks' geopolitical plans, Central Asia and Tibetan Buddhist areas played an auxiliary role, designated to become highways to carry revolutionary ideas into India, crown jewel of English imperialism.

At the same time, despite their idealism, the Bolsheviks were apprehensive about building large anticolonial alliances involving people of the same religion and the same language family. It was one thing to call the Eastern folk to unite in a holy war against the West; it was a totally different thing to handle large and motley coalitions that could be easily hijacked by enemies and turned against Red Russia. This explained the Bolsheviks' uneasiness about and even fear of such supranational units as pan-Mongolism, pan-Turkism, and pan-Buddhism. While working to anchor themselves in Asia, they were ready to tolerate such coalitions for a short while as an unavoidable evil. But as a permanent solution they were totally unacceptable.

For example, when in 1923 Red leaders of Tuva suggested to the neighboring Oirot Autonomous Region in the Altai that they merge into a united Soviet republic, the Moscow authorities were furious.[16] Paranoid about the specter of pan-Turkism, they placed the Tuvan fellow travelers who initiated this scheme on the secret police close-watch list. The Bolshevik leaders were equally mad the following year when several Tuvan revolutionary leaders suggested they join Red Mongolia. After all, before the collapse of the Chinese Empire in 1911, Tuva was formally part of Mongolia. A similar paranoia about pan-Mongolism drove Khoren Petrosian, deputy chief of the Eastern Division of OGPU, to treat with suspicion the attempts of Red Mongols to enlarge their state—a project advocated by Elbek-Dorji Rinchino, a Buryat socialist intellectual who ruled Mongolia as a dictator on behalf of his Moscow patrons. In 1924, this Bolshevik fellow traveler with large revolutionary ambitions speculated that after his country became totally Communist it should absorb the Buryat in Siberia and merge into a larger Soviet republic, with Tibet to be added later, upon conquest. The ultimate result would be the emergence of a vast Mongol-Tibetan Communist state allied with Red Russia. Petrosian called this idea very dangerous, fearing that "reactionary forces in Buddhism" could easily use this large state against Red Russia.[17] Rinchino, who did admit that pan-Mongolism might be a double-edged sword, nevertheless stressed, "In our hands, the all-Mongol national idea could be a powerful and sharp revolutionary weapon. Under no circumstances are we going to surrender this weapon into the hands of Mongol feudal lords, Japanese militarists, and Russian bandits like Baron Ungern."[18]

Bolshevik Affirmative-Action Empire

Petrosian's concerns notwithstanding, grand and ambitious pan-Mongol and pan-Buddhist projects such as Rinchino's were flawed anyway. They were mostly products of indigenous intellectuals' mind games. Ordinary people did not care about them whatsoever, if they heard about them at all. After the fall of the Chinese and Russians empires, local and ethnic concerns were dearer to the hearts of the Mongols, Tibetans, Buryat, Tuvans, and Oirot. Not without difficulty, the Bolsheviks understood that and learned how to exploit this reality to their own benefit. But some Bolshevik fellow travelers and also their enemies simply could not get it. For example, fighting for "united and indivisible"

Russia, the White counterrevolutionaries opposing the Bolsheviks had no room for local ethnic and national sentiments of non-Russians and sought to suppress these feelings. In Siberia, the charismatic admiral Alexander Kolchak, who joined the White cause in 1918, crushed independence movements in the Altai Mountain and Trans-Baikal area by throwing their leaders into prison. Even in those rare instances, as in the case of Baron von Ungern-Sternberg, when the White cause temporarily matched that of indigenous people, the Whites did not tap local nationalisms as a resource. The same situation existed in China, where, in the aftermath of the revolution, local warlords fought against Mongol and Tibetan autonomies, trying to crush them and bring them back to China. Thus, in 1919, the Chinese reoccupied Mongolia and eliminated its sovereignty, which stirred the national liberation movement among the nomads.

In contrast, the Bolsheviks began to massage indigenous nationalism, not out of love for multiculturalism but out of necessity. After all, the Reds were cosmopolitan and urban people who dreamed about building a working people's paradise without borders, religions, and national loyalties. At the same time, they were a practical gang who knew well that if they wanted to succeed they had to bend temporarily to ethnic and national sentiments. Moreover, the Bolsheviks realized they could use these feelings to their own advantage. Nikolai Bukharin, a prominent Bolshevik theoretician in the 1920s, was very explicit about the opportunity presented by nationalism, which he called "water for our mill": "If we propose the solution of the right of self-determination for the colonies, the Hottentots, the Negroes, the Indians, etc., we lose nothing by it. On the contrary, we gain, for the national gain as a whole will damage foreign imperialism."[19]

On the Marxist evolutionary scale of human development, nationalism was an unavoidable evil that all people had to go through before they merged into a global commonwealth of brothers and sisters. The remedy that Lenin and his comrades offered to deal with this natural evil was not devoid of logic. If nationalist feelings were surfacing all over the world anyway, let these sentiments flourish and exhaust themselves on their own instead of fighting budding nations and nationalities, which would only make things worse. Let them enjoy their folk cultures and languages, and give them their own indigenous bosses to make people happy. The early Bolsheviks assumed that such lenient attitudes to nationalism would surely help to merge humans into a global cosmopolitan commonwealth—which they assumed was the natural direction the whole world was moving toward. In the 1920s, Joseph Stalin declared, "We are undertaking the maximum development of national culture, so that it will exhaust itself completely and thereby create the base for the organization of international socialist culture."[20] Ironically, as early as 1917 this would-be dictator, who would preside over one of the most brutal dictatorships in history, was put in charge of the People's Commissariat for Nationalities Affairs, a special bureaucratic structure created by the Bolsheviks to draw non-Russians to their side.

In this nationalities scheme of the early Bolsheviks, the Russian population, which was held responsible for the sins of the old tsarist empire, was expected to humble itself and make room for non-Russians to even the social playing field. Formerly disadvantaged nationalities were to receive resources and more participation in Communist bureaucracy, government, and education. Simultaneously, in order to empower the less fortunate ones, Marxist historians began to rewrite history, turning indigenous historical characters into heroes, while their Russian counterparts were recast as villains. That is how the famous Bolshevik "affirmative-action empire" was born. Besides the noble goal of making all nationalities equal, courting local nationalist sentiments was a very handy tool of control. Essentially, it boiled down to the good old principle, divide and rule. This explains why in the 1920s the Bolsheviks tried to create a number of autonomies with their own languages, cultures, and Communist elites. Even miniscule tribes of hunters and gatherers in Siberia, some numbering less than two thousand people, were entitled to their schools, languages, and indigenous bureaucrats.

In the 1920s, the Buryat, Kalmyk, Tuvans, Oirot, Mongols, and many other groups received their own autonomies under supervision of the Bolsheviks. In 1921, Red Russia recognized the sovereignty of Mongolia, which formally was still considered part of China. Then in 1923 the Buryat-Mongol Autonomous Soviet Republic was created in Siberia, thereby splitting the Buryat and Mongols apart and casting aside the pan-Mongol dream of building up a great state for all people of Mongol stock. Later, a similar tactic was applied to Tuva, which was made a separate state with its own written language and Bolshevik-friendly indigenous elite.[21] The assumption was that it was safer to grant Tuva nationhood under Russian supervision than to merge it with Red Mongolia. Overall, the nationalities polices were a great coup for the Bolsheviks. Even though this strategy later backfired—in the early 1930s Stalin realized that nationalism did not want to exhaust itself, and therefore he had to wipe out indigenous elites and mute the affirmative action—in the 1920s, it did allow the Bolsheviks to draw non-Russian nationalities to their side.

Against the Grain: White Baron von Ungern-Sternberg

The success the early Bolsheviks enjoyed in hijacking ethnic and national sentiments becomes visible if contrasted with the failure of the pan-Asian project advocated by Baron von Ungern-Sternberg, a White general with occult leanings who briefly ruled Mongolia in 1920–21. Too much has been written both in English and Russian about this colorful baron and his sadistic deeds for me to go over it again here.[22] What is more interesting to explore is why he was initially so stunningly successful in winning over Mongolia and then failed so miserably by losing it in a few months.

The collapse of the imperial dynasty in Russia in 1917 and the advent of Communism was a personal tragedy for this psychotic Cossack platoon leader. His whole world was turned upside down. Like many of his Baltic German countrymen who were part of the old Russian imperial

Figure 5.4. "Mad Baron" Roman von Ungern-Sternberg, an occultist and runaway White Russian warlord from Siberia who briefly took over Mongolia in 1920–21.

elite, he felt uprooted, blaming international financiers, Jews, and Bolsheviks for all his troubles. From then on, Ungern would devote his life to eradicating these evils and to bringing monarchy back. For him, only kings and emperors were capable of providing order and stability. All other forms of government were unequivocally wicked and immoral.

In the beginning of the Civil War between Red Bolsheviks and White counterrevolutionaries, Ungern rose as a powerful warlord in the Far East, controlling a leg of the Trans-Siberian railroad. In charge of a wild bunch of more than six hundred Russian and Buryat Cossacks, drifters, and bandits, who tenderly called him "Grandpa," Ungern robbed passing trains, murdered Bolsheviks, and sabotaged supply lines of White colleagues he considered too liberal. By the end of 1920, when his fortunes were at low ebb, Ungern was fleeing southward from the advancing Red Army. Searching for a sanctuary, his hungry and freezing Asian Cavalry Division rolled into Mongolia. For him, this nomadic

Figure 5.5. Ragtag members of Ungern's Asian Cavalry Division.

country was a natural choice: by this time, he had become totally disgusted with the corrupt West and had fallen in love with Asia: "I am firmly convinced that the light comes from the East, where people are not yet spoiled by the West and where in a holy manner the foundations of goodness and honor, which were granted to us by Heaven, are still preserved untouched."[23] Ungern dreamed that from the heart of Asia, uncorrupted by modern life, he would advance westward, restoring monarchies all over Eurasia, first in China, then in Russia, and finally going farther to Central Europe.

In the meantime, taking advantage of the chaos caused by the 1917 Russian Revolution, Chinese warlord general Hsü Shu-cheng (Little Hsü) recaptured Mongolia, taking away the sovereignty the Mongols had enjoyed since 1913. In Urga, the Mongol capitol, Chinese troops drafted from the dregs of society lived by marauding the local population. The Bogdo-gegen, leader of Mongol-Tibetan Buddhists, was put under house arrest and publicly humiliated, and religious festivals were disrupted. The descendants of Genghis Khan came to hate the Chinese and were a gunpowder keg ready to explode.[24]

Into this explosive world rode Ungern with his hungry and freezing gang, eager to seize Chinese food supplies and ammunition. Storming into Mongolia, Ungern pledged to liberate it from the Chinese, and at first nomads cheered him as a redeemer who, as if by magic, descended upon them from the north, captured Urga, and squashed the despised aliens. The baron was pleased to observe how his cavalry unit became swollen with Mongol volunteers who flocked to join him.

The grateful Bogdo-gegen granted Ungern the title of Prince, and monks declared him a manifestation of Mahakala, one of the ferocious deities that protected the Buddhist faith. The clerics also interpreted Ungern's victory over the Chinese as the fulfillment of the Shambhala prophecy. Later, after the baron's demise, the Bolsheviks uncovered among his personal papers a Russian translation of a Tibetan text containing the Shambhala prophecy.[25] Ungern, who was always interested in occult things, gladly embraced his role as a legendary redeemer,

Figure 5.6. The eighth Bogdo-gegen, leader of Mongol-Tibetan Buddhists and head of the Mongol state from 1911 to 1924. Although considered a reincarnation of the great Tibetan scholar Taranatha, he was a heavy drinker and notorious womanizer, which seemed not to match his past life.

trying to act in an appropriate manner. He began wearing a long red-and-blue silk Mongol robe over his Russian officer uniform. In this outfit, with the Order of St. George received for his daring deeds during World War I and numerous Tibetan Buddhist amulets hanging on his chest, this descendant of Teutonic knights produced quite an impression on all who ran across him.

So Mongol independence was won. What was next? That was when the baron got into serious trouble and eventually lost the country. As it turned out, Ungern had nothing to offer the nomads, who wanted to see him not only as protector of the faith, but also as guardian of their national independence. First of all, the Mongols were greatly dismayed with the magnitude of the brutalities he committed. This is not to say that his nomadic colleagues acted nobly: the Mongols could be quite ruthless and brutal to their enemies. Yet some of Ungern's cruelties seemed too bizarre, excessive, and unnecessary; his nomadic allies could not understand why he punished his own officers by putting them on ice, burning them alive, or feeding them to wild beasts.

What especially puzzled the nomads was his pathological hatred of the "black Russians," the Mongols' expression for Jews. They could accept the massacre of some Chinese prisoners, enemies of their country and faith, but it was hard for them to rationalize the butchering of Jews, with whom the nomads never had any problems. There were not many of them in Urga anyway, no more than one hundred people, yet Ungern specially targeted all of them for annihilation. Before storming Urga, the baron gathered his officers and gave them an explicit order: "Upon taking Urga, all Jews should be destroyed, I mean slaughtered."[26] Back in Europe, budding German national socialists inspired by Alfred Rosenberg, a fellow Baltic-German expatriate, would have certainly applauded these words. Yet such scapegoating customized exclusively for the Europeans who were eager to build up their anger and hatred did not make any sense on the vast plains of Mongolia. In hindsight, Ungern would have made a better "national socialist" case by milking Mongol dislike of local Chinese merchants and the Chinese in general. Still, despite this opportunity, the baron was hopelessly trapped in the web of his European phobias, which he was determined to live by in Mongolia. It was certainly not the type of behavior the local people expected from Mahakala. In fact, some of them began to question Ungern's sanity.

However, this pathological anti-Semitism was not so much what alienated Ungern's nomadic allies. What really upset them was the future he envisioned for Mongols. After handing over power to the Bogdo-gegen, the baron began to pursue his most cherished dream—restoring monarchies. He would begin by resurrecting the Manchu dynasty that had controlled China along with Mongolia and Tibet for centuries before it was toppled by the 1911 revolution. Then he would proceed to Russia, bringing back the Romanovs' dynasty, and farther into Central Europe, restoring the Hapsburgs and their German cousins. As his short-term goal, Ungern set out to build a vast pan-Asian empire under the Manchu dynasty that would unite all people of Mongol stock, from China to Kazakhstan and from Mongolia to Tibet. It was hard to imagine a more senseless act than asking the Mongols who had just won their independence from the Chinese to go back under the Manchu-Chinese yoke.

Although he had some knowledge of the Mongols' culture, memorized several phrases in their language, and acquired at least a superficial knowledge of Tibetan Buddhism, Ungern did not grasp a simple thing: the nomads were craving independence. They were interested neither in building up a grand pan-Mongol state nor in restoring the Chinese Empire. Yet the eyes of the baron, with his medieval reverence for monarchies, remained blind. The borders he drew were between monarchs and their subjects, not between ethnic groups and nations. With his mind set in the glorious feudal past, Ungern could not comprehend what the Bolsheviks already grasped: the power of modern nationalism. That is why he lost Mongolia. The baron's faith in the divine power of kings and his obsession with feudal order, knighthood, and honor put him in the traditionalist camp—a motley group of like-minded contemporary Europeans who lamented the bygone aristocratic legacy and looked toward the Orient for inspiration.

General M. G. Tornovsky, one of Ungern's former officers, explained well why the Mongols gave up on Ungern so easily and switched to Red Russia: "The world of Buddhism will not say a good word about General Ungern. He was not committed to the Mongol national cause, being involved in correspondence with Chinese generals and aristocrats, trying to plot something with them. The Mongols could not forgive this and betrayed him. They realized that for General Ungern, Mongolia was not the goal but the tool to pursue his own goals, which were alien to the Mongols."[27]

Unaware that he was setting himself up for failure, Ungern wrote letters to various Mongol princes, chiefs of the Kazakhs in Soviet Central Asia, Muslims in western China, and even the Dalai Lama, asking them to join his grand enterprise of restoring the Chinese Middle

Kingdom.[28] Nobody replied to his messages, and the attempt to build up multinational coalition forces miserably failed. Even his clumsy attempt to invoke the Mongols' love for prophecies was so shallow and so Eurocentric that it did not resonate at all with the traditional oral culture of the nomads, let alone inspire them. Here is a revealing passage from his address to the Mongols:

> Not many people know the essence and principles of the Red Party but many believe in them. This is a secret Jewish party created three thousand years ago specially to seize power in all countries, and its goals are now being fulfilled. All European states secretly or openly followed this party, only Japan remains free now. Our god, who hears the torments and sufferings of people, guides us to crush the head of this poisonous snake. This must happen in the third month of this winter. This prophecy had been given more than two thousand years ago. So the Mongol people do not have to wait for too long.[29]

In desperation and losing the support of his Mongol hosts, Ungern decided to quickly boost his prestige through a military victory over the Red Russians in the summer of 1921. His plan was to thrust suddenly into Siberia and raise local Russians and indigenous folk against the Bolsheviks. Still, as always, Ungern could not overcome his virulent phobias. Before his suicidal leap into the Bolshevik trap, the baron released his notorious Order No. 15. This morbid flyer offered the Siberian populace only the familiar calls: restore monarchy and "murder all Communists, commissars, and Jews along with their families."[30] Refusing to fight for an alien cause on alien soil, his Mongol allies quickly deserted Ungern and scattered. In Siberia, nobody wanted to join him either. As a result, the Red Army quickly crushed his anti-Bolshevik crusade, and in June 1921 the baron found himself captured by a Red guerilla unit.

Ungern's Bolshevik opponents sincerely wondered why he disregarded a force as powerful and visible as nationalism. When Shumatsky, the Comintern boss in Siberia who personally interrogated the White general, asked him how on earth he planned to reconcile his support of Mongol independence with an alliance with Chinese monarchists, the baron frankly responded: "I did not think about the sovereignty of Mongolia, and talked about her independence in another sense, treating it simply as a slogan. I thought of the future fate of Mongolia only as subject of the Manchu khan."[31] The Bolsheviks brought the failed Mahakala to public trial in Siberia and counted a big propaganda coup: his brutal actions and medieval political philosophy helped the Bolsheviks compromise the entire White cause. Condemned to death, the Bloody Baron, who never cared about anybody's life including his own, calmly and with no visible emotions exposed the back of his head to the gun of a Bolshevik secret police officer.

Two kinds of medicinal herbs grow on the mountains there. One, called tu-janaya, is very sweet and has sharp thorns, leaves like the teeth of a battle-ax, and red flowers the color of sunset. It always grows on rocks that face toward the south.

—Taranatha, description of a route to Shambhala

In concealment lies a great part of our strength. For this reason we must cover ourselves in the name of another society. Do you realize sufficiently what it means to rule—to rule in a secret society? Not only over the more important of the populace, but over the best men, over men of all races, nations and religions.

—Adam Weishaupt, founder of the Illuminati, 1770s

Six

Red Prophecy on the March:
Mongolia to Tibet

O n October 29, 1920, in Irkutsk, Southern Siberia, in a thick cloud of cheap tobacco smoke in a spacious downtown house, a group of young people, mostly former students in their twenties, was making a revolution. The house, recently confiscated from a rich lady merchant, accommodated the headquarters of the Siberian branch of the Bolshevik Party, which set aside a few rooms for its Eastern Secretariat, a bureaucratic structure affiliated with Comintern. The secretariat was a motley crowd of Jewish, native Siberian, and Russian revolutionaries working to incite the Asian masses to revolt against colonial oppression and then to turn them toward Communism.

For the whole day, the group had been struggling to figure out how to bring Communism to Mongolia. They wanted to make sure the Mongol nomads themselves took an active part in the enterprise, knowing all too well they could not just impose their secular ideology on that country. Fortunately, there was a good opportunity to rally the nomads around the Bolshevik cause. Mongolia was occupied by Chinese troops, and the runaway White general Roman von Ungern-Sternberg threatened an invasion. So first the revolutionaries would help the nomads liberate Mongolia. Then they would link their cause to the religion of Buddha to reach out to illiterate shepherds and lamas, and bring this backward country into the golden age of Communism.

Like many other revolutionaries, those present liked to talk, dreaming aloud about how they would build the commonwealth of free toilers of the Orient. The talks went on and on; it was getting dark, and they could not come to a conclusion of what would be a better option: to storm into Mongolia right away before Ungern took it over or to wait and see when the nomads were ripe for a revolt.

It was time to wrap up the debates. Naum Burtman, a dropout student who had just returned from a reconnaissance trip to Mongolia and was chairing the meeting, had to interrupt one speaker after another. He was nervously playing with an empty pistol, tossing it like a top. At least everybody agreed that the liberation of the country should be done with as much Mongol involvement as possible. That was the key to success.

The most flamboyant speaker, who dominated the podium, was Sergei Borisov, a leader of the secretariat's Mongol-Tibetan Section. This

Figure 6.1. Sergei Borisov, head of the Mongol-Tibetan Section of Comintern. In 1925, disguised as a Tibetan Buddhist monk, he ventured into Tibet, trying to woo the thirteenth Dalai Lama to Red Russia's side.

intelligent tough-looking man with Asiatic features was the son of a famous Christian missionary priest, Stephan Borisov. He had come from the Altai, land of the Oirot, to study at Irkutsk Teachers College. Yet, like many of his comrades, he quickly caught the revolutionary fever and dropped out, devoting his life to bringing paradise on earth to the common people. Now, dressed in a workingman's blouse, Borisov, whose incipient baldness made him look older than his peers, insisted that they should immediately send Red Army troops to storm Mongolia before the counterrevolutionary Ungern snatched it.

Finally, around midnight, Burtman stepped in: "I ask all present to ask questions. Any questions? No questions. Do we consider it necessary to send the troops? Everybody agrees with the stipulation. Who is against it? Nobody. I suggest that Comrade Borisov, who came up with this idea in the first place, outline clearly the best way to bring the troops to Mongolia." Borisov explained that the invasion was to be presented as an indigenous Mongolian project and that the Mongols were to be an essential part. To accomplish this goal, the secretariat agreed to set up a Mongolian autonomous government and to mute for a while all talk about Communism, focusing instead on national liberation. Burtman again stepped in and finalized the debate in a high-pitched voice: "Thus, we all agree it is necessary to establish a provisional government from influential Mongols even though they are nationalists."[1]

Bolshevik Plans for Red Mongolia

In 1920 when the Reds were freely advancing through Siberia, finishing off pockets of the crumbling White resistance, the revolutionary frenzy among the Bolsheviks was so high that they were ready to roll immediately beyond Russian borders to liberate all Oriental people. The Eastern Secretariat set up by Boris Shumatsky and his Bolshevik brethren was the product of this revolutionary idealism. Soon this impromptu project of Siberian Bolsheviks was merged with Comintern and began to receive orders from Moscow. Four sections established within the new bureaucratic structure—Korean, Japanese, Chinese, and Mongol-Tibetan—were entrusted with igniting revolutionary fires in their respective regions.

The guidelines of the Mongol-Tibetan Section were clear: radicalizing the Mongol-Tibetan masses, extending the influence of Soviet Russia on those masses, and involving them in the struggle in Asia with world imperialism. Yet the same guidelines prescribed that the section's agents take into consideration cultures and traditions of the area. Because social and class sentiments were still dormant in these remote areas, Communism was not an immediate item on the Bolshevik agenda; Comintern agents were instructed to play on nationalism. The first task was hijacking national liberation movements to help oppressed nationalities win their freedom, to educate them, and to build up their industries. Only then would it be possible to turn the populace toward Communism.

The short-term goal for Mongolia was to "master ideologically the national movement of the Mongol popular masses, safeguarding and cleansing it of harmful layers that might shadow its social side." Muting their Communist zeal and restricting themselves to the national liberation of the Mongols from the Chinese and White Russians, Comintern agents were not to antagonize Mongol princes and especially lamas. Only when the country was free would Bolshevik fellow travelers step in and empower themselves by rallying common people and simultaneously phasing out princes and rich lamas. In the meantime, agents of the Mongol-Tibetan Section were to travel all over Mongolia and Tibet, educating people about the revolutionary prophecy from the north, building the network of Comintern cells, and recruiting new adepts.[2]

Elbek-Dorji Rinchino and Borisov, who ran this section, were socialists, but first of all they were ardent nationalists who dreamed about the liberation of their own people. When they realized that the Reds were winning and were promising self-determination for indigenous people, they cast their lot with the Bolsheviks and evolved from loyal fellow travelers into full-fledged revolutionaries. Rinchino, a Buryat intellectual with a law degree from St. Petersburg University, dreamed of uniting the Buryat and Mongols, who spoke similar languages and shared a similar culture, into a vast pan-Mongol socialist republic that would be a beacon for all Buddhists. In fact, he was the one who had created the Mongol-Tibetan Section, bringing along his friend Borisov. Rinchino would become the first Red dictator of Mongolia, and Borisov, who joined the Bolshevik Party in 1920, became deputy chair of the Eastern Section of Chicherin's Commissariat for Foreign Affairs.

The third leading member of the section, and the only one with hands-on knowledge of Tibetan Buddhism, was Choibalsan, deputy chair of the section and the only leading Mongol in Comintern at that time. As someone who knew how to read and write Mongol and could also speak Russian, this plump twenty-five-year-old was an excellent middleman and a great asset to the Bolshevik cause. Along with his partner Sukhe-Bator, Choibalsan was responsible for propaganda and publishing and was working closely with Rinchino and Borisov to recruit nomads to Red Russia's side.

Choibalsan had apprenticed to a lama as a teenager but tired of the drudgery of monastery life and escaped into the wider world, wandering into Urga, capital of Mongolia. There, by chance, a few compassionate Russians noticed his skill for languages and had him enrolled in the school for interpreters. The youth did not waste this opportunity and worked hard, and he was then sent to the Siberian city of Irkutsk to continue his education. Between 1914 and 1917 in Irkutsk, Choibalsan rubbed shoulders with Leftist students and eventually became close to them. By 1920 he was one of the two most important Mongol revolutionaries. The other was his friend Sukhe-Bator, a flamboyant show-off military man who was banding the nomads into an organized army and liked to pose for Russian photographers artistically holding a cigarette in his long fingers or sitting erect on his horse like an aristocrat observing his warriors from above.

Figure 6.2. Sukhe-Bator, a prominent Bolshevik fellow traveler in Mongolia, 1921.

Choibalsan did not do such foolish things, preferring to stay in the shadows. He still had things to learn from his Buryat, Jewish, and Russian comrades and would rather listen than talk. The modesty played well. His more flamboyant comrades felt it safe to make him a member of the Eastern Secretariat and deputy chief of the Mongol-Tibetan Section, which gave him the pleasant sense of a mission.[3] The former apprentice lama still had a hard time processing what his educated friends Borisov and Rinchino called socialism and Communism, and he could not yet digest some of the books they were reading. But he firmly grasped one simple truth: he was destined to help liberate his country from the hated Chinese and the Whites and then bring a new golden age of prosperity. Surely it would be a fulfillment of the glorious Shambhala prophecy that his monastery tutor had told him so much about. This was enough for now to empower Choibalsan. The details of what Lenin and Marx had to say about this new golden age he could learn later.

The union between the Mongol nationalists and Red Russians was formally consummated in August 1920 when Rinchino brought his friends Sukhe-Bator, Choibalsan, Danzan, Bodo, and several other men to Irkutsk to meet the chief Siberian Bolsheviks, Boris Shumatsky and Phillip Gapon. With Shumatsky as their chaperon, the nomadic revolutionaries then boarded a train to Moscow, where Lenin, Commissar for Foreign Affairs Georgy Chicherin, and other Bolshevik dignitaries welcomed them, promising to back up their nationalism and to deliver arms and ammunition. The visitors were pleasantly surprised when Chicherin greeted them wearing a traditional Mongol robe. These Bolsheviks surely could be good allies!

It was shortly after this that the young Bolshevik revolutionaries in Irkutsk, at Borisov's instigation, voted to send Red troops into Mongolia. In the meantime, Rinchino and several other Comintern agents were already in the field contacting discontented Mongol nomads and lamas. When everything was set up for a quick invasion and liberation of Mongolia, Shumatsky, as head of the Eastern Secretariat and the man who called the shots for Siberian Bolsheviks, changed everything.

Figure 6.3. Commissar for Foreign Affairs Georgy Chicherin (r.), who worked hard to woo Asians to the Bolshevik side, is shown wearing a Mongol robe during a reception for Mongol delegates.

Returning from Moscow, he ordered the revolutionary young Turks to hold on. Everyone was surprised. How could he leave Mongolia defenseless when Ungern, the mad White baron, was ready to roll into and take over the country? Wait and see, was Shumatsky's answer. This turned out to be a brilliant strategy. Shumatsky correctly assumed that by fighting each other Ungern's Whites and the Chinese would weaken themselves, and Mongolia would fall into the hands of Red Russia like a ripe fruit. His plan would work better than he expected.

Ungern's suicidal plans to restore the Chinese monarchy and to drag Mongolia into a war with Bolshevik Russia soon alienated the Mongols, and they turned away from the White general. The Bolsheviks quickly jumped in to encourage Mongol nationalism and help get rid of the "homeless Russians," the name the nomads gave to the émigré White Russians. In the meantime, Mongol soldiers who originally sided with the baron began to talk openly about switching sides and joining the Red Mongols. Bodo, Choibalsan, Danzan, Sukhe-Bator, and twenty other radical nationalists who had already been attracted to the message of national and social liberation coming from Moscow gathered in the borderland town of Kiahta. There, groomed by Borisov, Rinchino, and other Comintern agents, they were able to raise a small army of five hundred nomadic warriors. This indigenous detachment, the nucleus of the future Red Mongol army, embodied the Comintern strategy of "using Mongol national feelings for the defense of Mongol independence under the flag of a Mongol army." To give additional stimulus to the revolutionary spirit of this ragtag crowd of shepherds, drifters, and junior lamas, Borisov gave them food, warm underwear, and tobacco.[4] Simultaneously, assisted by Choibalsan and Sukhe-Bator, he worked hard to organize those who had at least some elementary education into the Mongol People's Revolutionary Party (MPRP). Beefed up by Buryat and Kalmyk revolutionaries imported from Siberia, MPRP was to become a Comintern tentacle ensuring that the nomadic masses were moving in the correct direction.

The Bolsheviks' plans proceeded smoothly. The Red Mongols' efforts received a handy theological backup when, at the end of 1920, Gutembe, a prominent lama oracle, conveniently went into a trance and came up with a prophecy that the Mongol state needed urgent help from outside. Comintern folk became so excited that they dispatched three Mongol agents to confirm the prophecy and to secure its power for the Red cause. Gutembe turned out to be very helpful, informing the visiting revolutionaries that just before their arrival one of the avenging gods had entered his body, told him how rotten the present state of society was, and also issued guidelines. As a special favor for the Red Mongols, the oracle went into trance again to ask the god more questions. Lighting his oil lamp and incense, reciting a ritual text, and brandishing a sword, he began raving and foaming from the mouth. After an assistant poured a glass of vodka into his mouth, the oracle relaxed a little and assured the Red Mongols that soon they would succeed.[5]

Meanwhile, Borisov was moving back and forth cementing and equipping the Red Mongols gathering on the Russian-Mongolian border ready for action. In 1921, the operational budget of the Mongol-Tibetan Section, which became the headquarters of the Mongol revolution, reached $112,000 Mexican dollars.[6] Of this amount, the bulk ($100,000) was spent to acquire weapons and supplies for the Mongol revolution. Borisov himself delivered much of this cargo in a caravan that reached the border in February of 1921. In addition, the Oirot revolutionary officially set aside $6,000 for bribes to be paid to various Mongol and Chinese headmen to smooth field trips of Comintern agents through Mongolia. Borisov neatly called it a special "engagement and counterintelligence fund" for "materials payments and gifts to people who are not yet revolutionized by our propaganda."[7] Bringing the Red Shambhala kingdom to Mongolia was not a cheap business.

The Triumph of Red Shambhala in Mongolia

On June 22, 1921, when Ungern was defeated and captured, the small Mongol army, beefed up by Buryats and Kalmyks, was already marching deep into Mongol territory. The arrival of the Red Mongol troops in Urga on July 7, 1921, was announced by the piercing sounds of trumpeters marching in front, blowing into traditional Buddhist shells. The trumpeters were followed by the Mongol cavalry in two lines. The squadron on the left rode with a red banner, while the one on the right carried a yellow banner. To nomadic revolutionaries the whole scene was very symbolic. The red banner stood for the rivers of blood they spilled in the cause of national liberation, which would eventually lead people to the "golden age kingdom," symbolized by the yellow.[8] The ceremony culminated in the ritual sacrifice of a White officer named Filimonov, chief of Ungern's counterintelligence service, to one of the avenging god-protectors of the Buddhist faith. His blood was used to smear the banners of the Red Mongols—an ancient ritual to appease the wrathful gods and secure new victories.[9]

The Shambhala army was coming again from the north, just as the legend said. Only now it was Red Shambhala. It was now time to engage old prophecies. Choibalsan, Sukhe-Bator, and rank-and-file Red Mongols were happy to portray the victory as a triumph of the prophetic Shambhala kingdom. In fact, when the five hundred nomadic warriors were waiting on the Russian-Mongolian border before the attack, they put together a song, "The War of Northern Shambhala," calling Mongol soldiers to rise up in a holy war against aliens, particularly the Chinese. One of the lines went, "Let us all die in this war and be reborn as warriors of Shambhala."[10] The nomadic warriors were convinced that if they participated in the sacred war they would be able to liberate themselves from samsara (the cycle of reincarnations) and end up in the happy Shambhala dreamland.

Figure 6.4. "Red lama" commissar of new Mongolia with his scribe, 1928. Note the sacred tanka scroll in the background with the face of Lenin, which replaced Maitreya and other Buddhist deities in the new Mongol iconography.

In the early 1920s, not only Shambhala but the entire Buddhist faith and existing prophecies were used by the Red Mongols to entrench themselves among the populace. For a while, Communism linked to Buddhism was advertized as some sort of Bolshevik liberation theology customized for common shepherds and lamas. Until at least 1928, Choibalsan, Rinchino, Sukhe-Bator, and their comrades deliberately tied their political and social reforms to messianic and prophetic sentiments popular among Inner Asian nomads.[11] Moreover, the political system of Red Mongolia briefly became a strange hybrid of Communism and Buddhism. In this Red theocracy, the Bogdo-gegen acted as the formal head of the country, while the government was run by Bolshevik fellow travelers, many of whom themselves came from the ranks of Buddhist clerics.

A major headache for the new Red Mongol regime was that the western part of their country was only loosely connected to Urga. There the notorious Ja-Lama, who had returned to "his people" in 1917 from his exile in Russia, was still running wild and free. The Avenging Lama and self-proclaimed grandson of the legendary Amursana had gotten a second wind. Ja-Lama held up a rich caravan of fifty Tibetan traders loaded with gold and silver, which gave him startup capital to build

Figure 6.5. Remains of Ja-Lama's magnificent fortress in the Gobi Desert, 1928.

another fiefdom and to lure supporters.[12] Soon with a small army of three hundred warriors, he settled in a desert area conveniently located near a trading route on the border between Inner and Outer Mongolia. Following his totalitarian dreams, Ja-Lama was turning this area into an orderly desert oasis, using slave labor of prisoners captured during his raids to erect a magnificent fortress. Canals and wells were dug, and aqueducts built. A group of Chinese prisoners tended opium fields, one of Ja-Lama's major sources of revenue.

At first Shumatsky, Borisov, and Rinchino had high hopes for Ja-Lama and thought about making him a guerrilla commander who could help them finish off pockets of White resistance. At one point, the Mongol-Tibetan Section sought "to establish urgently a formal connection with the partisan movement of western Mongolia by sending Dambi-Dzhamtsyn [Ja-Lama] a responsible representative of the [Mongol] people's party, who would steer this movement ideologically in a correct direction."[13] The Bolsheviks even offered the "lama with a gun" the official title of a national leader, Commander of Western Mongol Revolutionary Forces, and sent symbolic gifts: a Russian military cap and two small hand grenades.[14] Yet the reincarnation of Amursana was not a fool. As a former Russian subject who had rubbed shoulders with Marxist revolutionaries during his Siberian exile, he could easily figure out the Bolsheviks' true intentions. Besides, obsessed with a totalitarian dream of his own, Ja-Lama did not want to share power with anybody. His plan was to set up a large modern theocracy that would unite the Altai, western Mongolia, and western China—areas that had composed the glorious seventeenth-century Oirot confederation. So Ja-Lama flatly rejected the advances of Comintern agents.

Despite all his experience and cunning, the ruthless lama did not know how devious and imaginative his opponents could be. Unable to tame the unfriendly reincarnation, Shumatsky, Borisov, and their Mongol comrades decided to beat "Amursana" on his own spiritual ground by making up their own reincarnation in order to split Ja-Lama's flock and confuse local nomads. For the role of Red Amursana, the Bolsheviks picked Has Bator, a young lama priest and new convert to the Red Mongol cause, who, after a short training and indoctrination in Irkutsk, was sent to western Mongolia with two dozen Comintern agents and one thousand Red Mongol and Buryat troops. The goal of this "military-political expedition," as Shumatsky labeled it, was to put local anti-White and anti-Chinese guerrilla units under the Comintern wing.[15]

Bolsheviks and their Mongol fellow travelers initiated a sophisticated game of image making to bill Has Bator as the new and better reincarnation. They made him three luxurious felt tents decorated inside with antique weapons. Simultaneously, word was spread that the real Amursana had finally come from his northern land. Part of the game was creating an aura of mystery around the newly anointed one. Every day Red Amursana received mysterious packages from somewhere.[16] Several nomadic communities embraced this message and left Ja-Lama for Has Bator. Unfortunately, the new Amursana was not able to live up fully to Bolshevik expectations, lacking the courage to play his part well in a life-or-death situation. At one point, surrounded by a renegade band of cutthroat Whites, he lost his nerve, literally peed in his pants, and deserted his comrades by escaping into the fields, where the counterrevolutionaries quickly caught and shot him. The Whites chopped off the head of the poor revolutionary reincarnation and carried it around as proof that the Red pretender was destroyed.

The person who helped finish Ja-Lama was his own comrade-in-arms Hatan Bator (Hard Hero) Magsarjav (1878–1927). Ja-Lama and Hard Hero fought the Chinese together in 1913. Later General Magsarjav aided the Red Mongols to such an extent that they named him secretary of war in the new revolutionary Mongolia, which eventually secured him a spot in the pantheon of Mongol Communist heroes. What made the newly minted revolutionary general a dangerous opponent of Ja-Lama was that he was an oracle endowed with large spiritual power of his own. Hard Hero frequently went into a trance, predicting the dates and outcomes of his battles. Magsarjav was believed to be invincible to his enemies, and like his former friend Ja-Lama, he did not miss a chance to "prove" it. After a military clash, Magsarjav could be seen pulling from inside his robe a bullet or two that had "hit" him and was still warm. Like other oracles, during his trances Magsarjav merged with avenging Buddhist deities, building up his anger to fight enemies of the faith and nation. Besides, Hard Hero was equally ruthless and did not shy away from chopping off the heads and ripping open the chests of his opponents, whose blood he used to smear revolutionary banners.[17]

The Bolsheviks did not want to waste their time storming the totalitarian paradise erected by Ja-Lama. In 1923, the OGPU secret police along with State Internal Protection (GVO), its sister organization in Mongolia headed by Khaian Khirva, developed a special operation to dispose of Ja-Lama once and for all. Acting as religious pilgrims, a Mongol secret police agent named Nanzan, along with two other Red "lamas" went to Ja-Lama's headquarters to receive blessings. While talking to Ja-Lama, Nanzan suddenly pulled out a revolver and shot him point-blank a few times in the head. Like many others Mongols, the agent was under the impression that Amursana might somehow be invincible to bullets, so to make sure the notorious lama was finished, with trembling hands Nanzan emptied his Colt into Ja-Lama's neck and chest, severing his head.

The sudden execution of Ja-Lama so stunned and demoralized his flock that nobody offered any resistance, and the secret police pilgrims triumphantly left the compound carrying the head. Nanzan dropped it into a bucket filled with vodka for preservation and carried it to one of the major towns in western Mongolia, where it was placed on a lance at a central plaza to prove the famous Ja-Lama was finally gone. The new masters explained to the local populace that the new Red order in Mongolia was a fulfillment of the old Amursana prophecy.

In other parts of the country, Bolshevik fellow travelers similarly milked other epic tales and legends. "But of greatest appeal was the promise of achieving an earthly utopia with the aid of an apocalyptic army from the unearthly realm of Shambhala," as historian Larry Moses reminds us.[18]

Bolsheviks at the Gates of Lhasa

The romantic expectations of the coming worldwide revolutionary holocaust and their stunning success in Mongolia inspired the Bolsheviks to roll on southward to Tibet and farther to storm the Himalayan heights on the way to India. So Tibet was the next item on their agenda. Ideally, the goal was to replay in the Forbidden Kingdom the Mongol scenario: find a national liberation cause to latch onto, use existing prophecies, build up revolutionary cells, and stir the indigenous folk to rebel against an oppressor. In Mongolia, the oppressors were the Whites and Chinese merchants. In Tibet, the major candidate for this role was to be England.

In their revolutionary geopolitics, the early Bolsheviks never separated Siberia and Mongolia from the rest of Inner Asia. In their dreams, a map of the entire area was soon to be painted red. Chicherin, Commissar for Foreign Affairs, envisioned Mongolia as "a solid jumping ground in the advancement of revolutionary ideas to Tibet and India."[19] In this game of setting Inner Asia on fire, Sergei Borisov was again destined to become one of the major players. By 1921, senior Bolshevik comrades noticed the zeal of this Oirot fellow traveler, made him a member of their party, and, on top of this, awarded him a position of consultant at Chicherin's commissariat.

In fact, Tibet and her environs were already on the Bolshevik agenda as early as the fall of 1920, before Ungern stormed into Mongolia. The guidelines set by Comintern for the Mongol-Tibetan Section directed its agents "to gather data about the situation in Tibet and her relations with China and England, political sentiments, armed forces, and the extension of foreign influence." Comintern agents were also instructed "to find among Tibetans who live in Mongolia, particularly in Urga, persons who by their political convictions can be used by the section as interpreters both in Irkutsk and in Urga, and also be sent to Tibet for propaganda work." The next set of guidelines issued two weeks later instructed the agents to "urgently establish connections with Tibet" and to "urgently find among Tibetans who live in Mongolia" qualified people for propaganda work.[20] The Bolsheviks clearly shared a naive belief that all Tibetan Buddhist areas would soon fall easily into their hands.

Although the Bolsheviks were still working to secure their victory in Mongolia, Chicherin, Shumatsky, and Borisov were already contemplating a reconnaissance expedition to Tibet in the summer of 1921. In early July, amid information about progress in Mongolia and the capture of Ungern, Shumatsky reported in a secret cable to Chicherin and Meer Trilisser (then a Comintern boss, later chief of the foreign intelligence branch of OGPU): "We are now thinking about the best route for the expedition and gathering all necessary gear. As far as the machine gun is concerned, do not send it. I will get it here. If I receive all the items I requested from you, the Tibetan expedition will depart no later than August 1."[21] The most important item, which Shumatsky and Borisov were impatiently awaiting, was a wireless radio set they planned to leave with the Dalai Lama to set up a direct line of communication between Lhasa and Moscow. Two young Kalmyk revolutionaries, who were undergoing a crash radio course, were expected to stay and operate the device in Lhasa.

Yet the expedition had to be postponed because the silver set aside for the Tibetan venture was spent for urgent Mongolian needs. A few more months passed before Shumatsky raised new funds to get the project going. Finally the radio set arrived in Irkutsk, and the polyglot Bolshevik cabled Chicherin: "The radio transmitter has been received. I easily delivered it here by myself. Please make sure that those chaps who study radio and cable communication in Moscow know how this particular model works in order to be able to start it right away upon arrival in Tibet."[22] The former Dalai Lama tutor Agvan Dorzhiev, who was with Shumatsky and Borisov all this time, whetted the Bolsheviks'

Tibetan appetites, trying to sell them his cherished project of uniting all Tibetan Buddhists into a large theocratic state under Red Russia's protection.

But Tibet turned out to be a tough nut. It was not so easy to crack as Mongolia, and the Dalai Lama was not as submissive as the Bogdo-gegen. The Bolsheviks operated under a false impression that in Tibet they could easily milk the English threat, stretching out their helping hand and drawing the populace to their side. Unfortunately, the hated English imperialists did not even want to take over Tibet, preferring instead to keep it as a buffer between India and Russia-China. It took Moscow three expeditions to realize that there was no imminent threat to Tibet from England and that the Dalai Lama was simply a shrewd diplomat who skillfully played China, Russia, and England against one another without allowing any of them to get a foothold in his country. Given the traditional isolation of the Forbidden Kingdom, it was not hard for the Lhasa ruler to pursue this policy. After all, still in effect was the 1870s' decree, "If somebody penetrates our country, whoever he is, all possessions of this person shall be confiscated, and he shall be sewed into a skin bag and thrown into a river."[23] Even though the Dalai Lama used some knowledge of the English to make his nation a bit more modern, he always kept them at bay.

To reach out to Tibet, the Reds used two approaches. First, they tried to lure the Dalai Lama to their side. Second, they wanted to identify within the Tibetan populace discontented groups they could incite to ignite a revolutionary holocaust. First and foremost, the Bolsheviks needed reliable information about Tibet, which still remained terra incognita for Moscow revolutionaries. From Dorzhiev, Shumatsky found out that one of the secretaries of the Dalai Lama was a Kalmyk monk named Sharap Tepkin. This prompted Shumatsky, with some hesitation, to chose Vasilii Khomutnikov, a Red Army cavalry officer of Kalmyk origin who had fought against the Whites during the Civil War and then helped the Red Mongols build up their army, to lead the first mission to Lhasa. Although he was crude and could barely write, he was loyal to the cause and, most important, was a Kalmyk, which the Bolsheviks expected would ease access to the Lhasa ruler.

On September 13, 1921, Khomutnikov, with nine Kalmyk and Buryat comrades, traveled as part of a caravan of "peaceful" Mongol pilgrims and merchants, carrying fifteen hundred rifles, one million cartridges, machine guns, and grenades. This impressive arsenal had been seized from the bloody Baron Ungern. On top of this, using expedition funds, Khomutnikov continued to purchase rifles from local people en route. As a military man, he might have reasoned that soon his comrades would need all these weapons to bring revolution to the Himalayan kingdom. Alarmed by such hazardous cargo, Tibetan border guards blocked the pilgrims on the border, but a reference letter from Dorzhiev to the Dalai Lama unlocked the doors. Once in Lhasa, Khomutnikov did not hide his Bolshevik identity and openly tried to sway the Dalai Lama to his side. Yet, despite generous gifts of silverware, a golden clock, and a mysterious talking machine (the wireless radio), the Lhasa ruler was apprehensive about the cavalier advances of the Red emissary and did not want to take sides. Only after Khomutnikov repeatedly assured the Dalai Lama that the Bolsheviks respected Buddhism did he warm a bit and even asked the Moscow visitor for Red Russia to send military instructors and to help organize the manufacturing of gunpowder. (Creating a well-equipped modern army was a major concern of the Dalai Lama.) Khomutnikov answered that his government would be happy to accommodate the military needs of the Lhasa ruler. Still, the cautious Dalai Lama wanted to have more time to think this over, so it was decided to talk further about military cooperation as well as about establishing diplomatic relations during a second expedition from Soviet Russia to Tibet. Khomutnikov also received permission to look around, and he talked with several people from the government and with monks, some of whom expressed strong anti-English feelings. Encouraged by these talks and by the Dalai Lama's promises, the Bolshevik ambassador, who spent almost three weeks in Lhasa, left the Tibetan capital on April 9, 1922.

CHAPTER SIX

Comintern Agent Borisov Becomes a Lama Pilgrim

The Bolsheviks' hopes for Tibet rose in 1924 when they learned about clashes between reformers (a military faction) who favored England and conservative lamas who resisted modernization. Chicherin and Borisov saw this as the beginning of a class war in the Himalayan kingdom between the pro-English "capitalist" faction and "progressive" clergy. So it was time to send a second mission to find out what was going on in Tibet and to try again to win over the Dalai Lama. Borisov, now done with his job of turning Mongolia Red, could devote himself to Tibetan matters.

To smooth this new Lhasa mission, the atheist Borisov was to act like an influential Buryat lama pilgrim on a mission to reach out to His Holiness on behalf of both his Siberian brethren and the Soviet government. Updating the Soviet elite about the coming expedition, Commissar for Foreign Affairs Chicherin stressed, "Comrade Borisov and his travel companions will conduct this expedition in the capacity of religious pilgrims."[24] Besides Borisov and a few other fake lamas, the party was filled out with several genuine Buddhist pilgrims to make the masquerade more credible. The whole Buddhist showmanship was intended to hide Red Russia's advances into Inner Asia. A year earlier, aggressive efforts of the Bolsheviks to push the revolutionary tide to the Indian border had prompted the English government to threaten Moscow with shutting down all trade with Red Russia. In response, the Bolsheviks, hungry for Western technology and goods, promised to mute their revolutionary zeal.

In 1927, two years after his trip to Lhasa, Borisov revealed the details of this second Tibetan venture in a talk at the Communist University of the Toilers of the East (KUTV), which trained revolutionary activists for Eastern countries. Shumatsky, who headed this university in 1926–27, invited his old comrade-in-arms to share his experiences. Borisov stressed that, besides his attempts to draw the Dalai Lama to the Bolsheviks' side, he tried to court monks from several large monasteries that openly challenged Lhasa's modernization efforts. It was not a totally flawed strategy. Aside from the Panchen Lama's Tashilumpho, the hub of separatism that numbered four thousand monks, there were three other major monasteries, Drepung, Sero, and Ganden, that did not want to pay taxes either and hated to lose their privileged status. This conservative priesthood refused to cooperate with the Lhasa government, pointing out to His Holiness that universal taxation, the army reform, and the opening of an English school and a power station went against traditional Buddhism.[25]

Borisov found this monastery-grounded opposition very useful for the Bolsheviks: "Some of these heretical spiritual movements sometimes move as far as rejecting the holiness of the Dalai Lama. These lingering sentiments always existed, and monks are very susceptible to them." Under these circumstances, continued the Red Oirot, "the only thing that remains to be done is to make sure these sentiments move in an appropriate direction, become organized, and develop along revolutionary lines."[26] Borisov believed that planting revolutionary cells among junior-rank lamas was the way to organize them. In fact, he attempted to wiggle into the Drepung monastery, which had a large Buryat-Kalmyk colony with pro-Russian sentiments. The plan was to turn the monastery into a base for future Bolshevik operations.

The Borisov expedition left the Mongol capital at the end of January 1924 and after a long six-month trip finally reached Lhasa. Despite their Buddhist disguise, English intelligence agents quickly spotted and figured out the Red pilgrims through their own Kalmyk agents. After Khomutnikov's cavalier attempt to sway the Dalai Lama to the Bolsheviks' side, the English had become paranoid and started to monitor visitors coming from Red Mongolia. The person assigned to ward off Red pilgrims from this area was British intelligence agent Lt. Colonel Frederick Bailey, Political Officer in Sikkim from 1921 to 1928. The man was perfectly cut for this type of job. A fluent speaker of Tibetan and basic Russian, he was a born explorer and a daring adventurer. Among his hobbies were mountain climbing and butterfly collecting. In fact, he immortalized his name by discovering during his Asian ventures a few unknown specimens of butterflies. All in all, Bailey was a classical gentleman spy of the Victorian Age. A seasoned shadow warrior, he had already rubbed shoulders with his Moscow opponents, penetrating Russian Central Asia right after the 1917 revolution to find out what was going on in the Bolsheviks' backyard. Bailey did not restrict himself to gathering intelligence, but also took part in organizing White resistance to the Reds. At one point, playing with fire, through a trusted contact he was even able to get taken on as an agent for the Bolshevik secret police and was sent on a clandestine mission to Bukhara, a Muslim fiefdom challenging the Bolsheviks. One of his assignments was searching for the whereabouts of the English spy Bailey![27]

Like his predecessor, upon arrival in Lhasa Borisov showered the Dalai Lama with various gifts: porcelain vases, golden cups, silver plates, and many other items. Although Tibetan authorities realized those in the party were not true Buddhist pilgrims, they let the visitors wander around, take hundreds of pictures, and film military installations, gun workshops, communications, and other strategic places. The Dalai Lama did not mind playing the Russian card for a short while to tease his English neighbors a bit. He even called these "pilgrims" harmless. Worried about such a reckless attitude, Bailey worked hard, trying to use his intelligence information to wake up the Lhasa ruler to the danger. But the Dalai Lama had his own game to play. He received the Bolshevik ambassadors, smiled at them, assured his friendship, and gave numerous promises, but he did not bind himself by any agreement establishing military ties, as the Red Russians hoped. Thus, despite his long stay in Lhasa and persistent attempts to tie His Holiness to Moscow, Borisov returned to Moscow empty-handed in May of 1925.

It was obvious that the Dalai Lama's sympathy for Soviet Russia and the revolutionary potential of the Forbidden Kingdom were the Bolsheviks' wishful thinking. His Holiness, who never trusted the Red Russians, simply used them as a counterbalance to British and Chinese advances. Strange as it may sound, some in Moscow continued to believe in the

Dalai Lama's friendly disposition to the very end of the 1920s. In a 1928 memo the chief of the Eastern Department of the OGPU secret police still insisted that the "masses of Tibetan population" and their ruler looked favorably at Russia and Mongolia.[28]

"Mongol Embassy" to Lhasa and Cold Reception

In 1925, the Dalai Lama dismissed his war secretary, Tsarong Shape, head of the pro-English military faction, and several of his associates whom His Holiness suspected of plotting a conspiracy. This gave the Bolsheviks a second wind, and they were ready to continue their Tibetan advances. Chicherin optimistically predicted "the defeat of the Anglophile clique" and hoped that this time the Soviets would sway the Lhasa ruler to their side. To take advantage of the favorable political situation, a third mission would be sent to Tibet. Chicherin did not want to procrastinate with this project. The timing was too good to be missed: "An uprising has erupted in Tibet against the Anglophile clique which seized all power in the country. If we don't hurry up, some more developments might take place, so that Britain, by means of bribes and by attracting the material interests of the [Tibetans], can usurp power again."[29]

Learning from the previous experience of poor disguises, Chicherin and Borisov wanted to play it safe, keeping Red Russia out of the picture. Now, instead of playing Buddhist pilgrims from Siberia, the Bolsheviks were to become a Mongol religious mission sent to establish an embassy in Lhasa and discuss an important theological issue. The plan was to obtain Lhasa's permission to open a Mongol embassy, which the Bolsheviks could later use to organize a shipment of military hardware and to gradually hijack the Tibetan army by infiltrating it with loyal Kalmyk, Buryat, and Mongol advisors.

To lead this 1927 expedition, Chicherin and Borisov chose Arashi Chapchaev (1890–1938), a Kalmyk schoolteacher and recent graduate of the three-year Marxist program at the Communist Academy. Soviet dictator Joseph Stalin personally approved this choice. Since the Kalmyk

Bolshevik was an educator, he would pose as a Buddhist teacher under the assumed name Tsepag Dorji. Dressed in a red robe, he was to travel with his lama apprentice—the role assigned to another Kalmyk Bolshevik, Matstak Bimbaev. The party, which numbered fifteen people, included several other "Mongols," among them Jigme-Dorji Barduev, a Buryat lama priest who had taken part in the Borisov expedition, and Shagdur Landukov, a Kalmyk military advisor to the Mongol Red Army. At the same time, a few genuine Red Mongol fellow travelers with a good knowledge of Tibetan Buddhism were added to make the mission more credible.

A formal cover for the Mongol embassy was found in the important theological issue of recognizing a new reincarnation of the Bogdo-gegen, head of the Mongol-Tibetan Buddhists. When the old Bogdo had died from old age and numerous ailments in 1924, the Red Mongols and their Moscow patrons immediately sensed that this was a perfect occasion to end the Buddhist theocracy in Mongolia and replace it with a normal Red dictatorship. They forbade the search for a new reincarnation: lamas and the nomadic populace were surprised to find out that the deceased reincarnation was to be the last. The Red Mongols explained that Bogdo was now reborn as a great general in Shambhala, and there was no point in searching for a new reincarnation since henceforth Bogdo's permanent abode would be this magic kingdom, not the earthly realm.[30] Shrewd Red Mongols like Rinchino were not convinced their magic trick would work. Not wishing to completely antagonize the populace and the large number of lamas, they suggested an option to resolve the issue. Because all Bogdo's earlier reincarnations were traditionally found in Tibet and approved by the Dalai Lama, they would go to Lhasa and discuss this important matter with His Holiness. The Mongol embassy delegation headed by Chapchaev pursued this theological scheme when they arrived in Lhasa in April 1927. When the flattered Dalai Lama, who did not care much anyway about his junior counterpart (the deceased Bogdo had lived a rowdy life as a heavy drinker and womanizer), seemed to welcome this plan, the Bolsheviks thought they might kill two birds with one stone: pacifying Buddhist clerics in Mongolia and simultaneously receiving another chance to get a foothold in the Forbidden Kingdom.

The Lhasa ruler expected genuine religious pilgrims but, to his dismay, found out from his own sources and from Bailey that this group of pilgrims armed with twenty rifles and two Lewis machine guns were not even Mongols but once again Bolsheviks from Russia. Infuriated, the Dalai Lama at first refused to give Chapchaev a formal reception. The Red pilgrims were kept under constant surveillance and could not even relieve themselves without being watched. All their movements were now monitored by a double spy ring: the Dalai Lama's agents and Bailey's Kalmyk and Tibetan spies.

The situation was even worse than with the Borisov party. It did not help that the atheist Chapchaev and his friends were particularly lousy actors. Lhasa monks noticed that the visitors had a hard time following tedious Buddhist rituals.[31] Yet it was not entirely bad acting that showed up their Mongol disguise. One of them, Gomojitshin, a Buryat from Siberia working for the Mongol Department of Foreign Affairs, began having doubts about the Red cause. Disgusted with their pathetic Buddhist masquerade, he solicited and received a secret private audience with the Dalai Lama, during which he revealed the covert goals of the embassy.[32]

To make things worse, the most devastating and unexpected blow to the Bolshevik scheme was leveled by Dorzhiev, the Tibetan ambassador to Russia, whom both Chicherin and OGPU considered a loyal Bolshevik fellow traveler. By the mid-1920s, this old lama with sad eyes who dreamed about a vast Buddhist theocracy under Soviet protection had become increasingly frustrated with the Bolsheviks. For a short while, he had allied himself with them, hoping Communism could help return Buddhism to its original roots. Yet quite soon Dorzhiev saw that his faith did not gain anything from this alliance. Tibetan Buddhism in Russia was on the decline, and Bolshevik authorities in Siberia constantly harassed his brethren. Realizing that the Bolsheviks were simply using him to split the Buddhist community in Russia, the old monk started a double game. While still pretending to be loyal to the Bolsheviks, Dorzhiev secretly decided to do everything to safeguard his fellow believers in Tibet from Soviet advances.

In his formal letter introducing Chapchaev, Dorzhiev praised Russia and Mongolia for their treatment of Buddhists and asked the Dalai Lama to give the "Mongol pilgrims" the best treatment. Yet simultaneously, through a trusted merchant, he smuggled to His Holiness another letter in which he wrote: "I am an old man and will die very soon. Mongolia is not a peaceful country as it was formerly. The government is deadly against religions and monks, and they are helpless. Please don't have anything to do with the mission. I had to write a letter at their dictation to Your Holiness for these Bolshevik agents to take with them, but please do not take any notice of that letter."[33]

Although the Dalai Lama was angry, he did not dismiss Chapchaev and his company right away but, as always, played a good diplomat. After all, he did not want to endanger the large Tibetan community in Mongolia. Besides, the Lhasa ruler still held a large amount of money in the Mongol central bank and did not want to lose it. Still refusing to receive Chapchaev, the Dalai Lama nevertheless allowed the visitors to wander around, gather intelligence, and socialize with local Mongol and Buryat monks. Yet all their movements were monitored. Finally, the Mongol diplomats were permitted to have an audience with His Holiness. But in exchange for this favor, as the stunned visitors learned, they were to promise to leave Lhasa immediately after they finished their talk.

During this meeting, the Lhasa ruler played his favorite game of expressing friendship without promising anything. Trade between Mongolia and Tibet? Sure, let us trade; we might buy Mongol horses, they will be good for our cavalry. We Tibetans might even want to buy gunpowder from you. Opening a permanent Mongol mission in Lhasa? We would like to do it, but England, which does not have an embassy either, might be mad. Let us continue talking about it, and we will see. Chapchaev tried this and that, but he was not able to accomplish the major goal of the expedition—opening a permanent Mongol embassy.

At the same time, the Dalai Lama repeatedly shifted the conversation to the conditions of Buddhists in Siberia and Mongolia, surprising the Bolshevik visitors with his detailed knowledge of the situation. Chapchaev sensed that somebody had filled in His Holiness very well. Yet he never could figure out who.

Thus, the Bolshevik plan to tie Tibet to Red Russia through Mongolia completely fell through. Red pilgrims again had to leave Lhasa empty-handed. If they still had some expectations about the Dalai Lama before coming to Lhasa, now they realized that His Holiness could not be duped, played, or manipulated. The Lhasa ruler did not feel at all that his budding nation needed Russian, or for that matter English or Chinese, presence.

In December 1927, two months before the humiliated Chapchaev and his "Mongols" departed from Tibet, a messenger brought to Lhasa unpleasant news from the governor at Nagchu on the northern border: another group of pilgrims coming from Mongolia was about to enter the country. Not again, Lhasa officials might have thought in desperation. Yet there was something odd about this new party, which stood out among real and false pilgrims coming from Siberia and Mongolia. The head of the party, a sage-looking man with a trim beard, insisted that he and his European friends were Buddhists from the West. They also traveled under a strange flag covered with stars and stripes and called themselves Americans. Still, trusted people reported to His Holiness that the man in charge was a Russian. The Dalai Lama was also surprised to hear that this strange expedition carried another flag, a familiar sacred scroll with an image of Buddha Maitreya. The sage-looking man insisted that he and his people came to consummate the union between Western and Eastern Buddhists under His Holiness's leadership.

Who was this man? Whom was he working for? Was he a genuine ambassador or, like these recent Red Mongol visitors, a wolf in sheep's clothing? Welcome to the world of Nicholas Roerich, Shambhala warrior and one more pilgrim on a mission to unlock the Forbidden Kingdom.

Make no little plans, they have no power to stir men's souls.
—Daniel Burnham, American architect

Seven

The Great Plan:
Nicholas and Helena Roerich

On December 26, 1923, in eastern Tibet, one hundred heavily armed Buddhist monks, hidden in the morning fog, saddled their horses and quickly galloped northward away from Tashilumpho monastery, heading toward Mongolia. In the middle of the crowd, shielded on all sides by his bodyguards and followers, rode the ninth Panchen Lama (1883–1937), abbot of the monastery and the spiritual leader of Tibet. He was running for his life from the wrath of the Dalai Lama. In the eyes of Lhasa, the Panchen Lama, who ruled as a powerful local lord and refused to pay taxes, was a dangerous separatist defying the efforts of His Holiness to turn Tibet into a modern nation-state. The officer sent to chase the fleeing party was quite fond of the mild and friendly abbot and did not rush to fulfill his assignment. Pretending to be ill, he camped with his detachment for two days, and when the pursuit was renewed, it was too late: the Panchen Lama was far ahead of his pursuers, deep in Chinese Mongolia beyond the reach of the Dalai Lama. The runaway abbot settled into a self-imposed exile near the border with Red Mongolia.

After the Panchen Lama's escape, a prophecy spread throughout Inner Asia that the runaway abbot would come back to Tibet as the king of Shambhala and punish evildoers. The Panchen Lama's own grim predictions added to the general excitement:

The time has already arrived when it is rather difficult to escape such terrible sufferings. Dead bodies will fill the ravines and channels and rivers of blood will flow. Even if there will be roads, there will be no one to walk along them. Even if there will be yurts, there will be no one to live in them. Even if there will be clothes, there will be no one to wear them. Remember that the supreme nobles will be exterminated by diseases, and also the lower poor ones will be troubled by illness. Rich and poor will be equal. Only good ones and evil ones will be distinguished.[1]

The flight of the Panchen Lama stirred diplomatic and spy games that involved England, Japan, China, and Red Russia. Surprisingly, each, for its own reasons, wanted the Panchen Lama back in Tibet. China had plans to use him as a puppet to keep the Land of Snows in its orbit and disrupt nation-building in Tibet. Britain wanted to reconcile the runaway abbot with the Dalai Lama to make Tibet into a nation that would serve as a buffer between British India and Red Russia and China. The Bolsheviks were wary of the Panchen Lama hanging around the borders of Red Mongolia, where he enjoyed skyrocketing popularity and could present an ideological challenge to the sprouts of Communism. Added to this was a slim hope that he might be used to help the Bolsheviks get a foot into the Forbidden Kingdom. Finally, Japan, a latecomer to this game, wanted to use the Panchen Lama and his Shambhala war to squeeze the Chinese out of Inner Asia.

In the same fall of 1923, a peculiar, sage-looking European appeared in Darjeeling in the northernmost part of India near the Tibetan border. A plump man with a round face and a small Mongol-styled beard, he moved and talked like a high dignitary. He announced that he was a painter, and, indeed, from time to time people could see him here and there with a sketchbook, drawing local landscapes. Yet, even for an eccentric painter, he acted strangely. To begin with, he argued that he was an American, although he spoke English with a heavy Slavic accent. He also demonstrated a deep interest in Tibetan Buddhism, particularly in the Maitreya and Shambhala legends, which was not unusual—except that the painter had a ceremonial Dalai Lama robe made for himself and donned it occasionally, hinting he was the reincarnated fifth Dalai Lama, the famous reformer in early modern times. His behavior raised the eyebrows of local authorities, who passed this information along to the British intelligence service.

As strange as it might sound, the "sage" did strike a chord with some local Tibetan Buddhists, for several visiting lamas did recognized him as the reincarnated Dalai Lama by the moles on his cheeks. At that time, no one except several close relatives and disciples of the painter knew that he had a grand plan, which included dislodging the Dalai Lama, bringing the Panchen Lama back to Tibet, reforming Tibetan Buddhism, and establishing in the vast spaces of Inner Asia a new theocracy, which he planned to call the Sacred Union of the East. He saw the flight of the Panchen Lama as an occult signal of the coming Shambhala war that would bring to the world the new golden age of Maitreya. The name of this ambitious dreamer was Nicholas Roerich.

Education of a Practical Idealist

Roerich, who liked to call himself a practical idealist, came from a family with Baltic German roots on the paternal side; his father was a notary and his mother, a Russian, came from the ranks of city burghers. Nicholas had three siblings: an elder sister and two younger brothers. Since early childhood, his great passion was archaeology. As a nine-year-old, Roerich already took part in archaeological digs. This love for the past, legends, and fairy tales would remain with him for the rest of his life, and from the beginning he took legends and prophecies seriously, considering them reflections of actual events.

Another of Roerich's passions was art, for which he had a great talent. By 1917, he was already a famous and accomplished painter, working in the Art Nouveau style and portraying spiritual scenes, gradually shifting from Slavic primitivism to Oriental mysticism. Favorite subjects were various Buddhist and Hindu mythological characters depicted against mountain landscapes of blue, purple, yellow, and orange.[2] Many contemporaries noted one characteristic that united his canvases—they were cold and solemn. Devoid of emotion, Roerich's images were reminiscent of spiritual messages. A fellow painter and colleague described his art thus: "The world of Roerich represents a fairy tale clad in stone. He spreads colors on his paintings firmly like a mosaic. The forms of his art do not breathe and have no emotions at all. They are eternal like the rocks of cliffs and caves."[3] Roerich himself explained that his goal was to capture and depict the ideal forms of life and therefore he liked to paint from his head rather than from his heart.

In 1901 Roerich met and married his soul mate, Helena Shaposhnikova, the daughter of a famous St. Petersburg architect. It was a happy marriage: Helena and Nicholas were not only a couple but also fellow dreamers, which contributed to Roerich's conversion to the life of a spiritual seeker. They would share all their spiritual and geopolitical adventures. Their two sons, George and Svetoslav, who were made part of their Great Plan, later became scholars, explorers, and painters. The only troubles were the horrible headaches and fits that haunted Helena, the results of two serious head traumas. One was received during her childhood and another in adulthood when she fell on her head from an upper bunk in a train compartment. After the second trauma, Helena began to have visions of fire and flames that consumed her entire body. Another serious damage to her health might have been caused by prenatal trauma suffered when her mother had unsuccessfully tried to abort her.[4]

Everything changed when Helena reinterpreted those fits as an invitation to converse with otherworldly forces. Such an approach was unusual during that time when Freudian psychiatry was becoming a cultural fad and such things were treated as illness. Helena later claimed that a message came from her otherworldly teacher informing her that the fits were the result of the discovery of new energy centers in her body and that the work of these centers was what produced the excruciating pains.[5] The fire and flames she saw inside herself accompanied by visions and voices became the manifestation of Agni Yoga (Fire Yoga), a spiritual system the couple later worked into a new creed after they moved to the United States in 1921.

As soon as she converted her sickness into spiritual experiences, Helena's life became a bit easier. Now the headaches, horrific images, and visions that continued to haunt her became messages from otherworldly spiritual teachers. Moreover, Helena soon learned to put herself intentionally into a trancelike mood in order to receive information from the "other side." The other side was two spiritual masters who represented the Great White Brotherhood hidden in the Himalayas—spiritual baggage Helena borrowed from the famous Helena Blavatsky, founder of Theosophy. Just as in the case of Blavatsky, Helena Roerich's hidden masters were Hindu men who first appeared to her in London's Hyde Park. Eventually, the spiritual masters who visited Helena began to appear to Nicholas as well.

From early on, Nicholas Roerich nourished grand dreams. The painter was convinced that he was predestined for a great role in life. In fact, he never tried to hide his self-importance: "I have a big ego. Although this sometimes gives me moments of difficulty, I am glad that I have much of it. Like a good whip, my ego makes me move forward fast. Without such a source of energy I would not be able to accomplish many things."[6] Since childhood, Roerich was also fond of playing roles of imagined persons, usually great historical and mythological personalities. Eventually this habit became his second nature. His round face, pink cheeks, well-groomed hair, and small beard seemed like a mask that could be cast aside in an instant and replaced by another one.

This ability to wear different masks later helped him play different roles and cultivate useful people. The mysterious Roerich skillfully penetrated different spheres, including the court of the tsar. Smart, cunning, and polite, he knew well when and how to flatter and be courteous. His approach was usually very simple: "Make friends with a person" and "listen to him and let him speak." This talent in captivating useful people not only brought him many contacts and riches, but also enabled him to pursue his utopian projects. In fact, in their relations with people, Nicholas and Helena never thought in terms of emotions and friendship. The world was strictly divided into those who were useful and those who were useless. The people who surrounded them were just pawns in their schemes. Such an approach was natural, for the couple was not concerned about individuals—their goal was to bless all of humankind. Thus, one of their closest associates, Frances Grant, was a "good instrument." Rich and powerful philanthropists from New York, Washington, and Chicago were "useful for the future." Even the painter's own brother Vladimir was put on this grading scale: he would "be useful in our work."[7]

In 1909, another important event in Roerich's life aroused his interest in Tibetan Buddhism and triggered his quest for Shambhala. A group of Tibetan Buddhists in St. Petersburg headed by Agvan Dorzhiev, the Buryat Buddhist monk and envoy of the Dalai Lama to the Russian court, received Tsar Nicholas II's blessing to erect a Tibetan Buddhist temple in the Russian capital. Backed by bohemian spiritual seekers and cultural dignitaries fond of Theosophy and Buddhism, Dorzhiev was able to convince the tsar (who was prone to mysticism) that it would be good for both spiritual and geopolitical reasons. Playing on Russian-English rivalry in Asia in hopes of shielding Tibetan sovereignty from English and Chinese advances, the Dalai Lama's ambassador told the tsar that inhabitants of the Forbidden Kingdom viewed the Russian emperor as the king of northern Shambhala who would protect their country from the aliens' intrusions.

Roerich eagerly joined the project, designing stained glass for the temple. The painter also became fascinated with Dorzhiev's stories about Shambhala, the mysterious Buddhist paradise somewhere in the north. No less captivating was the Buryat lama's dream of bringing all Tibetan Buddhist people together in a united state under the protection of the Russian tsar. Roerich and the "learned Buryat lama," as the painter referred to Dorzhiev, had many cohorts among Russian intellectuals and aristocrats, whose cultural life was saturated with the occult. The early twentieth century in Russia was the time of the so-called

Silver Age—an incredible resurgence of humanities, music, art, and esotericism. Even some Marxists, to Lenin's dismay, paid tribute to this cultural renaissance, openly pondering how to elevate humans to the status of gods and how to turn communism into the religion of a new age. In St. Petersburg and Moscow salons, people were talking about the end of the Enlightenment era and its rationalism, turning away from Western civilization to the Orient. Theosophy, the first modern countercultural spirituality, which at that time was heavily loaded with Hinduism and Tibetan Buddhism, flourished among Russian people of arts and letters.

At the end of 1916, just on the eve of the Bolshevik takeover, Roerich and his family, as if sensing which way the wind would be blowing, conveniently left St. Petersburg and settled in a quiet summer cottage amid pine woods in Finland, away from the coming revolutionary storm. This turned out to be a very smart decision, allowing the Roeriches to avoid the bloodiest period in Russian history: the Communist Revolution of October 1917, mob attacks on "bourgeois" intellectuals, and the brutalities of so-called War Communism imposed by the Bolsheviks on Russia. This lack of hands-on experience with the "joys of Communism" might explain why later it became so easy for the couple to make friends with Red Russia.

Soon, invited by a rich admirer to exhibit Nicholas's paintings in London, the Roeriches moved to England. Here they could forget about everything and continue their Silver-Age lifestyle, joining the Theosophical Society and frequenting occult and spiritualist salons. In 1919, replicating experiences of her famous predecessor Helena Blavatsky, Helena Roerich had her spiritual breakthrough: in London's Hyde Park she "met" her Himalayan spiritual masters (mahatmas), named Morya and Khut-Humi. Later, Khut-Humi somehow dropped out, and the couple dealt only with Morya, who became their spiritual guide for the rest of their lives.

Although the Roeriches were able to rub shoulders with fellow spiritual seekers in England, they were not happy in London. Helena and

Nicholas wanted something bigger than just being a minuscule part of a large Theosophical crowd. There was no room for them to spread their wings to become spiritual teachers. The great occult celebrity Peter Ouspensky far overshadowed the newly arrived couple with budding mystical aspirations. Just across the English Channel in France, the flamboyant George Gurdjieff was a magnet drawing European seekers to his spiritual school. Even in the world of painting, Nicholas Roerich was relegated to a secondary role in the shadow of such European giants as fellow émigrés Wassily Kandinsky and Kazimir Malevich. Helena and Nicholas, who liked to compare themselves with Prometheus, could not stomach such a situation. Like this ancient Greek hero, they dreamed about storming heights, stealing fire to bring it to people.

For a while they played with the idea of moving to India and making that country a staging ground for their worldwide spiritual mission. In fact, they had already made contact with the famous Hindu writer and philosopher Rabindranath Tagore, who promised them "light, space and quietness, but not dollars." Yet the Indian option was swiftly cast aside. In one of her letters, Helena made a sarcastic remark about this offer: one could find such "treasures" in any desert.[8] The couple did need money and fame, and in this respect America sounded far more appealing. Again, like their prominent predecessor Blavatsky, they chose to move to New York City. Morya, the newly acquired spiritual guide from the Himalayas, backed up this decision. Before embarking overseas, Roerich confided to one of his friends: "He guides me and my family. Now he has given me a new assignment—to instill spirituality into American art and to establish an art school there named after the Masters."[9]

Soon after arriving in America in October 1920, the Roeriches pioneered their teaching, an offshoot of Theosophy called Agni Yoga that invoked fire, the recurrent image from Helena's visions and a symbol of destruction and creation. At the center of Agni Yoga was the idea of reincarnation, giving people the opportunity to improve and raise themselves to the level of the divine beings in the Himalayan Great White Brotherhood. These masters, who included Morya, guided humankind in its spiritual development and from time to time sent out sages to speed up this spiritual evolution. Of course, Helena and Nicholas were thinking about themselves as these sages-messengers sent to enlighten humankind. In his *Shambhala* (1930), the painter hinted about their historical mission: "Verily, verily, the people of Shambhala at times emerge into the world. They meet the earthly co-workers of Shambhala. For the sake of humanity, they send out precious gifts, remarkable relics. I can tell you many stories of how wonderful gifts were received through space. Even Rigden-jyepo [Rigden-Djapo, king of Shambhala] himself appears at times in human body. Suddenly he shows himself in holy places, in monasteries, and at time predestinated, pronounces his prophecies."[10]

Communication with the brotherhood was conducted through Morya, who began to issue detailed instructions regarding all aspects of the Roeriches' lives, from their political preferences to family matters. To get in touch with the master, Helena entered a trancelike state and recorded her messages by automatic writing, a technique popular among contemporary spiritualists. Although not blessed with divine headaches, Nicholas nevertheless learned how to get in touch with Morya, and from time to time he contacted the master, relying only on automatic writing. Turning his head aside and covering his eyes with the palm of one hand, the painter usually "talked" with Morya while simultaneously writing down the messages from the otherworld.

The new teaching drew initial converts: Frances Grant, a reporter, and a Russian Jewish couple, Sina Lichtmann-Fosdick and Maurice Lichtmann, two piano teachers who had moved across the ocean long before the revolution and had become almost fully Americanized. Soon another Jewish couple joined the group: Natty and Louis Horch, who had lost their first child and were searching for spiritual comfort. Louis, a currency speculator whose face was disfigured by a horrible trauma to his skull, turned out to be a treasure trove for Nicholas and Helena. By the early 1930s, he would blow more than one and a half million dollars funding Roerich's artistic and geopolitical ventures. In 1924, Nicholas Roerich added to this group George Grebenstchikoff, a writer and expert on Siberian geography and ethnography. Another prominent member of the inner circle was George Roerich, one of the Roeriches' two sons, whom they specially sent to Harvard and then to the Sorbonne in France to be groomed as an Orientalist. George was expected to learn about Tibetan and Hindu traditions—necessary assets for a future Shambhala warrior who was to assist his parents in their geopolitical plans.

Figure 7.1. Nicholas Roerich's inner circle, December 7, 1924. Left to right, sitting: Esther Lichtmann, Sina Lichtmann-Fosdick, Nicholas Roerich, Natty Horch, Frances Grant; standing: Louis Horch, Sofie Shafran, Svetoslav Roerich, Maurice Lichtmann, Tatiana Grebenstchikoff, George Grebenstchikoff.

There were other close contacts and associates who were never fully informed about the Roeriches' ultimate goals. Among them were industrialist and philanthropist Charles R. Crane; Frank Kellogg, U.S.

Secretary of State under Hoover; and later on Henry Wallace, FDR's Secretary of Agriculture, who was admitted into the painter's inner circle but at the same time was not completely devoted to his plans. The most trusted disciples received specially designed rings and esoteric names—symbols of belonging to the elect.[11] The rest of their friends and acquaintances, Nicholas stressed, should not be told of their long-term goals. For the general public, Roerich was to remain simply a painter and archaeologist interested in Oriental cultures. In 1922, after establishing his Master School of United Arts in New York, Roerich reminded the inner circle, "There are two sides of our school: the pretend illusionary one, which exists for all surrounding people, for many things must not be mentioned, and the real one—those wonderful events and miracles known only to us."[12]

Dreams of an Asian Spiritual Kingdom

The couple believed that World War I and the collapse of empires, along with bloody class and ethnic fights all over Eurasia, were a necessary purgatory: an Armageddon that would eventually bring a new golden age of universal happiness and spiritual bliss, which the Roeriches interchangeably called the Shambhala kingdom and the age of Maitreya. To Nicholas and Helena, the disorder that reigned in Inner Asia after the downfall of the Russian and Chinese empires and the expanding prophecies about mighty heroes that would come to deliver people appeared to provide an ideal stage for them to try out their role of saviors. Sometime by 1923, the Roeriches concluded the moment was right for them to plug into and use Shambhala and similar prophecies to build in Asia a powerful spiritual state based on reformed Buddhism: "For those who imagine Shambhala as a legendary invention, this indication is superstitious myth. But there are also others, fortified by more practical knowledge."[13] The Roeriches assumed that, if properly channeled, these prophecies might develop according to the scenario prescribed by the Great White Brotherhood.

The flight of the Panchen Lama from Tibet in December 1923 was seen as another powerful sign from the otherworldly brothers for them to step up. Without an assertive spiritual leader, thought Roerich, Tibetan Buddhists would "become prey to the intrigues of the retrograding lamaistic parties." To signal the coming of the new age, the painter would act as that assertive leader by bringing the Panchen Lama to Lhasa, fixing the situation, and making sure that the thirteenth Dalai Lama would be the last. The authority of the Yellow Pope (a derogatory nickname Roerich frequently used to refer to the sitting Dalai Lama) was to be erased: "The sacred army will purge Lhasa of all its nefarious enemies," and "the realm of righteous will be established." Roerich was convinced that all Tibetans were just awaiting "the prophecy that a new ruler from Shambhala, with numberless warriors, shall come to vanquish and to establish righteousness in the citadel of Lhasa."[14] An expedition to Inner Asia, headed by the painter and disguised as a scientific archaeological enterprise, was to accomplish this task.

The final goal of this venture gradually crystallized into what Helena and Nicholas called the Great Plan—an idea to bring all Tibetan Buddhist people of Asia, from Siberia to the Himalayas, together into the Sacred Union of the East with the Panchen Lama and Roerich presiding over this future theocracy. This state was to be guided by reformed Buddhism cleansed from what the painter and his wife considered "shamanic superstitions," adjusted to the original teachings of Buddha, and injected with the Roeriches' Agni Yoga. The couple envisioned this utopia as a commonwealth of people who would live a highly spiritual life and work in cooperatives—the economic foundation of this new state.[15] Their theocracy would stir a spiritual revival in the rest of the world. This grand dream certainly did not spring up overnight. For Helena and Nicholas, the Great Plan was a work in progress that continued from 1921 to 1929 and then was renewed in 1933–35.

Although they were dreamers, the Roeriches were not totally out of touch with reality. In fact, Nicholas and Helena's geopolitical scheme would not have sounded outlandish to their contemporaries, as many of them, both on the left and on the right, seriously believed there were absolute solutions to the world's problems, and that political and cultural messiahs were capable of delivering salvation. These solutions were usually based on collectivism and suppression of individuals to the will of a nation, class, or religion. With their grand geopolitical scheme designed to guide humankind to the correct spiritual path, the Roeriches perfectly fit their time.

At the end of 1921, the otherworldly teacher Morya gave his first hints on how to proceed with the unification of Inner Asian peoples into a spiritual kingdom: "In this life, without a fairy tale, you must visit us in Tibet, then go teach in Russia. I witness this by those happy events that take place in America" (August); "Think about Tibet, help to bring about harmony" (September); and finally, "Urusvati [Helena], I lead thee to the revealed Lhasa" (December).[16] The master also recommended they reread such spiritual classics as Ouspensky's *Tertium Organum* (1922) and Blavatsky's *Secret Doctrine* (1888) in order to be armed philosophically for the grand Asian journey

On July 29, 1922, when "conversing" with Helena and Nicholas, Morya delivered a stunning revelation: in his past life, Nicholas had been the fifth Dalai Lama (1617–82), one of the most prominent Tibetan leaders, who brought the people of the Forbidden Kingdom together and had the famous Potala Palace built in Lhasa. On that same day, the painter learned that the Great White Brotherhood had chosen him to go to Tibet as a spiritual ambassador and then to proceed farther north to Russia. The otherworldly master added that when they went to Tibet the couple would have to shed their European dress and replace it with Oriental garments. After Tibet, upon their arrival in Russia, Maurice Lichtmann would welcome them with the Torah in his hands and on behalf of the Jewish nation would "deliver a welcoming address to the East." At the end of their journey, prophesized Morya, representatives of various Inner Asian and Siberian peoples would come together and consummate the Sacred Union of the East. Eventually, out of this

Asia-centered theocracy the superior race of people would spread the light of true spirituality all over the world.[17]

Like many Western intellectuals, including contemporary Theosophists, Helena and Nicholas were convinced that humankind's enlightenment and salvation would come from the East. This habit of looking to the Orient as the source of high wisdom has a long history. It started during the Enlightenment and then received an additional boost from Romanticism in the first half of the nineteenth century. By the beginning of the twentieth century, quite a few intellectuals had built up in their minds an idealized ancient Orient soaked in rich spiritual life and contrasted it to the imperfect contemporary West that scared Western seekers with its materialism, industrialization, and individualism.

Much like contemporary Theosophists, the Roeriches merged their Asia-centered geopolitical utopia with Charles Darwin's evolutionary theory, which had become fashionable at the end of the nineteenth century not only in the sciences, but also in the humanities and popular media. Following their predecessor Blavatsky, the Roeriches talked about a coming superior race that would dislodge spiritually degenerate races in the process of evolution. The Great White Brotherhood from the Himalayas and its messengers (the Roeriches) could speed up this evolution by navigating human beings toward the better future beyond materialism. To be exact, both Blavatsky and the Roeriches meant a spiritual evolution, not a biological one. At that time in the West, this kind of talk about superior and inferior species and races, as well as grading cultures into primitive and advanced ones, was common, taken for granted, and never raised any eyebrows. Politicians, writers, scholars, and scientists all shared this mindset.

Besides Blavatsky's Theosophy, another powerful out-of-Asia source for the Roeriches was the Siberian autonomist movement. For some reason, all existing writings about the Roeriches somehow downplay this movement's influence on their geopolitical ideas. Autonomists were a small but outspoken group of Russian writers, artists, and scholars in Siberia, headed by the folklore scholar Grigorii Potanin (1835–1920), who worked to boost the status of their area within the Russian Empire. These men and women of arts and letters were convinced that their vast northern Asian homeland was a colony of European Russia. To them, Siberia was destined for a better role than to serve simply as a dump for common criminals and political prisoners and as the source of raw materials. At one point, when they became too vocal in demanding autonomy for Siberia, the Russian tsar condemned Potanin and several of his friends to exile in the European part of Russia. The emperor surely did not want to give these cultural rebels such a treat as an exile to Siberia.

Of special interest to the autonomists were the indigenous cultures of Siberia and Inner Asia. Potanin and his comrades were on a mission to use archaeological, folkloric, and ethnographic materials to show that Siberia, with its ancient Asiatic legacy, was a land steeped in rich culture more ancient than that of European Russia. The Russians in Siberia were not counted. As Europeans and newcomers to the area, they did not have ancient roots. What counted were lore, legends, and the ethnography of the indigenous folk of the Altai, Tuva, Buryat, and Mongolia. Like any cultural separatists living on the periphery, autonomists argued that their land was better and more ancient than other places: "The older the better" is the mantra of all nationalists and separatists who try to empower themselves. Talking and writing about the creative role of Inner Asian nomads were an important part of the autonomists' agenda. As if anticipating present-day politically correct historians, Potanin and his friends worked hard remaking the Mongols from ruthless barbarians and conquerors into noble cultural heroes and civilization carriers. At one point, Potanin went as far as arguing that Bible stories and Anglo-Saxon lore originated from Mongol and Siberian legends carried to the West and conflated with Middle Eastern and European oral culture.

Nicholas Roerich equally liked to indulge in such talk about nomads as cultural heroes. Moreover, for him, the Inner Asian nomads were potential foot soldiers in the coming Shambhala kingdom. Not spoiled by

Western civilization, they would become the spearheads of the world's liberation. Potanin's books about Turkic and Mongol legends became must-reads in the curriculum of Roerich's arts and humanities Master School in New York. The painter especially liked how Potanin worked with facts, finding links other writers somehow did not see. For example, if the Hebrew name Solomon sounded similar to Solmon, a character from the old epic tales of the Mongol and Altaian people, Potanin quickly concluded that Hebrew mythology had been affected by Asian nomads.

Although Roerich read Potanin's works and from them picked up many Asia-centric ideas, the only autonomist he had a chance to interact closely with was George Grebenstchikoff, whom he met while visiting Paris. This fellow émigré and struggling writer from southern Siberia was one of Potanin's close followers. Grebenstchikoff bragged about traces of Mongol blood in his veins and struck a chord with Roerich by expounding on the special historical role of his "ancestors" in world civilization. Roerich was drawn to Grebenstchikoff's stories about the traditions and mysteries of Siberia and Inner Asia. His stories about the landscapes and legends of the Altai sounded especially fascinating, and Roerich began to dream about this picturesque mountain country at the intersection of Siberia, Mongolia, and Kazakhstan as the center of his future spiritual kingdom. He and Helena contemplated erecting Zvenigorod (the city of bells), the capital of their future Pan-Asian state, in the Altai. The Siberian writer turned out to be so useful to the Great Plan that Nicholas concluded, "Grebenstchikoff knows everything."[18]

Special efforts were made to bring Grebenstchikoff from Paris to New York to keep him around as an expert on the area. The writer, who lived a miserable life in France, was more than happy to join the Roeriches' inner circle. Roerich gave him money (that came from Horch), helped him to settle in America, and endowed him with a new esoteric name: Tarukhan (from Tarlyk-khan, supposedly a Mongolian great grandfather of Grebenstchikoff). Helena and Nicholas made sure that Grebenstchikoff felt comfortable and secure in his new home. Once Helena instructed one of her sons, "Be close to Tarukhan. It is not only our request, it is also Mahatma Morya's order. Help our American friends understand the complexity and power of his character and the beauty of his visions. He is absolutely necessary for our project. I want them to trust him more. They will not be able to accomplish anything without him!"[19] In exchange, the writer eagerly fed the geopolitical fantasies of the painter and his wife with his ethnographic tales.

The painter spent many hours with Tarukhan, inquiring about landscape, particular sites, and prophecies of the Altai. Grebenstchikoff's stories about the mysterious Belovodie (White Waters Land) layered well on what the painter read about Shambhala. Belovodie was a prophecy shared by Altai Russian Orthodox schismatics who envisioned a utopian land of plenty where they could worship freely without being harassed by the tsarist government. The painter was equally captivated by Grebenstchikoff's talks about the Oirot prophecy that sprang up at the turn of the 1900s among indigenous nomads of the Altai; the legendary chief Oirot was a personification of the glorious seventeenth-century nomadic confederation of Oirot tribes and their prince Amursana. Local nomads expected this legendary character to resurrect and save them from the Russian advance into their land and culture. For Roerich, both Belovodie and Oirot were local versions of the Shambhala prophecy. In hindsight, Roerich turned out to be more useful to Tarukhan than vice versa. After 1929, Grebenstchikoff gradually and politely disentangled himself from the adventurous couple and their dangerous projects and eventually built up a successful career in the United States as a writer and college professor.

Not a small influence in stirring the Roeriches' geopolitical dreams was the book *Beasts, Men and Gods* (1922) by Ferdinand Ossendowski, a former Russian-Polish reporter in St. Petersburg exiled by the tsar to Siberia in 1905 for his revolutionary activities. There he became a professor of chemistry at Tomsk Polytechnic College and later secretary of finance for the White government of Siberia and a leader of the White resistance against the Bolsheviks. Ossendowski's action-packed book, which reads as half adventure story and half esoteric thriller, is a hair-raising account of his escape from the Bolsheviks southward through Tuva and Mongolia after the White cause collapsed in Siberia in 1921. En route, the professor got stuck with the bloody sadist Baron Roman von Ungern-Sternberg, who, as we have seen, dreamed, like Roerich, about building a grand pan-Asian empire.

In breathtaking style, Ossendowski described his actual life-and-death adventures as well as local landscapes, cultures, and prophecies of Asian nomads. A central theme is how the Bloody Baron hijacked Mongol prophecies. Roerich, who read and reread the book, certainly noted how quickly Ungern, an ordinary cavalry officer with average intelligence, by chance happened to liberate the Mongols from the Chinese and was elevated by the nomads to semidivine status. The painter might have assumed that if such a mediocre and mean individual was able to stir indigenous prophecies and to entrench himself in the Tibetan Buddhist world, it surely would be easier for a person of a higher intellectual caliber like himself, who knew more about cultures of the area and, unlike the crazy baron, had a noble agenda, to do the same. The Roeriches took very seriously what they read in Ossendowski's book. Unlike bashers of *Beasts, Men and Gods* who unwarrantably accused Ossendowski of making up all his stories (critics could not forgive him for weaving into his text Alexandre d'Alveydre's myth of subterranean Agartha), the Roeriches knew exactly what Ossendowski was talking about. After all, the couple had their own personal source to check the facts in Ossendowski's book: Nicholas's brother Vladimir was the White officer in charge of the supply train in the Bloody Baron's army. After Ungern's demise, Vladimir escaped from the Reds, made his way to China, and settled in Harbin.[20]

Obstacles, Magic Stone, and Reincarnation as the Dalai Lama

Early in 1923, armed with ideas of spiritual advancement, brotherhood, and collectivism, the Roeriches concluded the time was right for

172

them to go and build their new-age kingdom of peace, love, beauty, and spirituality in the heart of Asia. Their teacher Morya instructed them along the same lines: "It is time for the fairy tale to become real."[21] Yet, George, who had purposely been sent to Paris to be trained in Tibetan and Hindu studies, nearly ruined the Great Plan with his reckless behavior. At the end of 1922, when Master Morya kept sending his messages preparing the family for the Asian venture, George suddenly announced that he was going to get married. Away from the watchful eyes of Nicholas and Helena, George had fallen in love with a fellow Russian émigré, a beautiful and highly intelligent brunette named Marcel Mantsiarli, a Theosophist and follower of Jiddu Krishnamurti.

George was excited and wrote to his parents that his beloved was not only a beautiful girl but also a mystically inclined and sensitive person, and, "most importantly, she is devoted to our cause."[22] Helena and Nicholas were infuriated. A marriage on the eve of such a grand enterprise? This was a disaster! Helena was so mad that she immediately showered George with letters denigrating Marcel: the girl was five years older than George and simply wanted to trap her innocent boy. Even Master Morya interfered, giving Helena an alarming warning: "The reputation of the son that I need so much is being shattered." For George, the uncompromising position of his parents became a real drama. Marcel's mother, who specially came to New York to fix the problem, could not convince Helena to change her mind. The son desperately pleaded, "I beg you, I ask you, do not break my happiness."[23] Despite all of his pleas, nothing was able to melt the hearts of the messengers of the Great White Brotherhood. The spiritual crusaders who were about to bring enlightenment to Asia and then to all of humankind could not afford to have such a trivial thing as love meddle with their Great Plan. Eventually, George's parents took him away from Paris on a trip across Europe. Under their pressure and brainwashing, George broke up with the girl—a choice he regretted for the rest of his life.

Ironically, as soon as they settled "George's problem" another potential Shambhala warrior fell into precisely the same trap. Colonel Nikolai

Kordashevsky, an eccentric Lithuanian aristocrat of Polish descent from Lithuania whom the Roeriches had similarly groomed as part of their future Asian venture, suddenly fell in love as well. Surely the devil's forces were at work here, putting obstacles before the forces of light. Kordashevsky, a former White officer who had fought the Reds in Siberia, was a die-hard romantic and spiritual seeker. He loved monarchy and, like Baron Ungern, toyed for a while after the collapse of the Whites with the idea of moving to Tibet to serve the last true monarch—the Dalai Lama. But he changed his mind and returned to Europe. After a brief and disappointing experience with the celebrity occult teacher Gurdjieff, who exhausted the officer-aristocrat with his rigorous physical training, Kordashevsky wandered around Europe seeking new spiritual experiences. While in Paris in 1923, he stumbled upon Nicholas Roerich, who mesmerized him with his Asian plans. Soon, Kordashevsky was introduced into the painter's inner circle by receiving a ring and the esoteric name Chakhembula.

Bored to death on his Lithuanian estate, the colonel craved action and was ready to depart for Tibet right away. Helena and Nicholas had to restrain him. Waiting for orders from his new guru in New York, Kordashevsky was killing time by reading Theosophical books and Nordic legends and composing a novel about Joan of Arc when he suddenly fell in love with a local high-school teacher, a soul mate fascinated with the mysteries of ancient Egypt. This development presented a new challenge for the Roeriches, and it took another batch of letters to convince the romantic colonel to drop the girl. How could Kordashevsky afford such childish nonsense, Nicholas Roerich chastised him, when soon he was to saddle a horse, draw his sword, and ride into the heart of Asia? Kordashevsky followed the advice of his guru and forced himself to drop the girl.

Although the Roeriches were contemplating building an Inner Asian theocracy based on reformed Tibetan Buddhism and Agni Yoga, they had not settled on an exact itinerary of their activities. A tentative plan was to enter the area as an embassy of Western Buddhists, then somehow to contact the Panchen Lama and bring him to Tibet. After that they hoped to play by circumstances, going farther northward to Mongolia and Russia, stirring up en route Shambhala and other local prophecies. To finalize their plans, the family decided to make a reconnaissance trip to Sikkim, a small Indian principality in northern India conveniently located on the southern border of Tibet.

The Roeriches did not simply buy tickets and casually depart to India. Since theirs was a historical mission sponsored by the otherworldly forces of the Great White Brotherhood, they needed an occult blessing, at least in the eyes of their friends and associates. On the way to Sikkim, the couple stopped in Paris to secure identification documents. The Roeriches still held Russian passports issued before the Bolshevik revolution, and they did not want to draw too much attention to themselves in India by using passports of a nonexistent state. France aided the White Russian émigrés, providing them with necessary papers.

The occult blessing arrived, as Nicholas and Helena explained to their adepts, on the morning of October 6, 1923, when someone knocked on the door of their room at Lord Byron Hotel. George Roerich opened the door. The visitor introduced himself as a clerk from the Paris Bankers Trust, handed him a mysterious package, and immediately departed. When Helena, George, and Nicholas opened the package, they found a small box inside decorated with silhouettes of a man, woman, kingfisher, and four gothic letters engraved "M" on the edges. However, the real surprise was inside the box—a black shiny aerolite. The next day telegrams flew to all associates of the Roeriches in various countries: lo and behold, the Great White Brotherhood had entrusted the Roeriches with the sacred Chintamani stone. This magic jewel, which possessed incredible power, was to be carried on their Asian expedition and delivered to the Shambhala kingdom.

In Tibetan Buddhist tradition the Chintamani stone is known as a wish-granting gem. Ferocious deities, protectors of the Tibetan Buddhist faith, were frequently portrayed on sacred scrolls holding this stone. On these scrolls the Chintamani is depicted as either an ordinary jewel or a stone engulfed in flames—this theological link to the Roeriches' Agni Yoga might have been why they were attracted to this sacred item. The Roeriches described the Chintamani as a powerful occult weapon that would help their Asian mission. Now they could act not only as prophets who could fulfill wishes by using the wish-granting gem, but also as protectors of the Buddhist faith: "The stone draws people like a magnet. Entire nations can rise up if one lifts the stone. An enemy can be destroyed if you say his name three times looking at the stone. Only people who are pure in their spirit and thought can look at it."[24] It is highly probable that George Roerich, a professional student of Tibetan Buddhism who was shrewd in intricacies of this tradition, fed the Chintamani legend to his parents, who layered on it their own personal mythology and then manufactured the entire story about the mysterious gift.

The couple's fantasy moved further. The Roeriches wrote to their friends that the Chintamani was not only about Asian tradition: the magic gem was also known to the ancient Druids and to European Meistersingers as *Lapis exilis*. The stone delivered to the Roeriches was wrapped in a piece of old fabric; on it was an image of the sun with mysterious Latin letters inside the sun circle: I.H.S., which might be rendered as *In hoc signo* [*vinces*] (by this sign [you will win]). The same Latin abbreviation was inscribed on the banner of Constantine the Great, the famous Roman emperor who first legalized Christianity. Weaving Buddhist and European mythology together, the Roeriches said that the Chintamani magically disappeared and then reappeared at crucial historical moments to be handed to the righteous ones who would guide humankind to a better future. Of course, the righteous ones were the painter and his wife.

Armed with the power of the sacred stone, George, Helena, and Nicholas, the three Shambhala warriors, reached Bombay on December 2, 1923. By railroad, the family quickly traveled to northern India, where they stopped in the town of Darjeeling (a corrupted version of *dorje lingam* [hard penis]),[25] the capital of Sikkim. Here, in the town famous for the tea that grows in the area, the Roeriches established their temporary base. For their residency they picked not just any house, but a small summer cottage called the Palace of Dalai, on the southern slopes of the Himalayas; the place was once used by the thirteenth Dalai Lama when he had to flee from the Chinese in 1910. The painter and his wife feasted their eyes on the picturesque site surrounded by mighty cedar trees. From their windows they could enjoy a divine view of the Himalayan ridges and valleys.[26] Somewhere north of these mountain ranges lay mysterious Shambhala and its prophecies, waiting to be stirred and awakened.

The reconnaissance trip to Darjeeling turned out to be very stimulating. Nicholas spent his time not only painting awesome Himalayan landscapes and contemplating the coming Shambhala war, but also rubbing shoulders with visiting Tibetan Buddhist monks. A group of them from the Moru monastery visited the painter in April 1924; stunningly, they recognized him as the reincarnation of the great fifth Dalai Lama by the moles on his right cheek, which formed the shape of Ursa

Figure 7.2. Nicholas Roerich with visiting Buddhist monks, who recognized him as a reincarnation of the fifth Dalai Lama, Darjeeling, India, 1924. Standing, right to left: George Roerich, Lama Lobzang Mingyur Dorje, Nicholas Roerich, Helena Roerich.

177

Major, thereby confirming what Master Morya had already revealed to the couple. But Nicholas had not simply sat waiting to be discovered as the reincarnation. Rather he had actively worked for this by donning lama vestments when entertaining his native and nonnative visitors. By all his demeanor and talk, Roerich emanated high dignity and spiritual wisdom. The strategy worked.

Figure 7.3. Nicholas Roerich, wearing his Dalai Lama robe.

Yet, not everything was going well for him. British intelligence noted the strange Russian and put him under close watch. The painter sensed this attention and diplomatically never bragged about that miraculous recognition or his historical mission in Asia. Instead, he let other people do the talking. It was here in the "hard" tea town of Darjeeling that Roerich first heard about the Panchen Lama's flight from Tibet—news that prompted the painter to speed up his Great Plan. The escape of the spiritual leader of Tibet was a sure occult sign that the Shambhala war was coming. The prophecy was hot, and he needed to move quickly to unleash its energy in order to bring about the new age.

Every century the Arhats make an effort to enlighten the world. But until now, not one of these efforts has been successful. Failure has followed failure. It is said that until the day when a lama will be born in a Western body and appear as a spiritual conqueror for the destruction of the century-old ignorance, until then there will be little success in dissolving the snares of the West.

—Nicholas Roerich, *Altai-Himalaya*

Eight

Shambhala Warrior in a Western Body: Nicholas Roerich's Asian Ventures

In the spring of 1924, the Reds, previously viewed as nothing more than the servants of Satan, suddenly turned into allies. Nicholas and Helena Roerich realized that the success of their plan to build their Sacred Union of the East needed backing by one of the great powers in the area. Red Russia was their choice: what if they linked their project to the Bolsheviks' attempts to stir national liberation in the East? Besides, Nicholas did not like the British anyway because they had been trying to disrupt his attempts to enter Tibet. Their teacher Morya blessed this political turnaround: "Now business needs to be done with the Bolsheviks."[1]

Soon, the master unveiled the following political itinerary for the couple: "A trip to Moscow, where the one who will come from the East will be received with honors. From there, he will travel to Mongolia. In the middle of 1926, you can be in Mongolia in the center of the Orient, since, from now on, this country is the center." After receiving these revelations, Helena noted in her diary, "Now everything has changed. Lenin is with us."[2]

Inspired by this new turn of events, Nicholas Roerich did not stay in India for long. Leaving his wife in Darjeeling, he and George rushed to Europe, where they showed up at the gates of the Soviet embassy in Berlin and were welcomed by Nikolai Krestinsky, Bolshevik ambassador to Germany. Roerich began by explaining that he was planning an expedition to Inner Asia to paint local landscapes and do some archaeological digs. Since the envisioned route would go through southern Siberia and Mongolia, the painter needed Soviet diplomatic and logistic backup. In exchange, Roerich volunteered to promote the Bolshevik cause and to gather intelligence information on British activities in the area. Like his idealistic comrades, Krestinsky lived in expectation of the world Communist revolution—the Marxist second coming. Well aware of this revolutionary prophecy, Roerich readily massaged the diplomat's Bolshevik ego. In Tibet and in the caves of the Himalayas, the painter confided, hundreds of thousands of Hindu mahatmas and Buddhist lamas looked with hope to Red Russia. All these people, Roerich continued, circulated militant prophecies and preached the triumph of communism, for it matched the ancient teachings of Buddha, who had advocated equality and communal living. These Oriental folk hated the British and were eager to join the Bolshevik cause.

Roerich also played on the Bolsheviks' anti-England paranoia, exaggerating British activities in Tibet: "The occupation of Tibet by the English continues uninterrupted. English troops infiltrate the area by small groups, using all kinds of excuses."[3] In reality, there was no English occupation of Tibet or of any other area north of the Himalayas. In fact, the thirteenth Dalai Lama skillfully played one great power off another and did not allow anyone to make inroads into his theocracy. The cost-saving British never actually planned to take over the Forbidden Kingdom, even during their 1904 invasion of Tibet. Their goal was to open up the country for trade and keep it as a territorial cushion between India and Russia/China.

Haunted by the specter of the British threat and lacking reliable information about Inner Asia, Bolshevik diplomats were susceptible to Roerich's bluff. In fact, before the painter visited the Soviet embassy in Berlin, Georgy Chicherin, Bolshevik Commissar for Foreign Affairs, was already convinced that Tibet was almost a colony of England. Satisfied with the talk, Krestinsky promised to support Roerich and immediately sent a report to Chicherin, knowing that his Anglophobe boss would be pleased. Before the two parted, they agreed that Roerich would send intelligence briefs and sign them using the alias Ak-Dorje, which means "White Hard Arrow" or "White Hard Lightning" in Tibetan. Chicherin became excited and wrote back to Berlin, stressing that through Roerich Red Russia could get a foothold in Tibet: "Dear comrade, please do not lose from sight that half-Buddhist and half-Communist you wrote me about earlier. So far we have not had such a good bridge to these important centers. Under no circumstances should we lose such an opportunity. How we are going to use this opportunity, however, will require very serious consideration and preparation."[4]

In October 1924, the painter and his son stunned their American associates by suddenly resurfacing in New York and announcing that from then on the Bolsheviks should be treated as comrades. Roerich also revealed he was planning to take a land concession in the Altai in southern Siberia, officially for mining and agricultural purposes, but actually he planned to set up the capital of his Sacred Union of the East in this area. Krestinsky was not Roerich's only Bolshevik contact. On the way to New York, he had stopped in Paris where he met Leonid Krasin, a Bolshevik ambassador to France, and discussed with him the Altaian concession. Back in the United States, the painter got in touch with Dr. Dmitri Borodin, a plant physiologist and rather shady character whom the painter and his friends nicknamed Uncle Boris. After the Bolshevik revolution, Borodin moved to the United States, where he represented the Soviet Commissariat for Agriculture. A few years later he became an immigrant, working first as a zoology instructor at Columbia University and then as a researcher in a biology laboratory in Cold Spring Harbor, New York. A well-rounded but very unscrupulous individual, Borodin served as Roerich's Bolshevik liaison, helping the painter stay in touch with Soviet diplomats in Montreal, Paris, Berlin, and Moscow. Uncle Boris not only assisted Roerich in securing the concession in Altai; he also became involved in his Great Plan.

It appears that through Borodin, Roerich tried to probe how the Bolsheviks would react to his scheme to blend Tibetan Buddhism with

Communism and to the whole idea of the Sacred Union of the East. An entry from the diary of Roerich's secretary on December 7, 1924, is very revealing:

> Borodin told N. K. [Roerich] that now the most important thing for them is the unification of Asia. As for the business [the concession] they have been recently discussing, it is a secondary matter. N. K. asks him if he is aware that the unification of Asia can be accomplished through religion. Borodin responded that he knows. Does he realize that this unification can be accomplished by using the name of Buddha? Borodin agreed. Will those in Paris [Soviet diplomats] agree with this? Borodin responded that they are not stupid and understand everything. So both men came to a complete agreement, which made this day very important.[5]

Why did Borodin, a plant physiologist, suddenly become so concerned about this geopolitical scheme? It is highly likely that he worked either for Comintern or for OGPU, or for both, as Comintern was rapidly turning into an informal arm of OGPU. As a representative of the Soviet Commissariat for Agriculture, an ideal cover for any spy, Borodin traveled widely throughout the United States and Canada. Through him, Roerich's name might have showed up on Comintern and OGPU radars. It is little wonder that during Roerich's 1926 visit to Moscow OGPU was most supportive of the painter's Tibetan expedition. The Roeriches did not care who Uncle Boris was and what he actually did for a living. The most important thing was that Borodin was useful for the Great Plan. In one of her letters, Helena instructed her son Svetoslav: "Be nice and decent in front of Uncle Boris. It is important to make a good impression on him. Do not forget that all rich people like to spy on their associates, and our Uncle especially excels in this."[6]

The Bolsheviks' interest in the Roeriches' venture could have been twofold. First, the painter was useful as a source of information on Tibet and surrounding areas. Second, his Shambhala scheme contained a promising opportunity. If successful, it could give Red Russia a chance to navigate political developments in the Forbidden Kingdom according to the Mongolian scenario. Although Chicherin cautioned against reckless behavior in Asia that could provoke England to seize Tibet, by supporting Roerich's expedition, the chief Soviet diplomat and his more adventurous associates from Comintern and OGPU had nothing to lose. The Roeriches' party was going to travel as a scientific expedition under the American flag and the Buddhist sacred banner (tanka), a handy, cheap, and safe option for the Bolsheviks to penetrate the area without exposing themselves.

After all, with a total lack of the industrial working class (which Bolsheviks considered the chief mover and shaker of the Marxist prophecy) in Tibetan Buddhist areas, anything and anybody that could wake up Asian masses for revolution sounded attractive, whether this be lamas' antiforeign sentiments or prophecies like Shambhala. In any case, for the Bolsheviks the Roeriches' Sacred Union of the East was a political gift, which, if they played their cards right, could draw Tibet closer to Red Russia. If the Roeriches got involved in an international scandal or any other trouble, they could be safely cast aside as an American expedition.

In the early 1920s, still dizzy from their success in Mongolia, the Bolsheviks were ready to roll on to Tibet and farther southward to India, but they were not yet fully aware that Tibet was not Mongolia. The Forbidden Kingdom was not occupied by a foreign power that gave Red Russia an excuse to go there and milk national liberation sentiments. Rumors about the British threat to Tibet that the Bolsheviks lived by turned out to be false. Unlike his Mongolian neighbors, the Dalai Lama had no intention of appealing to Red Russia for help, preferring to play off one great power against another and keeping all of them at bay. Precisely because of this smart strategy, Tibet managed to survive as an independent nation from 1912 to 1951, before it was overrun by Communist China.

Gradually the Bolsheviks began to realize that it would be hard to sway the Forbidden Kingdom to Red Russia's side. Under these circumstances, the Roeriches' plan to bring the Panchen Lama back to Tibet and to stir the Shambhala war might have looked appealing to the them. In any case, Red Russia wanted to see the Panchen Lama back in Tibet and away from Mongolia. The man was hanging around with two hundred armed nomads along the southern border of Red Mongolia, performing collective Kalachakra initiations for local Mongols and inducting them into the ranks of Shambhala warriors. It was hard to predict what would come out of that.

The Bolsheviks became worried when the Mongols began looking at the Panchen Lama as their new shepherd after they lost Bogdo-gegen in 1924; the reincarnated head of the Mongol Buddhists died from old age and numerous ailments, and the Bolsheviks forbade searching for his new reincarnation. At any time, even against his will, the Panchen Lama could become a dangerous spiritual weapon in the hands of anti-Bolshevik forces; this became especially true in the second half of the 1920s after Red Mongols began cracking down on religion. Though the abbot of the Tashilumpho monastery was not a die-hard anti-Communist, he did allow himself anti-Bolshevik statements, rebuking the Reds for harassing top lamas. At the same time, always cautious, the abbot refused to join or even support any active resistance to the Bolsheviks. In fact, the Soviet secret police never considered him an enemy, believing there was a good chance to draw the spiritual leader of Tibet to Moscow's side at least as a temporary ally.[7] But still the Bolsheviks were wary of his presence among the Mongols and felt they could sleep better with the Panchen Lama back in Tibet.

No doubt Roerich treated his Bolshevik contacts in the same pragmatic manner as useful and disposable allies. Although, like many contemporary intellectuals, Roerich was captivated by then-popular ideas of collectivism and social evolution and had a strong leader-redeemer complex, it is highly unlikely that he was totally in love with Soviet Communism. The flirt with the Bolsheviks appeared to be a smokescreen to accomplish his occult goals of building his own totalitarian theocracy. After all, from his otherworldly abode, Master Morya, Helena and Nicholas's alter ego, explicitly encouraged a healthy opportunistic approach to the Bolsheviks: "One can grow wonderful nuts by putting one's own seed into an alien shell," and, "Talk about Lenin and Marx without mentioning drawbacks of Marx. I guarantee your success, but you have to be patient."[8] The Roeriches rendered these commands of the master into instructions for their associates: "Talking about legends and prophecies, one needs to draw more attention to practical life, stressing how good life will be in the New Country under cooperatives. We need to point out that Buddha built communist commonwealth, and Christ propagated communist order. Moreover, it will be useful if we recognize that Lenin is the most important Communist."[9]

To Inner Asia with a Detour to Moscow

Roerich was so impatient to embark on his Sacred Union of the East project that he could not even wait for his Soviet visa. In the summer of 1925, the painter was already back in Darjeeling, ready to make a leap into the heart of Asia. Master Morya was equally excited, hurrying the Roeriches to move and shake the whole area:

The teacher believes the invasion of Tibet is useful. The flow of events will affect religion, and you will succeed by responding to religious complaints. Therefore, do not waste your time; note all signs related to religious feelings. Each sign is valuable. Find out to what extent monks are now discontent. Learn how many people do not accept the new order [a reference to army and police reforms in Tibet assisted by the English]. Alien uniform disgraces holy places. A strike will thunder over the desert. Udraia [George Roerich] should think about wearing a lama robe. Only the robe will defeat the uniform. The new times require a new shell. A correct route will lead to a bloodless victory. It is not our plan to shoot from cannons. One good sure shot at Buddha might make up for an entire battle. Behold, the sons of Israel will come back to those who wait for M [Maitreya] and turn the holy dream into a reality.

The otherworldly teacher encouraged the Roeriches to stir Tibetan monks against the power of the Dalai Lama: "Mold is growing in Lhasa, and an old lama who is sitting by an altar is thinking about galloping to the north."[10]

After travelling by automobile and rail from Darjeeling to Srinigar in Kashmir, the Roeriches' expedition set out in August 1925. It looked more like a religious procession than a scientific-archaeological enterprise. Passing through Ladakh and then into western China, the party engaged local people in talks about Shambhala and Maitreya, dropping here and there hints about the coming Armageddon followed by a new age. The Buddhist robes that Nicholas and George donned from time to time enhanced the importance of the mission in the eyes of locals. The elder Roerich presented himself as a sage named Ak-Dorje—the same name he used in his reports to Soviet diplomats in Berlin. Helena became the messenger of the goddess White Tara, and George was acting as the Mongolian prince Narukhan.

Ak-Dorje distributed dozens of flyers written in Tibetan to the lamas they met en route. Some of these texts included only the phrase "Maitreya is coming," while others contained a more elaborate text:

> Thus the prophecies of ancestors and the wise ones come true. Behold what is predestined when in the fifth year [1925] the messengers of northern Shambhala warriors appear. Meet them and accept the new glory of Tibet and Mongolia. I will give Thee my sign of lightning. May all remember: where one receives Tara's blessing, there will be the ray of Maitreya, where one hears the name of Ak-Dorje, there will be a wheel of justice, and where the name of Narukhan appears, there will be the sword of Buddha. Shambhala will show the galloping horse and give arrows to all loyal sons of Buddhism. Behold and wait.[11]

A batch of these flyers was sent to the Tashilumpho monastery to be distributed among the Panchen Lama's followers. The purpose of all this showmanship was obvious: the painter and his wife wanted to arouse rumors among the indigenous folk about their party being messengers of the great northern Shambhala and the coming age of Maitreya. In other words, the Roeriches were spreading propaganda in an attempt to stir a religious war in Inner Asia. And sure enough, word began to spread about a strange and mighty prophet.

In April 1925, the expedition reached the capital of Sinkiang: Urumchi. Here Roerich met and befriended Alexander Bystrov, the local Soviet consul general. The painter immediately confided to him that he had ambitious plans to merge Buddhism and Communism. Roerich also informed Bystrov that from China he would be going straight to Moscow to meet Stalin and Chicherin and hand them two important messages on behalf of thousands of Hindus and Buddhists. On the evening of April 16, 1926, after meeting Nicholas and Helena, the consul wrote in his journal:

Today Roerich along with his wife and son visited me and mentioned many interesting details of their journeys. They say they study Buddhism and are in touch with mahatmas, from whom they often receive guidelines about their future plans. By the way, they stated they are carrying letters from these mahatmas to Comrades Chicherin and Stalin. They say the goal of these mahatmas is the unification of Buddhism and Communism and the creation of the Great Eastern Union of Republics. The Roeriches told me that Tibetans and Hindu Buddhists share a popular prophecy that their liberation from foreign yoke will come from Russia, from the Reds (Red Northern Shambhala). The Roeriches carry to Moscow several of these prophecies. According to the Roeriches, their trips to India, Tibet, and Western China are the fulfillment of an assignment given by the mahatmas, who supposedly also instructed them to go to the USSR and then to Mongolia, where they should get in touch with Panchen Lama (Dalai Lama's assistant responsible for spiritual life who escaped from Tibet to China) and bring him to Mongolia. From Mongolia the Roeriches plan to organize a spiritual march to Tibet to free it from the English yoke.[12]

With the assistance of Bystrov and the OGPU secret police agents, the Roerich expedition safely crossed the Soviet-Chinese border, by-passing customs. In the Siberian town of Omsk the party was placed on a train. The painter wrote in his diary: "A train arrives at midnight. An OGPU agent passes by and with his eyes lets me know that everything is in order. We are passing under the Sign of the Rose [in other words, secretly]."[13] On June 10, 1926, the Roeriches were in Moscow, where they met Chicherin, Meer Trilisser, head of the foreign espionage branch of the OGPU secret police, and several other Soviet dignitaries. The most promising meeting was the reception at OGPU. Sina Fosdick, Roerich's secretary who prepared this event, was happy to record in her diary: "The most memorable meeting was in GPU, where the names of Maitreya and Shambhala were pronounced and where we came with the name of the Master. The offers of cooperation were met with enthusiasm. Several times we met with those who have all power."[14]

The adventurous couple also presented their Moscow hosts "mahatmas' messages" calling for advancement of Communism into Asia and beyond. Manufactured by Helena and Nicholas and translated into Tibetan by George to make them look authentic, then "translated" into Russian for the Bolshevik leaders, these letters were infested with sugarcoated flattery: "In the Himalayas we know about your deeds. You demolished churches that became dens of lies and superstition. You destroyed mercantilism that became the conduit of prejudices. You eliminated the outdated prison of education and marriage based on hypocrisy. You squashed the spiders of enrichment and closed the doors of night brothels. You relieved the earth from the traitors and money-makers. You recognized that religion is the teaching about the matter. You recognized the ephemeral nature of private property and saw the evolution toward the future world commune."[15]

Without beating around the bush, Roerich laid out for the Bolshevik leaders his program to secure the alliance between Communism and Tibetan Buddhism:

1. Buddha's teaching is revolutionary.
2. Maitreya represents the symbol of Communism.
3. The millions of Buddhists of Asia can be drawn into the movement to support the idea of the commune.
4. The basic law of Gautama Buddha easily penetrates the minds of the masses.
5. Europe will be shattered by the alliance between Buddhism and Communism.
6. The Mongols, Tibetans, and Kalmyk now expect the fulfillment of Maitreya prophecies, and they are ready to apply them to the current evolution.
7. The escape of the Panchen Lama from Tibet provides an incredible opportunity to stage a revolt in the East.
8. Buddhism explains the reason for the negation of God.
9. The Soviet government needs to act quickly, taking into consideration cultural conditions and prophecies of Asia.[16]

Posing as a representative of Hindu and Tibetan masses, the painter painted with wide strokes on a vast Asian geopolitical canvas: "If the Soviet Union recognizes Buddhism as part of the Communist teaching, our communities will furnish active assistance, and hundreds of millions of Buddhists scattered over the world will provide necessary and unexpected power. We need to adopt measures to introduce Communism as the step in the coming evolution."[17] The Roeriches nourished hopes that the Bolsheviks would embrace this scheme and attach to their expedition a Red cavalry unit that would accompany them on the second leg of their journey through Inner Asia.

Although they swallowed some of the Roeriches' bluff, Chicherin and other Bolshevik leaders were not so naive as to immerse themselves totally in such a reckless plan. Chicherin and Trilisser made it clear that direct involvement of Red Russia in their Tibetan venture was out of the question. Besides, the Bolsheviks had mixed feelings about the painter himself. They certainly enjoyed his praises of Communism as well as his utterances about the evils of private property and the joys of communal living. However, as atheists and materialists, they were not thrilled about Roerich's talk of Buddhism, Theosophy, and spirituality. It was little wonder that Trilisser, while supporting the Roeriches' expedition, flatly refused to give them permission to print in the Soviet Union their books about the foundations of Buddhism and Agni Yoga. To the chief of the Bolshevik foreign espionage network, this stuff was pure idealistic propaganda.

Despite the ideological differences, Chicherin and OGPU gave Nicholas the green light and also promised logistic and diplomatic support. Trilisser instructed one of OGPU's colorful characters, Jacob Bliumkin, to provide assistance of all kinds to Roerich's party. This young operative, who came from the Jewish quarters of Odessa in southern Russia, joined OGPU at the tender age of seventeen, right after the revolution. His favorite pastime was dining, wining, and bragging among Moscow's bohemian poets and writers. Occasionally, this revolutionary romantic and "man of theater" (as one of his sweethearts called him) liked to toy with verses himself. By the early 1920s, Bliumkin was already a seasoned terrorist, provocateur, hit man, and master of disguise. He even managed to leave a visible trace in modern European history by murdering in 1918 a German ambassador to Russia in hopes of provoking a new round of war between Russia and Germany. Relating this episode to his friends, this revolutionary adventurer always stressed how he confidently pulled out his Colt revolver, like characters from his favorite silent movies. At the same time, he usually omitted how, while escaping from the embassy, he received a bullet in his buttocks.[18]

In 1926, Bliumkin was conveniently assigned to Mongolia as the chief advisor to the sister secret-police structure and arrived in the country of nomads simultaneously with the Roeriches. It is also highly probable that Trilisser or Bliumkin verbally gave the painter assignments. Dr. Konstantin Riabinin, a participant of the second expedition, later remembered, "Since the time we left Urga [capital of Mongolia] and all the time en route, I was under the impression that Moscow had entrusted the professor [Roerich] with an important assignment related to Tibet."[19]

Back to Asia: Altai to Mongolia

On July 22, 1926, Roerich and his party were on their way back to southern Siberia. There, from the Altai, they planned to launch the second leg of their Asian venture. In the middle of August, the expedition crossed the borders of the Oirot Autonomous Region, an autonomy set up for the local Turkic-speaking nomads (half Buddhists and half shamanists) by the Bolsheviks to foster the nationalistic feelings of local nomads. This was the Mountain Altai, the homeland of the Oirot prophecy that the painter viewed as a local version of Shambhala.

Roerich was especially thrilled to learn that in this area, on the fringes of the Mongol-Tibetan world, many nomads were shedding shamanism and switching to Buddhism. He believed this shift confirmed his spiritual forecast regarding Inner Asia: people were phasing out dark rituals and moving toward the ancient teachings of Buddha. Of course, he too would ride this movement. As earlier in Darjeeling, Roerich could not resist the temptation to step into the local prophecy. He started toying with the idea of impersonating Oirot, the legendary redeemer of the Altai nomads. He listed the places he had visited during the first leg of his Asian journey as if they were sites visited by Oirot and then hinted that local nomads already knew that "the Blessed Oirot is already traveling throughout the world, announcing the great Advent." Another hint was even more explicit: "About the good Oirot all know. Also they know the favorite Altaian name—Nikolai."[20] Blindly loyal to her guru, Roerich's secretary, Fosdick, immediately caught the mood of the teacher when they entered the Altai and suddenly began referring to Roerich as Gegen (a reincarnated one).[21]

As the reincarnate Oirot, Roerich would proceed through the Altai, then enter Mongolia from the north (from northern Shambhala!), and, accompanied by the host of legends, triumphantly continue his route southward to Tibet. The "Blessed One" was convinced that all pieces of his occult puzzle were placed incredibly well. What he did not see behind the Oirot prophecy, taking it as a local version of the Shambhala legend, was naked Altai nationalism wrapped in spiritual garb. Singing hymns to Oirot and Burkhan (the face of Buddha), who commanded Oirot, nomads of the Altai craved unity and sovereignty. Since they shared a similar culture and fate, the Altaians tried to empower themselves by dropping clan-based shamanism with its impromptu rituals and rallying around the Oirot prophecy familiar to all of them, then layering traits of Buddhism on top of this. In other words, it was an unconscious effort of these people to help bond themselves into an Oirot or White Altai nation, as they sang in their hymns.

Unlike Roerich, the Bolsheviks knew better. They understood that the Oirot people were restless, awaiting the legendary redeemer who would shield them from Russian advances into their land and culture. The Bolshevik answer to this explosive spiritual brew was simple and clever. The Communist Revolution, they explained to the nomads, was a fulfillment of the prophecy, and Lenin was the reincarnation of Oirot. To sugarcoat this message, autonomy was offered to the people of Oirot with their own indigenous Oirot Bolshevik leaders at the top. Many frustrated nomads, who at first did not trust the Bolsheviks and were about to leave the Altai for Mongolia and China, swallowed this bait and stayed home. By the end of the 1920s, the explosive prophecy would gradually subside.

As Roerich proceeded, a few months later the same blinders prevented him from detecting pure nationalism behind the Shambhala prophecy, which the Red Mongols milked during their fight against the Chinese. Still worse, not only did Roerich not understand the demonic power of nationalism over people, but also, as a true citizen of the world, he refused to acknowledge it, thinking only in terms of global humanity. Quoting the song of northern Red Shambhala composed by Mongol revolutionary soldiers in 1921, but dropping the first lines that mentioned a mortal fight against Chinese infidels, Roerich retained only its "spiritual" verses: "We march to the holy war of Shambhala. Let us be reborn in the sacred land."[22]

At the end of August 1926, the party safely crossed the Mongolian border. Again, on orders from the Bolshevik secret police, their baggage safely bypassed customs. In Mongolia, an unpleasant surprise awaited the painter and his wife. They had to wait for seven more months for permission from Chinese and Tibetan authorities to enter their countries. Yet, as always, the couple did not lose their spirits and did not waste time. While Roerich worked on his paintings, his wife was able to publish a small book on the basics of Buddhism, one of the texts Trilisser would not allow them to print in Red Russia.

There is also circumstantial evidence that while in Mongolia Roerich did get in touch with the Panchen Lama. With the help of his Bolshevik benefactors, he might have made a quick automobile trip to Beijing to meet the runaway Tibetan abbot, who resided in the Chinese capital at that time. A Soviet diplomat named Boris Pankratov remembered meeting the painter in Beijing in the spring of 1927: "Roerich nourished a hope to enter Tibet as the twenty-fifth king of Shambhala, of whom people would say that he came from the north and brought salvation to the whole world and became king of the world. For this purpose, the painter was dressed in a ceremonial lama priest robe."[23] Since Roerich was prone to all kinds of adventurous tricks, one cannot totally exclude the possibility of a secret visit to the Chinese capital and talks with the Panchen Lama. Still, whether Roerich met him or not, the cautious abbot never became involved in the painter's scheme.

While in Mongolia, the Roeriches were in close contact with Bliumkin, their guardian angel from OGPU, and with Leo Berlin, another secret police officer working in Mongolia under the cover of the Soviet Commissariat for Foreign Affairs.[24] Roerich's son George, who spoke Tibetan fluently, helped Bliumkin close an arms deal with a representative of the Dalai Lama. Moreover, the two spies helped the Shambhala warriors with logistics and supervised the departure of the "artistic and archaeological expedition" from Urga.[25]

The Tibetan Venture: High Hopes and Grand Failure

When all permissions were finally secured, the party departed on April 13, 1927. The Soviet embassy provided automobiles, which allowed the Roeriches to quickly reach the southernmost border of Mongolia. There they switched to camels and entered western China, an area populated by warlike tribes, infested with bandits, and contested by several Chinese warlords. Moscow OGPU sent a radiogram to a warlord friendly to the Bolsheviks, asking him "to provide all possible help to Roerich's expedition."[26] The party again took the form of a spiritual march. In addition to the Stars and Stripes, the expedition proceeded under the Maitreya banner, a sacred tanka attached to a flagpole. Anticipating the grand historical mission that awaited them, Roerich wrote, "With this holy banner, we can reach the most beautiful lands and we can awaken ancient cultures for new achievements and for new splendors."[27]

The expedition was not just a family business anymore. A few more people had joined the couple and their son George: Dr. Riabinin, an enthusiast of Tibetan medicine the Roeriches knew from their pre-revolutionary days in St. Petersburg; a young Theosophist from Siberia named Pavel Portniagin; and the lama Danzan Malonov from Agvan Dorzhiev's Buddhist Kalachakra temple in Leningrad. Malonov was a seasoned "Red pilgrim" who, two years earlier, had participated in the Bolshevik Lhasa venture headed by Sergei Borisov. Malonov was most likely attached to the party by OGPU or Chicherin to perform special tasks. Two more members, aristocrat-romantic Colonel Nikolai Kordashevsky and Alexander Golubin, a merchant who worked for an English trade company, joined the party in Chinese territory. As former White officers who fought against the Reds in Siberia, the two had not wanted to risk their lives entering Red Mongolia. The expedition also included twenty Buryat and Mongol armed guards.

On the way, Nicholas Roerich watched for signs of the Shambhala prophecy, noting various anomalous phenomena and observing the behavior of the nomads. In the evenings, he conducted instructive

Figure 8.1. Nicholas Roerich holding tanka depicting Maitreya. Urga, Mongolia, March or April, 1927.

Figure 8.2. Onward to Lhasa under the Stars and Stripes and the sacred Maitreya banner: the Roerich camp at Sharagol Valley, Inner Mongolia, December 1927– January 1928.

spiritual talks, enlightening his comrades about the coming evolution of humankind, the advent of a spiritually superior sixth race, the world commune, cooperative labor, the evils of private property, Maitreya, Shambhala, and the sacred Great White Brotherhood. In the meantime, in her tent Helena engaged in dialogues with their otherworldly teacher, Master Morya. Occasionally, to boost the spirit of the Shambhala warriors, Roerich turned on an American gramophone, and over the mountains flew the tunes of "Forging of the Sword," "Call of the Valkyrie," and "Roar of Fafner" by Richard Wagner, the painter's favorite composer. Wagner's pieces resounded high in the mountains, "radiating heroic realism."[28]

As before, special efforts were made to promote rumors among local nomads about the party as messengers of Shambhala and the new age of Maitreya. The painter constantly reminded his travel companions to remember that now they were all walking heroes: "All our steps

Figure 8.3. Nicholas Roerich with his Shambhala seekers on the eve of their departure to Tibet. Left to right: Konstantin Riabinin, George Roerich, Nicholas Roerich, Pavel Portniagin, Sina Lichtmann-Fosdick, Maurice Lichtmann. Urga, Mongolia, March or April, 1927.

are destined to become legends, which people will compose about our journey. And who knows, they might be great legends. On the threshold of the coming of the sixth race, all events are destined to become special."[29] Morya was pleased with how the legend making was developing and encouraged his earthly students: "The legend is growing. You need to proceed to Tibet without hurry, sending around rumors about your Buddhist embassy. The appearance of the embassy under the banner of Buddha is something that has never been seen before in the history of humankind. In the name of Maitreya Commune, you need to topple false teachings. . . . Each evening talk about Shambhala! Shambhala prepares the coming of Maitreya. . . . Plan your movement to make sure that each phrase you utter turns into a legend. Remember, you already stand above regular human beings."[30]

Figure 8.4. A last photo in the company of Red Mongol troops before the Roerich expedition moved southward across the Mongolian border. Konstantin Riabinin is in white hat; on his right is George Roerich; Sina Lichtmann-Fosdick, second from left, has a holstered gun on her belt. Altan-usu, Gobi Desert, May 1927.

Part of this legend making was the erection of a Buddhist stupa (*sub-urgan*) in the Sharagol valley in Inner Mongolia. Into the foundation of the structure devoted to Maitreya the Roeriches placed a specially minted order of *All-Conquering Buddha*, the text containing the Shambhala prophecy, in Tibetan, a silver ring with the word *Maitreya*, and a blue silk scarf (a traditional goodwill gift in Tibetan Buddhism). Local Mongol chiefs accompanied by crowds of nomads flocked to the Roeriches' camp to take part in a consecration ceremony officiated by a local Gegen (reincarnated one). That same evening, from the other world, Master Morya expressed his approval: "The erection of the suburgan affirms the legend, and therefore it is useful. The Teacher is happy with this."[31]

Overcoming various natural obstacles and brandishing their rifles to scare away bandits they met en route, the travelers proceeded through western China, then crossed the most dangerous leg of the journey—the vast salt desert of Tsaidam—and finally, in October, reached the Tibetan border in the Nagchu area. Here the Shambhala warriors had to face a formidable problem, which eventually ruined their hopes to conquer Lhasa. Despite an official permission to enter the Forbidden Kingdom issued by a Tibetan envoy in Mongolia, the party was detained by armed border guards. The Roeriches could not figure out what was going on. Although not formally arrested, they were blocked and not allowed to proceed further. Playing by the script he had prepared in advance, Nicholas explained to the local governor that they were emissaries of Western Buddhists on a mission to bring Western and Eastern believers under the benevolent wing of His Holiness. Yet all was in vain. Roerich's high talk and all his inquiries were brushed aside with the advice to stay and wait for Lhasa's instructions.

Little did the travelers know that the formidable wall on their way to Tibet was erected not only by the Lhasa officials but also by Lt. Colonel Bailey, the English spy stationed in Sikkim entrusted with monitoring all Bolshevik activities in Inner Asia. In 1925 he had figured out the Borisov "Buddhist pilgrims" mission sent to Lhasa by Comintern, OGPU, and the Commissariat for Foreign Affairs. Then, in 1927, through his Kalmyk and Buryat agents, Bailey had exposed another Moscow mission to Tibet, the one headed by Arashi Chapchaev, which had departed from Urga just before Roerich launched his own expedition.

To the seasoned English shadow warrior, Roerich, whom Bailey already knew from the painter's stay in Sikkim, was no different from such disguised Bolsheviks as Borisov and Chapchaev. And, besides, like his Red predecessors, Roerich was coming from the same place, Red Mongolia. In Bailey's eyes, Roerich's Buddhist trappings—vestments, sacred scrolls, and his Shambhala and Maitreya talk—were simply part of a devious and more sophisticated Bolshevik conspiracy to dislodge Britain from Asia. For his part, the Dalai Lama, who had just gotten rid of the phony Mongol pilgrim Chapchaev, again had to deal with another intruder of the same caliber. The Lhasa ruler definitely did not want such a headache. The English spymaster recommended that Tibetan authorities immediately block the movement of the "American" expedition, and Lhasa followed this advice. Although Bailey was not totally wrong about Roerich's mission, at that point he did not yet realize that the painter was playing his own game. All in all, it did not matter. The lieutenant colonel would have hardly changed his plans had he found out Roerich was not actually a Bolshevik.

After halting the Roeriches at Nagchu, the Tibetans did not know what to do with them. To allow these suspicious folk to proceed farther was dangerous. Yet forcing them back to Mongolia in the middle of winter would surely have killed all members of the expedition. The Dalai Lama certainly did not want to place this sin on his shoulders. While Lhasa was mulling over what to do, the party of Shambhala warriors was literally marooned for five months in freezing weather and thin air on a high-altitude plateau. At one point, George Roerich blacked out, narrowly surviving a heart attack, which did take the life of one of them: Lama Malonov, the alleged secret police informer. On November 8, 1927, Portniagin wrote in his diary: "Temperature is minus 27 Celsius. This morning the doctor said, 'From the viewpoint of medical science and physiology, our situation is catastrophic, and we all shall die. Only a miracle can save us.'"[32]

Besides suffering from cold and oxygen deficiency in the high altitude, the travelers were forbidden to purchase food from the locals. Yet Nicholas and Helena never lost their spirit. Obstacles only empowered them, and the painter cheered up his comrades: "Occult work must be done in fresh air and in the cold."[33] While Helena continued to conjure Master Morya in her tent, Nicholas inspired the party with stories about the beauties of the Shambhala kingdom they would eventually reach. For his companions, shivering from piercing winter winds, he drew pictures of a beautiful mountain valley blossoming with subtropical vegetation. It would be as magnificent as the Grand Canyon in Arizona, he told them.

On February 17, 1928, after prolonged deliberations, Lhasa officials finally worked out a solution. The Roeriches would proceed quickly through Tibet, bypassing the capital, and going straight to Sikkim to Bailey's home. Let the English spy deal with them.

When they finally arrived in Sikkim in mid-May, Lt. Colonel Bailey welcomed the exhausted travelers into his residence, acting as if nothing had happened. He even hosted them for a while, offering hot baths and good foods. It took the experienced operative only a brief chat with the painter to figure out that Roerich was not a Bolshevik but simply a dangerous eccentric.[34] Yet, as a professional spy, he had no remorse about what he had done to Roerich and his companions. Better to be on the safe side.

Figure 8.5. In "friendly" hands: English spy Lt. Colonel F. M. Bailey, Political Officer in Sikkim, hosts his unsuspecting opponent Nicholas Roerich. Left to right, sitting: Mrs. F. M. Bailey, Nicholas Roerich, Helena Roerich; standing: Nikolai Kordashevsky, George Roerich, Konstantin Riabinin, name not recorded, F. M. Bailey. Bailey residence, Gangtok, Sikkim, May 24–25, 1928.

After parting with the hospitable Bailey, the Roerich party was nearing the end of its journey. The long Asian odyssey, which cost $97,000 and took the Roeriches all over Eurasia, was finally over. The Shambhala war the painter wanted to unleash in Inner Asia had fallen through miserably. So had his plan to bring all Tibetan Buddhists into the Sacred Union of the East. But the couple did not want to simply say good-bye to their comrades and go their separate ways. The grand magic drama that had started with the miraculous manifestation of the Chintamani stone required at least a magic ending. And the Roeriches provided it. The painter suddenly announced to his friends that he, along with Helena and George, would leave the rest in order to proceed straight to the forbidden Shambhala kingdom: the Great White Brotherhood was calling them. Exclaiming "It is nice to believe in the fairy tale of life," the Roeriches parted with their comrades.[35] Dr. Riabinin sadly watched how the three riders galloped away and soon blended in with the horizon, lowering the curtain of mystery behind them: "We Europeans who accompanied Nicholas and Helena must say good-bye to them, for we are not supposed to know their future path. Will the messenger of Shambhala accompany them?"[36]

Botanical Expedition with an Occult Spin, 1935

The major result of the Roeriches' mission to Inner Asia was their complete disillusionment with official Tibetan Buddhism. The painter and his wife became equally frustrated about the Bolsheviks, who did not wholeheartedly support their Great Plan, so they decided to delete the Reds from their lives as well. Their otherworldly teacher shared these frustrations, and in his usual cryptic manner stated that in the future city of knowledge there would be nothing red, not even red flowers. Only blue, white, and violet would remain. Trying to close this page of his life, the painter had all mention of the Bolsheviks, including his Moscow visit, purged from further editions of his books.

Figure 8.6. Nicholas Roerich's Master Building, intended to become a spiritual beacon for humankind. It featured brickwork that gradually shifted from dark to light as the building rose.

The failures they experienced only hardened the couple's determination not to give up on their dream: "Blessed obstacles, through you we grow."[37] By that time, the Roeriches were so firmly entangled in their visionary world controlled by Master Morya that there was simply no way back. Roerich's books, and especially Helena's spiritual diaries, clearly showed that the two spiritual seekers were not opportunistic actors. The couple came to truly believe in their own theater of magic, becoming totally convinced they had been chosen by hidden masters of the Great White Brotherhood to speed up human spiritual evolution. The symbol of this grand mission became a skyscraper that Louis Horch, the Roerich's major donor, built in 1929 to accommodate spiritual and artistic projects of the painter. Located at 310 Riverside Drive in Manhattan, this twenty-four-story Master Building (a reference to Master Morya) was to become a cultural and intellectual beacon for humankind.

What the Shambhala warriors needed now was a new sponsor to back up their Great Plan. The United States became their natural choice, and the ocean of flattery that the Roeriches earlier showered on the Bolsheviks was now redirected toward America and particular politicians: President Herbert Hoover, the influential Republican senator from Idaho William Borah, and later President Franklin Delano Roosevelt. In the pages of Nicholas Roerich's books published after 1929, Mongol and Kalmyk nomads share legends about the "generous Giant," the "one who feeds people"—references to Hoover's American Relief Association, which fought famine in Soviet Russia in 1921–22. The most ridiculous statement was a flattering remark addressed to Borah: "A letter from him is considered a good passport everywhere. Sometimes in Mongolia, or in the Altai, or in Chinese Turkestan you can hear a strange pronunciation of his name: 'Boria is a powerful man.'" "This is so precious to hear," added Roerich without a hint of irony: the sweeter the talk the better.[38]

The biggest coup was making friends with Henry Wallace, a rising politician from Iowa, the Secretary of Agriculture and later Vice President in the FDR administration. Wallace came to the political spotlight during the Great Depression, when millions of unemployed workers, bankrupt farmers, and the majority of intellectuals came to the firm conclusion that the days of capitalism were over and that the future belonged, if not to communism, then definitely to a greater welfare state that would take care of people and tame unruly profiteers. Like many on the FDR team, the Iowa politician became disgusted with the free market going wild. Yet unlike his comrades, Wallace looked beyond social and economic change, contemplating a spiritual transformation of the human being. A deeply religious man, he attributed many social evils to the materialism of Western civilization. Thus he joined the growing tribe of Caucasian people who searched for redemption in Native American, Oriental, and Western esoteric traditions. This quest drew him to Indian shamans and Theosophy and led him to explore the influence of stars on Iowa cereal crops. In the early 1930s, Wallace was still looking for his spiritual niche. The plant physiologist Borodin, who had taken Roerich's project of the Sacred Union of the East so close to his heart, helped the seeker find the "correct" path. Sharing with Wallace a common interest in drought-resistant plants, Uncle Boris had courted the future Secretary of Agriculture since the end of the 1920s. Hearing of Wallace's spiritual side, Borodin revealed that in New York City there lived a man who would be able to quench his spiritual thirst. Thus, Wallace was drawn into Roerich's circle.

The painter immediately saw that the highly positioned seeker could be very useful for his Great Plan and began to gently cultivate this valuable contact. Massaging Wallace's ego, Roerich prophesized that he was destined to become the next president. Soon Wallace was admitted into the inner circle, receiving a ring and the esoteric name Galahad—a reference to the legend that Galahad, along with Parsifal, took the Holy Grail to the Orient. Fascinated with Roerich's prophecies and stories about travels to Buddhist areas, Wallace withdrew from the mainstream Theosophical Society and took up the Roeriches' cause. When Wallace became Secretary of Agriculture, the couple was eventually able to reach out to FDR, who already knew about the painter and his Master Building through his mother, Sara, a woman with esoteric leanings.

Soon Helena Roerich corresponded directly with the president, sending FDR her "fiery messages" peppered with advice about domestic and international politics.[39] In February 1935, she finally felt comfortable enough to reveal to the chief executive the details of the Great Plan, hinting that the United States might help this noble project: "Thus, the time for reconstruction in the East has come, and let us have friends of the Orient in America. The Union of Asian peoples is envisioned. The unification of the tribes and nationalities will proceed gradually. They will have their own federation. Mongolia, China, and the Kalmyk will counterbalance Japan. Mr. President, in this project of unification we need your good will."[40]

Meanwhile, rubbing shoulders with Wallace, Roerich suddenly saw an opportunity to use this friendship for his occult geopolitics. In the wake of the horrible drought that hit the Central Plains, the Department of Agriculture started looking for drought-resistant grasses and cereals, sending out its people to various parts of the globe, including Central and Inner Asia. When Roerich found out about it, he was quick to offer himself as an expert on Asian plant life. According to the painter's occult calendar, it was a good time for him to step out of the shadows and attempt to launch again the Sacred Union of the East: on December 17, 1933, the thirteenth Dalai Lama died. This "happy news," surmised the painter, would surely trigger a chain of events. To his circle of the elect he announced, "Now we have reached the future!"[41]

By the end of December Wallace was already in Roosevelt's office, trying to sell his boss on the idea of an Asian botanical expedition that would include Roerich and his son George. The president, who would soon take a personal interest in Roerich's cause, liked the project and gave his go-ahead. At the same time, the Secretary of Agriculture indirectly tried to prepare FDR for something bigger than simply a botanical venture, vaguely hinting that the political situation in Asia was always quite intriguing because of various ancient prophecies and legends. At the last moment, Wallace's worried subordinates convinced their boss to attach two actual plant scientists to the expedition. The Roeriches did not like this idea at all and immediately dissociated themselves from the agriculturalists by traveling separately.

Instead of going to Tibet and western China, the areas that earlier were so dear to his heart, the painter now rushed to northeastern China: Manchuria and Inner Mongolia. Why such a sudden change of itinerary? At first glance this choice did not make much sense, but if we look closely at the geopolitical situation in northeastern China at that time, all pieces of the puzzle fall in place.

The death of the Dalai Lama was surely an important occult sign. Yet there was no popular turmoil and discontent in Tibet at that time. At the same time, Manchuria, Chinese (Inner) Mongolia, and Red Mongolia were all on fire. In 1931, Japan, a rising imperialist giant, suddenly invaded China and occupied the northeastern part (Manchuria). From there, Japan now threatened the Soviet Far East, Mongolia, and central China, reviving in the Mongols' hearts hopes of liberation from the Chinese settlers and indigenous Bolsheviks who now crusaded against Tibetan Buddhism. In an apparent gesture of goodwill, Japan stimulated these hopes by setting up for the Mongols an autonomous region within Manchuria called Hsingan. Meanwhile, in 1929, the Soviets and their indigenous fellow travelers stopped courting lamas in Mongolia and unleashed merciless attacks against these former allies. Many monasteries were shut down, their properties confiscated, and lamas along with the rest of the nomads forced onto collective farms. A spontaneous rebellion of common Mongol shepherds and lamas against this assault began in 1931 simultaneously with Japan's invasion of Manchuria. Red Russia faced a real risk of losing Mongolia to Japan, and the Far East quickly became one of Stalin's major security concerns.

As they always did in times of great troubles, the Mongols tried to empower themselves with familiar prophecies. Rebellious lamas looked at the advancing Japanese army as legions of the legendary Shambhala king finally coming to deliver them from misery.[42] The venerated Panchen Lama added his voice to these sentiments: "The happiness will come from the East. Japanese and Mongols are people of the same kin, and Mongols should worship the Japanese emperor. One needs to struggle against the Red menace." Samdin, a Mongol Comintern spy who was hanging around the runaway Tibetan abbot, alerted his Moscow bosses that it was the first time Panchen brought up the Japanese in his talks, which was dangerous. Soon word spread all over Red Mongolia that the Panchen Lama himself would come and lead the Mongols in a war against the Red infidels. Although he did not provide any practical help to the rebels, his spiritual presence was powerful enough to arouse concerns. The Panchen Lama was traveling back and forth along the southern border of Mongolia, initiating nomads into the ranks of Shambhala warriors. The same Comintern agent worriedly reported, "The Panchen Lama spreads around holy prophecies, which speak of the holy yellow war of Shambhala."[43] The talk about the Shambhala holy war disturbed not only the Bolsheviks, but also Chinese settlers who had seized nomads' lands in Inner Mongolia and now had to face their wrath.

This was the explosive situation that Roerich craved to step into, and word about the coming Shambhala war in and around Mongolia was welcome news for him. Again it was time to set in motion the Great Plan: "Imagine, suddenly an invincible Mongolian army shows up and begins to win and to act—amazing!"[44] If successful in Manchuria and Red Mongolia, the painter could easily make an alliance with Japan and, drawing the Panchen Lama to his side, advance northward to Siberia and then southwest to Tibet. While dreaming about riding the Mongol revolts against the Bolsheviks and the Chinese, Roerich also planned to tap into the manpower of thousands of White Russian émigrés who resided in eastern China by offering as a spiritual role model St. Sergius of Radonezh, a medieval Russian Christian saint and patron of the military. The irony of the situation was that this saint had spiritually mobilized the Russian princes against the Mongol yoke. But the painter never mentioned this uncomfortable fact.

As usual, Roerich imagined himself as the head of the whole movement. On one of his canvases, he portrayed himself as St. Sergius

Figure 8.7. Nicholas Roerich's image of himself as St. Sergius the Builder in charge of a mighty army and under protection of the all-seeing eye of Master Morya.

surrounded by an army of warriors with spears ready for an attack. The painting also shows the face of Jesus Christ at the feet of the saint and the familiar all-seeing eye of the Great Architect of the Universe, an image borrowed from Freemasonry. Moreover, in conversations with his American associates Roerich began to talk openly about himself as leader of the future Asiatic theocracy. If other painters, musicians, and humanities professors could be politicians and even heads of states, the painter remarked, he could be too.[45]

Helena fed these ambitions by constantly saying that it was a time of the assertive politician, pointing out that all over Asia, Europe, and even in the United States people were opting for strong-willed leaders. Observing the megalomaniacal dreams of his friend, George Grebenst-chikoff, Roerich's expert on Siberia, now cautiously stepped aside, re-fusing to back up a new geopolitical venture. In fact, the writer could not resist making fun of the painter in his poem about the false tsar Dmitri, a seventeenth-century pretender who, backed up by a Polish king, tried to claim the Russian throne. Roerich was so angry that he excluded Grebenstchikoff from his inner circle.

As during his journey to Tibet, troubles pursued the Shambhala war-rior from the very beginning. In August 1934, on their way to Man-churia, the painter and his son stopped in Japan. There, without any official credentials, the painter began to act as a high American digni-tary, meeting the Japanese secretary of war and praising him for the job the Japanese occupation army was doing in China. Three years earlier, the United States had condemned Japan for invading China, and Roer-ich's behavior now looked very embarrassing. Roerich, who did not like that the United States favored China over Japan, viewed the Land of the Rising Sun as a positive force because it backed up the Mongols.

As soon as the botanical expedition stepped on Chinese soil, George Roerich got in touch with a representative of the Panchen Lama. But, surrounded by a tight ring of intelligence agents from various coun-tries, the spiritual leader of Tibet exercised extra caution and again re-fused to get involved in any grand scheme or conspiracy. Accompanied by several armed guards recruited from the ranks of Russian émigrés, the Roeriches then made a blitz visit to Manchurian Mongols right on the border with Red Mongolia, mingling with local princes and lamas. From Manchuria, Roerich and his son drove to Inner Mongolia, where they met Teh Wang, leader of the Mongol national liberation movement against the Chinese, promising him American support—another reckless step that further raised the eyebrows of U.S. diplomats in China and Japan.

En route, George kept a detailed diary, which seems more of a military journal than travel notes. He carefully scanned the topography of places they visited, measured hills and distances between various sites and towns, noted major intersections, and provided detailed information about the Japanese military transportation system, the movement of Japanese troops, and the plan of Teh Wang's headquarters. In short, this was a blueprint for developing future defensive and offensive plans.[46]

Figure 8.8. Nicholas and George Roerich during their "botanical expedition" to China with an occult spin. Manchuria–Inner Mongolia, 1934–35.

Simultaneously, at a monastery press in Inner Mongolia, Roerich had his brief biography printed in Mongolian to be distributed among local lamas. Again, as during his abortive Tibetan venture, the goal was to build up his image as the divine messenger of a new era with links to the Tibetan Buddhist tradition. This silly text filled with praises for the painter was written in 1926 by Tseveen Jamtsarano, a former cultural leader of Red Mongolia who befriended the Roeriches during their long stay in Urga in 1926. Jamtsarano, a Bolshevik fellow traveler, who, like Roerich, toyed with the idea of marrying Buddhism and Communism, endorsed the painter as a new Asian messiah: "Spreading all over the world, the name of the great Teacher Roerich, became the greatest in all countries. In future, if trouble happens somewhere, he will teach us and light our path."[47]

Besides this spiritual propaganda, the Roeriches explored Buddhist manuscripts in the monasteries they visited and collected samples of herbs used in Tibetan medicine. With such an intensive geopolitical, cultural, and medicinal agenda, there was hardly any time left for drought-resistant plants. During the sixteen months of their expedition, the Roeriches were able to produce specimens of only twenty plants, whereas the two botanists sent by the Department of Agriculture brought home more than two thousand plant samples, including 726 soil-conserving grasses.[48]

Red tide: a brownish-red discoloration of marine waters that is lethal to fish.

—Random House Dictionary of English Language

Epilogue:
The End of Red Shambhala

Roerich's careless steps and his megalomaniacal taste for adventure again backfired. First of all, he was noticed by the Japanese intelligence service and put on their close-watch list. Spies from the Land of the Rising Sun tried to figure out whom the painter worked for. Was he an American or Russian agent? In fact, the Japanese had been monitoring him on and off since the mid-1920s, reading his correspondence to his brother Vladimir, who had settled in Harbin in eastern China after escaping from the Bolsheviks.

Despite Nicholas Roerich's warm gestures to Tokyo supporting Mongol independence, the Japanese did not trust the painter. They became alarmed when, during his side trip to Harbin, a city that accommodated thousands of White Russian refugees, Roerich suddenly began acting as the future leader of the entire Russian émigré community. The Japanese were especially mad at the painter for speaking harshly against Konstantin Rodzaevsky, head of the Harbin-based Russian Fascist Party, whom Japanese intelligence was grooming as the chief of all Whites.

Thinking the Americans had purposely planted Roerich to disrupt this plan, Japanese intelligence unleashed a smear campaign in the press against the painter. The intercepted letters that Nicholas wrote to Vladimir in 1926 on the eve of his Tibetan expedition were excavated from the intelligence archives and made public.[1] Although in a heavily distorted form, parts of his Great Plan were now exposed. The press wrote that Roerich was a Mason, which was not true, and a messenger of the mysterious Great White Brotherhood that sought to establish a great Siberian state—which did contain elements of truth. Several newspapers drew attention to his brief romance with the Bolsheviks, wondering if it was still going on. Meanwhile, the American press raised hell, speculating about some hidden U.S. governmental agenda linked to the Roerich Manchurian expedition. So again the painter was caught in the crossfire of diplomatic, spy, and media games.

Still worse, the State Department informed his patron Wallace that the Soviets had sent a confidential protest to the American government, complaining that the dangerous émigré Roerich was wandering along the borders of Red Mongolia. The Bolsheviks were worried that "the armed party is now making their way toward the Soviet Union ostensibly as a scientific expedition but actually to rally former White elements and discontented Mongols."[2] To the last moment, Wallace backed up Roerich and dismissed all insinuations against his "botanist." Only when he realized that the painter had become a diplomatic embarrassment for the government and that his own career was now on the line did the Secretary of Agriculture call off the expedition, cut funding, and terminate all contact with his former guru. Eventually, along with Louis Horch, another sponsor who dropped Roerich, Wallace turned against the painter, initiating a tax-evasion lawsuit against him and seizing all his properties in the United States. FDR felt embarrassed about the whole situation and personally interfered, promising Horch and Wallace to call the judge who handled the case in order to guarantee the "correct" verdict. And sure enough, Roerich, who trusted Horch to do his finances, was indicted. Betrayed and humiliated by his esoteric partners Logvan and Galahad, Roerich never came back to the United States, wisely choosing to settle in India.

Manchurian Candidate: The Conclusion of Roerich's Odyssey

What went unnoticed at the time was that in January 1933 in Leningrad, right on the eve of the Manchurian expedition, Boris Roerich, another brother of the painter who remained in Red Russia, was suddenly released by OGPU for good behavior before his sentence expired; in May 1931, the Bolshevik secret police had set up and then arrested Boris for attempting to smuggle his own antique items to the West. Yet, there is an interesting detail here. Boris's three-year sentence seems more a house arrest. An architect by profession, he was confined to work at the secret technical bureau, designing the Big House, which headquartered the Leningrad branch of the secret police and Stalin's summer cottage! Here Nicholas Roerich's brother worked under Nikolai Lansere, the Soviet architectural star who received a similar sentence.[3]

Figure E.1. Left to right: Konstantin Riabinin, Boris Roerich, Sina Lichtmann-Fosdick, Nicholas Roerich. Urga, Mongolia, April 1927.

From Boris's recently declassified secret police file it is clear OGPU was using him as a tool in some sophisticated game that most certainly involved Nicholas Roerich. As early as February 1929, the secret police searched Boris's apartment, trying to find materials that might implicate him in espionage. Two months later he was recruited by OGPU and began working as its secret informer. Then two years later OGPU suddenly framed and arrested him for smuggling, sentencing him to three years in a concentration camp. Yet, hardly had two months passed before this draconian sentence was miraculously waived and replaced by benevolent confinement in the golden cage of the secret technical bureau.[4]

But this strange story does not end here. From 1936 to 1937, now in Moscow and again with Lansere, Boris Roerich worked on the monumental project of the All Union Institute of Experimental Medicine (VIEM), the notorious "new age" Stalinist research center described in chapter 4. What followed was even more stunning. From 1937 to 1939, during the period of the Great Terror when hundreds of thousands of Soviet intellectuals, including Lansere, and numerous Bolshevik bureaucrats were either shot or locked in concentration camps for a good deal less than being relatives of "enemies of the people," Boris continued his career as if nothing was happening and even improved his material conditions by moving to an elite neighborhood in Moscow, where he quietly died a natural death in 1945.[5] It is notable that during the same time when the architect lived safely in Moscow, Dr. Konstantin Riabinin, who never fought or spoke against the Bolshevik regime, was rearrested and placed in a concentration camp for fifteen more years simply for his association with the "English spy" Nicholas Roerich during the Tibetan expedition!

The facts of Boris Roerich's biography look shocking. Even without having such a "dangerous" brother, Boris, simply as a former White officer who fought against the Bolsheviks during the Civil War, was a prime candidate if not for execution then at least for a twenty-five-year sentence in a concentration camp. Still, by some providential force, the Bolsheviks' vengeance never reached him. How to explain this miracle? What was the magic shield that protected Boris Roerich? The most obvious answer is that this magic guardian was his adventurous brother. Remembering that the use of relatives to guarantee the cooperation of victims and the loyalty of OGPU agents was standard practice for Stalin's secret police, all pieces of the puzzle fall in place.

It is quite possible that Boris was a bargaining chip in some devious and sophisticated spy game that involved Nicholas Roerich. I will not repeat here the far-fetched argument made by Moscow writer Oleg Shishkin that after 1919 or 1920 the painter was always a paid Bolshevik spy and that his Master School in New York City was a cover for a Soviet spy ring.[6] There is simply no credible evidence to support such a case. At the same time, one cannot totally exclude the possibility that at some point Roerich was simply blackmailed by the Soviet secret police and forced to perform occasional clandestine assignments, especially during his Manchurian venture. These assignments might not have necessarily contradicted his Great Plan. They could include monitoring Japanese military activities near Red Mongolia's border, the location of their troops and military hardware, the status of Manchuria as a puppet state, and the general geopolitical situation in the area, a major concern for the Soviet Union in the 1930s. Bolshevik intelligence threw a tremendous amount of resources and manpower into the Far East, recruiting hundreds of unemployed White émigrés to spy on the Japanese. Besides, putting on a leash as a possible agent of influence the prominent Russian émigré who worked to unite White Russians and Mongols in a sacred crusade against Communism was not a bad idea. Viewed from this angle, the protest quietly delivered by the Soviets to the United States in 1935 regarding Roerich's "armed and dangerous party" might have simply been a good smokescreen to smooth the mission of the reluctant agent.

As long as Boris remained in the hands of the Soviet secret police, the painter's cooperation could be safely solicited anytime. There were signs that after their failed Tibetan venture Nicholas and Helena Roerich wanted to drop the Bolsheviks and find another sponsor. The couple probably thought their involvement of Moscow in their 1920s' geopolitical scheme was a one-time thing. If they thought so, they made a fatal mistake. If Nicholas Roerich wanted to drop the Bolsheviks, most likely they did not want to drop him. At the least, we know that Boris

Roerich, who in 1922 was ready to leave Russia to join his brother in New York, never got his chance.

After his second attempt to launch the Sacred Union of the East from Manchuria failed and after the Master Building was seized by Horch, Nicholas and Helena, along with their two sons, settled in northern India in the picturesque Kulu Valley. Right next door, beyond the Himalayan ranges, loomed the Tibet these "Shambhala warriors" failed to conquer. Immersing himself in painting local landscapes and entertaining occasional visitors, Roerich finally had to lay to rest his grand dreams of becoming the spiritual redeemer for humankind. Here in Kulu, the painter peacefully died in 1947 from prostate cancer. His wife followed him eight years later.

Yet before he died, during the Second World War when Russia was attacked by Nazi Germany, Roerich suddenly again became openly pro-Soviet and patriotic. Moreover, after the war ended, he approached the Soviet government, asking permission to return to Russia. Did the old man expect some special treatment from Stalin for occasional services he might have provided to the Bolshevik regime? Or was he simply an old, naïve idealist nostalgic for his motherland? Who knows? Fortunately for him, Red Russia refused to issue such permission. Roerich, who did not know anything about real life in the Bolshevik utopia, was certainly unaware how lucky he was. What could await him in Stalinist Russia in case he returned? The atmosphere of total suspicion, suffocating propaganda, and possibly a prison sentence.

In 1957, after the death of Stalin, George Roerich, a linguist and Tibetan scholar who was always part of his parents' Great Plan, followed his father's footsteps; he asked for and did receive permission to immigrate to the Soviet Union. The Soviets not only let him in but also awarded him a prestigious job as a senior research fellow at the Moscow Institute of Oriental Studies. Three years later he died from natural causes. The younger son, Svetoslav, an architect, lived a long life and died in 1993 at his estate in Bangalore, India. None of them left any offspring. It surely looked as if some divine punishment was inflicted on the Roerich clan for their attempts to meddle with human evolution and to elevate themselves above God.

Shambhala the Sinister:
The Fall of Gleb Bokii and His Red Merlin

In 1925, when their Shambhala expedition to Inner Asia fell through, the cryptographer Gleb Bokii and Alexander Barchenko began looking for traces of the mysterious kingdom within the Soviet Union. Using Special Section money, Barchenko traveled all over the country, contacting esoteric and occult groups and gathering prophetic lore. By the turn of the 1930s, it was getting harder to do such things. The dictatorship Stalin had been patiently building since the 1920s had matured, turning into a full-fledged totalitarian state. The dictator, rapidly being turned into a Red messiah to be worshipped and obeyed, was ready to phase out all his old comrades, the early Bolsheviks who, like Bokii, sometimes questioned things and for whom Stalin was not an authority.

Bokii's Special Section was gradually stripped of its functions, which were delegated to other departments of the secret police. Moreover, research into occult and paranormal phenomena and into engineering better human beings was now shifted to VIEM. By 1934, Bokii's section was relegated to its original tasks, ciphering and deciphering, and it even lost its name. It was no longer Special, but simply Section Nine. Although Bokii now occupied the prestigious rank of Commissar of State Security, the secret police equivalent of an army marshal, he did not have as much power as earlier. It was just a matter of time before the chief cryptographer would find himself on Stalin's hit list. By 1934, when all dissenting voices were silenced, it became dangerous to talk about things that did not fit politically correct and officially sanctioned lines. All occult and esoteric societies had already been wiped out, and their members were laboring in concentration camps. The general atmosphere in Red Russia forced people to become mute and invisible. Now Bokii had to think twice when meeting his friends and acquaintances, and especially before indulging in talks about the mysterious, occult, and paranormal. Such behavior could be easily interpreted as subversive. So the cryptographer caved in and began to avoid Barchenko.

Oblivious to what was going on around him, Barchenko, the aspiring Red Merlin, did not want to give up. He was still compulsively obsessed with his dream to enlighten the Bolshevik elite about Shambhala and Kalachakra and to teach them how to model and predict the future. In early 1936, he tried to press his OGPU patron to put him in touch with Viacheslav Molotov and Kliment Voroshilov, Stalin's two closest advisors. But Bokii wisely ignored this request. Barchenko then turned to Little Karl, Feodor Karlovich Leismaier-Schwarz, one of the former secret police officers who had introduced him to Bokii in the first place. Probably driven by the same desire to partake of the great cause, Leismaier-Schwarz, now working as a photojournalist in Leningrad, foolishly agreed to Barchenko's request. Both naively believed that Leismaier-Schwarz's brief stint as a secret police officer during the first days of the revolution would open doors to the corridors of power. Although Little Karl was not able to reach any Bolshevik dignitaries, he was able to hand the synopsis of Barchenko's ancient science to Voroshilov's secretary.

Barchenko waited for a year and, having received no answer, made a more dangerous move. He decided to go straight to Stalin to enlighten him about Shambhala and Kalachakra. Turning again to Little Karl, he gave him a hazardous assignment—to get into the Kremlin and prepare a personal meeting between Barchenko and the Red dictator! A few months later, when interrogated by Stalin's agents, Leismaier-Schwarz remembered, "Barchenko complained to me that it was very hard to penetrate party and state leadership. He was frustrated with Bokii, who was not active enough to fulfill Barchenko's guidelines and who could not set up a meeting with Stalin. So I volunteered to fulfill this task. Barchenko accepted my offer and said, 'Try to meet Stalin personally.'"[7] This time, not only did Little Karl fail to reach Stalin, but he also attracted the attention of the secret police.

EPILOGUE

It is hard to explain what drove Barchenko and Leismaier-Schwarz to such reckless behavior. In 1937, when people all over Russia, especially in capital cities, lay low, paralyzed by fear of the Great Terror, and when everybody carefully tried to exercise self-censorship, Barchenko still boldly dreamed about upgrading Communism through the wisdom of Shambhala and Kalachakra. He might simply have become a prisoner of his grand delusion to the point of obsession and conveyed this virus to the spineless Leismaier-Schwarz. Another possible explanation is that, after losing Bokii, who generously funded his esoteric trips, he felt the need to latch on again to a powerful sponsor (the higher the better) to continue his quest. In all fairness, the advent of the totalitarian state would have sooner or later consumed Bokii, Barchenko, Leismaier-Schwarz, and the like anyway. They simply stood out too much with their suspicious esoteric agenda. Still, by his careless behavior Barchenko sped up the process. In the atmosphere of total suspicion and mistrust that reigned in 1930s' Russia, his paranoid zeal to reach out to the Bolshevik elite backfired.

The final judgment came on May 16, 1937. On that day, the "Bloody Dwarf," Nikolai Ezhov, the new secret police chief appointed by Stalin to purge old members of the Bolshevik Party, summoned Bokii to his office. The cryptographer was always surprised why his former wife, Sofia, and her husband, Moskvin, welcomed this five-foot-tall, not-very-educated, mediocre underclass fellow to their apartment. What did they find in this petty bureaucrat with the watery eyes of a sadist? Maybe it was his agreeable nature and good voice: the dwarf excelled in singing ballads. Moskvin had stupidly promoted him as a secretary of the Central Committee of the Bolshevik Party, where Stalin noticed the obedient workaholic clerk and took him under his wing.

When Ezhov demanded that Bokii turn over all compromising files Bokii had kept since the 1920s on top Bolshevik bosses, adding that this was Comrade Stalin's order, the cryptographer could not restrain himself: "Who cares about your Stalin. It was Lenin who put me into my position."[8] By saying this, Bokii signed his own death warrant. For the next two days the cryptographer was interrogated by one of his colleagues, Commissar of State Security Lev Belsky,[9] assisted by a semiliterate senior lieutenant from Kazakhstan, Ali Kutebarov, a product of the Bolshevik affirmative-action program.

Bokii was originally accused of espionage for England and of being a member of a secret Freemason society that tried to predict the future—a reference to the long-defunct esoteric commune United Labor Brotherhood (ULB) created by Barchenko. The cryptographer did not hide his doubts and frustrations about the revolution, and he also described how his interest in esotericism drove him to Barchenko's ancient science and the Shambhala quest. Trying to save his life, Bokii revealed the names of friends and acquaintances who took part in their esoteric talks and classes. A few days later, all of these people were rounded up and arrested. Based on their stories, Belsky eventually made up a case about a subversive religious and political Freemason order called Shambhala-Dunkhor with branches all over the world, including Red Russia. According to his scenario, this sinister secret society was used by England to penetrate the minds of top Bolshevik leaders and control them. It was obvious that the compulsive grand dreams nourished by Barchenko now boomeranged. In the hands of this Stalin henchman, Shambhala, the resplendent and peaceful Tibetan Buddhist paradise, was turned into its opposite—a sinister destructive force that threatened Red Russia.

The transcript of Bokii's interrogation, which was heavily edited by Belsky, reveals the process of the invention of the counterrevolutionary Shambhala-Dunkhor society:

Belsky: Give me detailed testimony about the spy activities of Barchenko.

Bokii: The spy activities of Barchenko were mainly focused on building up a network of espionage. The work proceeded in two directions. First, it was the organization of a spy network on the periphery. Second, it was a penetration into the party and governmental circles. The latter was done to take over the minds of leadership and, following the example of Masonic organizations in capitalist countries like, for example, in France, guide their activities in a needed direction. For the work on the periphery, Barchenko used various religious and mystical sects of Eastern origin. For this purpose, he made frequent trips to different areas of the Soviet Union, establishing connections with local sects and meeting their foreign emissaries. To penetrate the Soviet ruling circles, Barchenko tried to make some of them interested in his scientific research, its significance for the country's defense, and so forth. Getting somebody interested in this scientific side, he gradually disclosed his teaching about Shambhala. Then, wrapping his victims in the web of mysticism, he used them for espionage purposes. That is how he brainwashed me and penetrated OGPU.[10]

Belsky's imagination notwithstanding, in the 1930s Shambhala indeed became somewhat of a threat to Soviet leadership. Lamas who revolted in Mongolia against Communism linked this legend to the Japanese army that advanced into Manchuria, viewing it as the army of Shambhala. Besides, in Stalin's Siberian backyard Buryat clergy, furious about the forced Soviet collectivization and assault on their faith, began to send around chain letters with the same prophecy about the coming Shambhala war against Red enemies of the Buddhist faith. As early as 1929, right at the beginning of the Stalin "revolution," Agvan Dorzhiev and his lama friends, before erecting a new Kalachakra prayer site in the Trans-Baikal area, placed in its foundation nine hundred thousand steel needles, symbolizing the iron warriors of the future Shambhala king. In 1937–38, when the last Buddhist monasteries were shut down in Siberia, Soviet media began to link the Shambhala prophecy to fascism and Japanese militarism.

Although Belsky pressed Bokii hard to provide specifics of his spy activities, he was not able to dig anything up except for Bokii's mysticism and his membership in the long-defunct ULB. Moreover, even the

Figure E.2. Lev Belsky, the Bolshevik secret police investigator, who in 1937 manufactured the case about a sinister anti-Soviet worldwide clandestine organization
named Shambhala-Dunkhor.

edited transcript of the interrogation shows that, while playing to Belsky's script, Bokii nevertheless tried to water down the accusations of
espionage in order to break the whole case. Moreover, at one point he
flatly rejected all espionage accusations:

Belsky: Why did you seek contacts with counterrevolutionaries and
spies?

Bokii: I never sought any special contacts with spy elements. I sought
contacts with the abovementioned sects and cults because I was lured
by Barchenko's mystical teaching. I do admit that I placed mastering the
mysteries of this teaching above the interests of the Communist Party and the state. In my eyes, the high task of mastering the scientific-

mystical mysteries of Shambhala justified the deviation from the Marxist-Leninist teaching about classes and class warfare. However, I did not specially plan to do any harm to the party or the Soviet power, and not a single member of our order was known as a spy or a person who had links to spies. . . .

Belsky: What spy activities did you conduct personally, and what particular spy assignments did you receive from Barchenko?

Bokii: I never received direct espionage assignments from Barchenko. By being immersed in Barchenko's mysticism, I simply neglected interests of the state and covered his activities by the name of the Special Section, which assisted him to conduct spy work.

Belsky: The investigator does not trust you. Trying to shift the investigation away from your spy activities, you want to move it in the other direction. I suggest that you sincerely confess your spy work. . . .

Bokii: I cannot add anything to what I have already told you.[11]

To make the cryptographer look creepier, the stories about Bokii's naturist commune and group sex were added, along with the collection of mummified penises found in his apartment. So the cryptographer looked like a perfect degenerate and a pervert through and through. Still, all this did not make a spy case convincing enough to please Stalin. It seems that at this point the crude Kutebarov entered the game. During a second interrogation in August 1937 (one wonders what happened to Bokii during the previous three months), the cryptographer suddenly confessed that, on top of other evil things, the Shambhala-Dunkhor order planned to blow up the Kremlin and assassinate the Red dictator at his retreat on the Black Sea.

A second interrogation usually took place when a victim did not cooperate. The arsenal of tools of persuasion varied. They included beatings, squeezing of genitals, breaking ribs, burning with cigarettes, and urinating on detainees. Yet the most effective and "cleanest" method was the practice of using victims' relatives as hostages. One of Bokii's daughters suffered from asthma and could have been a good bargaining chip for his interrogators.[12] Whatever methods they used, Belsky and Kutebarov cracked the cryptographer along with other members of the Shambhala-Dunkhor "ring." It is essential to note that Bokii was disposed of not because he was involved in mysticism and the esoteric Shambhala quest that did not fit Marxism, but because he belonged to the old revolutionaries who never viewed Stalin as the Red messiah. With or without Shambhala, merely by belonging to the old Marxists, Bokii was doomed to be exterminated, as were thousands of his colleagues. On November 15, 1937, after a closed trial, which was conducted by three secret police officers and took only fifteen minutes, Bokii was condemned to death, executed, and cremated on the same day.[13]

All the other people who had unfortunately associated themselves with Bokii and Barchenko were also executed in 1937, including Kondiain, Leismaier-Schwarz, Moskvin, and others. Bokii's former wife, Sofia Doller, was also zealously interrogated and after a "sincere" confession was promptly shot. Yet she was not included in the ranks of the Shambhala-Dunkhor culprits. Ezhov ordered that she be made part of a separate but no less exotic case. Belsky and Kutebarov assigned her and the doctor of Tibetan medicine Nikolai Badmaev to the role of Japanese spies. According to the secret police script, the Japan ordered Doller and Badmaev, her and Moskvin's close friend, to dispose of Ezhov by using exotic herbal poisons delivered from Tibet.[14]

Two years later Stalin ordered the execution of the executioners themselves. "Bloody Dwarf" Ezhov, who, to stretch his muscles, once in a while liked to descend to a secret police cellar to perform an execution, now himself was shot by his colleagues in the same cellar after listening to false accusations of terrorism, spying, and homosexuality. A year later, Belsky and Kutebarov followed their boss.

The last one of these Shambhala seekers to be shot was Barchenko, chief of the "spy ring," who fought for his life to the very end. The failed

Red Merlin eagerly cooperated with the investigation and played to the changing scenarios of his investigators, implicating himself and others in all kinds of crimes and adding more details from his life as early as 1917. Already condemned to death, he still struggled to extend his days, resorting to familiar "scientific" tools. On December 24, 1937, he wrote directly to Ezhov. In this last pathetic appeal he masochistically pleaded, "I was informed that my case has been completed. I fully disarmed myself with no loophole for retreat and revealed to the investigation all details, events, and names from my past. I clearly understand that I am responsible for what I did and do not ask you to soften my fate. Yet, let me draw your attention to the fact that I discovered a physical phenomenon unknown to modern science." The rest of his long letter was designed to awe the chief of Stalin's secret police with another miraculous scientific story. Now it was a legend about the secret of energy regulation used by bacteria—a discovery that promised to arm Red Russia with an "extraordinary powerful weapon" to fight epidemic diseases and protect the country from bacteriological attacks.[15] The message was obvious: please, save me, I still can be useful.

Yet nothing helped, and on April 25, 1938, with a bullet in the back of his head, the Red Merlin followed his brethren from the Shambhala-Dunkhor order. Who was Barchenko? A sincere, naive spiritual seeker who became the prisoner of his compulsive dream or a talented scientist, as his Russian biographer Alexandre Andreyev hinted.[16] Probably the former. A dropout medical student and an occult-fiction writer, he never had a systematic knowledge of biology, physics, or other sciences. Contrary to his claims, neither was he an expert on Tibetan Buddhism. Even in the field of esotericism, Barchenko unfortunately did not create anything new, simply adjusting Alexandre d'Alveydre's "subterranean blues" to the Communist utopia. What he definitely excelled in was trumpeting his ancient science, a smorgasbord of Kalachakra, d'Alveydre's Agartha, and Eliphas Levi's books. Clearly a charismatic spiritual adventurer, Barchenko convinced himself and several dozen people around him that he knew how to scientifically engineer a society free of social ills, and in this capacity he kept offering himself to the Bolshevik elite.

Red Pilgrims to Ashes: Shumatsky, Borisov, and Others

No less tragic was the fate of those romantic Bolsheviks who in the 1920s rushed into Mongolia, western China, and farther to Tibet to build the Red Shambhala paradise by stirring indigenous prophecies and instigating lamas to revolution. By 1930, after nationalist movements in China, India, and other Eastern countries failed to mutate into a Communist revolution, the Bolsheviks realized that the project of world Communism was going no farther than Mongolia. Soviet fortunes were at low ebb, and Stalin ordered all outreach ventures to be halted, concentrating on his domestic agenda.[17] It was clear that Communism could not win over nationalism, which showed no indication of exhausting itself as the Bolsheviks expected. In a decisive move, the dictator cracked down on the Communist indigenous elites that had expanded their influence in the 1920s. He also slowed down affirmative-action programs for indigenous ethnic groups and stopped flirting with religions. The brief romance with Tibetan Buddhism was over.

Red Russia was quickly turning into an isolated Communist fortress, shutting down contacts with the outside world. Comintern, an organization specially created to sponsor worldwide revolution, became an unnecessary appendix. Crippled by arrests of its agents, it was eventually shut down. Commissar for Foreign Affairs Georgy Chicherin, a Russian noble turned Bolshevik diplomat, was quickly losing his power. At first, he retreated to Germany to relax from the suffocating police-state environment Stalin was creating. Then, not wishing to betray the cause, Chicherin returned and quietly retired in 1929, then conveniently died in 1936 on the eve of Stalin's Great Terror, which mowed down all of Chicherin's team.

Sergei Borisov was one of the first to go down. This Oirot Bolshevik, who helped to foment revolution in Mongolia and then as a "lama" led an expedition to Tibet, made a good career in the foreign affairs commissariat, serving as deputy chair of the Eastern Department. On September 10, 1937, Borisov was tried and shot along with hundreds of other early Bolsheviks working in the Soviet Foreign Service. Elbek-Dorji Rinchino, the Buryat intellectual and first Red dictator of Mongolia who dreamed about the vast pan-Mongol Communist empire, was executed a year later. At least, unlike Borisov, who was simply shot for no reason as a Japanese spy, Rinchino was disposed of with a good official excuse as an unreformed proponent of pan-Mongolism. Agvan Dorzhiev, another player in the great Bolshevik game in Inner Asia, ended his Shambhala quest in a secret police prison morgue. By the 1930s, futile compromises with the Bolshevik regime morally broke down this former Dalai Lama ambassador to Russia. In 1937, with the advent of Stalin's Great Terror, secret police shut down his Kalachakra temple in Leningrad as a "counterrevolutionary cell," and Dorzhiev decided to return to his home in Siberia, hoping to spend his last years in peace and prayer. Yet once there the feeble eighty-four-year-old Buryat lama was immediately arrested as a Japanese spy. The Shambhala seeker did not even live to see his execution, dying from a heart attack after his first and only interrogation.

Boris Shumatsky, the polyglot Bolshevik organizer equally at home with his Yiddish-speaking kin, Russian workers, and Buryat or Mongol nomads, followed his former comrades-in-arms. This revolutionary who wanted to bring Communism to all of northern Eurasia constantly clashed with Stalin when trying to secure more self-government for indigenous people in Siberia. As early as the 1920s, Shumatsky was already out of favor with the budding dictator, who did not like this assertive Jew from Siberia. After a brief stint as president of the university that trained Comintern agents, Shumatsky was made the chief Bolshevik censor supervising the emerging Soviet cinema. In 1938, he was sentenced to execution for the crime that perfectly fit his latest position: Shumatsky found out he was planning to assassinate Comrade Stalin during a movie screening for the dictator.

Of all the Bolsheviks and their fellow travelers who conjured Red Shambhala in Inner Asia, the most prominent one to survive Stalin's slaughterhouse was the chubby Mongolian Choibalsan, former member of Comintern's Mongol-Tibetan Department. In 1937, this short and shy former junior lama was elevated by Stalin to the position of Mongolia's dictator. His predecessor had lost his life for wondering aloud how it was possible to eliminate one hundred thousand lamas—a goal the Russian dictator set for his Mongol comrades. Choibalsan, who preferred listening and doing to asking questions, took this assignment seriously. He cracked down on his former brothers, wiping out those who resisted and sending those who were mute and submissive into his army to serve as soldiers or to concentration camps to perform hard labor. By 1940, the Mongol Buddhist clergy was decimated.[18] When rounded up to be sent to Siberian camps, many lamas could not comprehend the magnitude of the whole event, believing they were being shipped to northern Shambhala, the cherished land of spiritual bliss. Thus came true the dream of the lama bandit Ja-Lama, who in his small totalitarian paradise in the Gobi Desert dreamed about making "lazy" lamas perform productive labor.

In the summer of 2009, I was returning to the United States from Moscow, where I had completed gathering archival material for this book. Having a ten-hour wait before my flight, I decided to go to downtown Moscow to find sites linked to major characters in this book. The place where in the 1920s Bokii and Barchenko conjured their Shambhala project was not difficult to find. The four-floor structure at 21 Kuznetsky Bridge then belonged to the Commissariat for Foreign Affairs. The two upper floors, which to Chicherin's chagrin accommodated Bokii's Special Section, are now apartments. In an adjacent building around the corner on Lubyanka Square, Chicherin, Shumatsky, and Borisov worked out their Mongol and Tibetan schemes.

I came to enjoy my small tour of Red Shambhala sites, and upon landing in New York I decided to continue it. Now my destination was

310 Riverside Drive, Nicholas Roerich's skyscraper. The Master Building is still there, solid and sound. In fact, now it is a historic landmark. Somewhere down below in the foundation is a treasure chest containing Tibetan coins and a letter with the prophecy of a new golden age. A young, intelligent-looking fellow wearing earphones came out of the building. He explained that the building was now completely occupied by apartments and that he had heard some weird Russian painter once owned the skyscraper. He looked surprised (if he actually understood what I was talking about) when I said that the weird painter designed this magnificent tower-like structure to become the Master Building, beacon of knowledge and highest spirituality for all humankind.

I was about to add a couple of words about Roerich and his wife, but the man was already walking away. I smiled to myself: Busy people, both in Moscow and New York, are deeply immersed in their twenty-first-century hectic lifestyles. Why should they care about forgotten ideological alchemists who tried to engineer noble human beings and build a perfect society in which all problems would be solved once and for all—a quest that took them, along with millions of their contemporaries, on a path of self-destruction?

Notes

Abbreviation

RASPH: Rossiiskii Arkhiv sotsial'no-politicheskoii istorii, [Russian Archive of Social and Political History], Moscow

Preface

1. Emanuel Sarkisyanz, *Russland and der Messianismus des Orients-Sendungs-bewusstsein und politischer Chiliasmus des Ostens* [Russia and Oriental Messianism: Sense of Mission and Political Chiliasm in the East] (Tübingen: J. C. P. Mohr, 1955); Emanuel Sarkisyantz, "Communism and Lamaist Utopianism in Central Asia," *Review of Politics* 20, no. 4 (1958): 623–33.
2. "Shambhala," in *The Oxford Dictionary of World Religions*, ed. John Bowker (Oxford: Oxford University Press, 1997), 885.
3. Chogyam Trungpa, *Shambhala: The Sacred Path of the Warrior* (Boulder, CO: Shambhala, 1984).
4. An example of this type of criticism is Donald S. Lopez, *Prisoners of Shangri-La: Tibetan Buddhism and the West* (Chicago: University of Chicago Press, 1998). In contrast, two recent books have provided an unbiased account of the cultural history of Buddhism in the West: Lawrence Sutin, *All is Change: The Two-Thousand-Year Journey of Buddhism to the West* (New York: Little, Brown and Co., 2006); Jeffery Paine, *Re-enchantment: Tibetan Buddhism Comes to the West* (New York: W. W. Norton, 2004).
5. See, for example, Christopher Hale, *Himmler's Crusade: The Nazi Expedition to Find the Origins of the Aryan Race* (New York: Wiley, 2003).
6. Gary Lachman, *Politics and the Occult: The Left, the Right, and the Radically Unseen* (Wheaton, IL: Quest Books, 2008), xv.
7. Helena Roerich (E. I. Rerikh), *Vysokii put'* [High Path], vol. 1 (1920–1928), vol. 2 (1929–1944), (Moscow: Sfera, 2006). These two volumes present extensive excerpts from her journals, now scanned and posted at http://urusvati.agni-age.net. The other valuable sources on the activities of the

Roeriches, particularly on their Inner Asian expedition, are the Tibetan journals of their travel companions Dr. Konstantin Riabinin, Pavel Portniagin, and Colonel Nikolai Kordashevsky. These journals have all been published and now are available on the Web at http://aryavest.com/journals.php.

8. Alexandre Andreyev, *Vremya Shambaly: okkultizm, nauka i politika v Sovetskoi Rossii* [Time of Shambhala: Occultism, Science, and Politics in Soviet Russia] (St. Petersburg: Neva, 2004); Alexandre Andreyev, *Soviet Russia and Tibet: The Debacle of Secret Diplomacy, 1918–1930s* (Leiden and Boston: Brill, 2003).

9. Vladimir Rosov, *Nikolai Rerikh vestnik Zvenigoroda* [Nicholas Roerich: Messenger of Zvenigorod], vol. 1 (Velikii plan) (St. Petersburg: Aleteiia, 2002); vol. 2 (Novaia strana) (Moscow: Ariavarta-Press, 2004).

10. Oleg Shishkin, *Bitva za Gimalaii: NKVD, magiia i shpionazh* [Fight for the Himalayas: NKVD, Magic, and Espionage] (Moscow: Olma-Press, 1999), 316–75.

11. John McCannon, "Searching for Shambhala: The Mystical Art and Epic Journeys of Nikolai Roerich," *Russian Life* 44, no. 1 (2001): 48–56, and "By the Shores of White Waters: The Altai and Its Place in the Spiritual Geopolitics of Nicholas Roerich," *Sibirica: Journal of Siberian Studies* 2, no. 3 (2002): 166–89; Markus Osterrieder, "From Synarchy to Shambhala: The Role of Political Occultism and Social Messianism in the Activities of Nicholas Roerich," www.harrimaninstitute.org/MEDIA/00741.pdf (accessed Feb. 5, 2010). About the occult side of Roerich's activities, see Richard Spence, "Red Star Over Shambhala: Soviet, British and American Intelligence & the Search for Lost Civilization in Central Asia," *New Dawn Magazine* July-August (2008), http://www.newdawnmagazine.com/article/Red_Star_Over_Shambhala.html (accessed Nov. 1, 2009).

12. Sarkisyanz, *Russland and der Messianismus des Orients*; Terry Martin, *The Affirmative Action Empire: Nations and Nationalism in the Soviet Union, 1923–1939* (Ithaca: Cornell University Press, 2001).

Chapter One

1. John R. Newman, "A Brief History of the Kalachakra," in *The Wheel of Time: The Kalachakra in Context*, ed. Beth Simon (Ithaca, NY: Snow Lion Publications, 1991), 54–58.

2. Edwin Bernbaum, *The Way to Shambhala: A Search for the Mystical Kingdom Beyond the Himalayas* (Los Angeles: Tarcher, 1980), 25.

3. Sergei Tokarev, *History of Religion* (Moscow: Progress Publishers, 1989), 314.

4. "Predskazanie sviashchennosluzhitelia Lobsan Palden Yeshe," [Lobsan Palden Yeshe Prophecy] in *Baron Ungern v dokumentakh i materialakh* [Baron Ungern: Documents and Materials], ed. S. L. Kuzmin, (Moscow: KMK, 2004), 1:150–51.

5. Victor Trimondi and Victoria Trimondi, *The Shadow of the Dalai Lama: Sexuality, Magic and Politics in Tibetan Buddhism*, part 1 (2003), http://www.iivs.de/~iivs01311/SDLE/Part-1-10.htm (accessed Dec. 6, 2009).

6. Johan Elverskog, *Buddhism and Islam on the Silk Road* (Philadelphia: Pennsylvania University Press, 2010): 96–98; Alexander Berzin, "Holy Wars in Buddhism and Islam: The Myth of Shambhala," http://www.berzinarchives.com (accessed Dec. 5, 2009); Trimondi, *Shadow of the Dalai Lama*.

7. Helmut Hoffman, *The Religions of Tibet* (London: Allen and Unwin, 1996), 125–26; Roger Jackson, "Kalachakra in Context," in *Wheel of Time*, 33.

8. Newman, "Brief History of the Kalachakra," 85. The Tajiks are Turkic-speaking seminomadic people in Central Asia who embraced Islam in the early Middle Ages.

9. Ibid., 78–80.

10. Berzin, "Holy Wars in Buddhism and Islam."

11. See Lokesh Chandra, ed., *The Collected Works of Bu-ston* (New Delhi: International Academy of Indian Culture, 1965).

12. Bernbaum, *Way to Shambhala*, 123–24.

13. Trimondi and Trimondi, "Kalachakra: The Public and the Secret Initiations," chap. 6 in *Shadow of the Dalai Lama*, part 1.

14. Edward A. Arnold, ed., *As Long As Space Endures: Essays on the Kalacakra Tantra in Honor of H. H. the Dalai Lama* (Ithaca, NY: Snow Lion Publications, 2009), 58, 83, 98.

15. David Snellgrove, *Indo-Tibetan Buddhism* (Boston: Shambhala, 1987), 1:125–26.

16. Trimondi and Trimondi, "The Law of Inversion," chap. 4 in *Shadow of the Dalai Lama*, part 1.

17. Robert Beer, *The Handbook of Tibetan Buddhist Symbols* (Boston: Shambhala, 2003).

18. The Kalachakra deity is the personification of Kalachakra tantra.

19. For a detailed description of protective gods in Tibetan Buddhism, see Alice Getty, *The Gods of Northern Buddhism* (Rutland, VT: Charles E. Tuttle Co., 1974), 142–64.

20. Emil Schlagintweit, *Buddhism in Tibet* (1863; reprint, New York: Augustus M. Kelly, 1969), 112–13.

21. Romio Shrestha and Ian A. Baker, *Celestial Gallery* (New York: Fall River Press, 2009), 16.

22. Rene de Nebesky-Wojkowitz, *Oracles and Demons of Tibet: The Cult and Iconography of the Tibetan Protective Deities* (Graz, Austria: Akademische Druck-u. Verlagsanstalt, 1975), 343.

23. Walther Heissig, *A Lost Civilization: The Mongols Rediscovered*, trans. from German D. J. S. Thomson (New York: Basic Books, 1966), 86.

Chapter Two

1. A bodhisattva is one who has attained perfection and is ready to become Buddha but instead chooses to stay in this world to help other humans.

2. Albert Grünwedel, ed. and trans., *Der Weg nach Sambhala* [The Way to Shambhala] (Munich: G. Franz in Komm, 1915).

3. Owen Lattimore, *Nationalism and Revolution in Mongolia* (Leiden: E. J. Brill, 1955), 51.

4. Gavin Hambly, "Lamaist Civilization in Tibet and Mongolia," in *Central Asia*, ed. Gavin Hambly (New York: Delacorte Press, 1969), 258.

5. M. Huc, *Travels to Tartary, Thibet, and China during the Years 1844–1846* (London: National Illustrated Library, 1854), 2:158.

6. Rebecca Empson, introduction to *Time, Causality and Prophecy in the Mongolian Cultural Region: Visions of Future*, ed. Rebecca Empson (Kent, UK: Global Oriental, 2006), 2, 5, 8.

7. Huc, *Travels to Tartary*, 158–59.

8. Bernbaum, *Way to Shambhala*, 81 (see chap. 1, n. 2).

9. Besides Gautama and Maitreya, other chief Buddhas are Dipankara, the Buddha of Fixed Light; Kasyapa, the Keeper of Light; Manla, the Buddha of Medicine; and Amitabha, the Buddha of Infinite Light.

10. Alice Sarkozi, *Political Prophecies in Mongolia in the 17–20th Centuries* (Wiesbaden: Otto Harrassowitz, 1992), 130–31.

11. Lattimore, *Nationalism and Revolution in Mongolia*, 57.

12. Ferdinand Ossendowski, *Beasts, Men and Gods* (New York: Dutton, 1922), 113–21.
13. Andrei Znamenski, "Power of Myth: Popular Nationalism and Nationality-Building in Mountain Altai, 1904–1922," *Acta Slavica Iaponica* 22 (2005): 45 (http://src-h.slav.hokudai.ac.jp/publictn/acta/22/znamenski.pdf).
14. The conflict between the Dalai Lama and the Panchen Lama as well as the story of Panchen's escape from Tibet is detailed in Melvyn Goldstein, *A History of Modern Tibet, 1913–1951* (Berkeley: University of California Press, 1989), 110–20.
15. Ja-Lama at first modestly declared himself the grandson of Amursana. Then, after his popularity increased, he announced that he was in fact the reincarnation of the legendary prince. For a biography of Ja-Lama in English, see Don Croner, *False Lama: The Life and Death of Dambijant-san* (2009), http://dambijantsan.doncroner.com/index.html (accessed Aug. 31, 2009). For the most complete account of his life story, consult *Golova Dzha-Lamy* [Ja-Lama's Head] (Ulan-Ude and St. Petersburg: Ecoart, 1993) by Inessa Lomakina, a Russian writer and historian of Mongolia.
16. Boris Vladimirtsov, *Raboty po istorii i etnografii mongol'skikh narodov* [History and Ethnography of the Mongol People] (Moscow: iz-vo vostochnoi literatury, 2002), 276.
17. Ossendowski, *Beasts, Men and Gods*, 119.
18. The German photographer Hermann Consten, who happened to spy for the Russians in and around Kobdo, left a vivid description of the event in *Weideplätze der Mongolen* [Mongol Pastures] (Berlin: Dietrich Reimer, 1920), 2:214–17.
19. Inessa Lomakina, *Groznie makhakaly Vostoka* [Avenging Mahakalas of the East] (Moscow: Eksmo-Iauza, 2004), 127, 130.

Chapter Three

1. The Soviet secret police went through numerous name changes. Originally, it carried the long name Extraordinary Commission for Combating Sabotage and Counterrevolution, which was immediately abbreviated as Cheka. In the 1920s, it was known at first as GPU (State Political Administration) and then as OGPU (Ob'edinnnoe politicheskoe upravlenie, United State Political Administration). For the sake of clarity, I use OGPU.

2. By 1917, Russian Marxists who wanted to bring Communism to Russia were split into two groups, Mensheviks (people of minority) and Bolsheviks (people of majority). The Mensheviks, moderate socialists, relied more on parliamentary democratic methods. Lenin and his militant Bolshevik comrades, on the contrary, considered such democratic practices as parliaments and elections a bourgeois fraud and worked to bring about a Communist revolution in Russia and beyond.

3. "Iz protokola doprosa G. I. Bokia, May 17, 1937" [Minutes of Interrogation of G. I. Bokii, May 17, 1937], in Andreyev, *Vremya Shambaly*, 210 (see preface, n. 8).

4. Martin McCauley, *The Rise and Fall of the Soviet Union* (Harlow, UK: Pearson, 2008), 54; Jörg Baberowski, *Der Rote Terror: die Geschichte des Stalinismus* [Red Terror: History of Stalinism] (Munich: Deutsche Verlags-Anstalt, 2003), 28–29.

5. Donald Rayfield, *Stalin and His Hangmen: The Tyrant and Those Who Killed for Him* (New York: Random House, 2005), 67.

6. Igor Minutko, *Iskushenie uchitelia* [Master's Temptation] (Moscow: AST Press, 2005), 109–12.

7. Andreyev, *Vremya Shambaly*, 76 (see preface, n. 8).

8. "Protokol doprosa A. V. Barchenko, sledovatel' Ali Kutebarov" [Minutes of Interrogation of A. V. Barchenko, Interrogator Ali Kutebarov], in Oleg Shishkin, *Bitva za Gimalaii*, 353 (see preface, n. 10).

9. Alexandre Saint-Yves d'Alveydre, "Missia Indii v Evrope" [Mission of India in Europe], in *Mezhdu Shambaloi i Agarthoi: orakuly velikoi tainy* [Between Shambhala and Agartha: Oracles of Great Mystery], ed. Alexandre Andreyev and Oleg Shishkin (Moscow: Eksmo-Iauza, 2005), 59–60.

10. Adolph Erman, *Travels in Siberia* (London: Longman, 1848), 2:38.

11. Eduard Kudriavtsev, "Novoe ob okkultiste strany Sovetov," [New Materials about a Soviet Occultist] *Neva* 12 (2006): 280–81.

12. "Protokol doprosa A. V. Barchenko," 354.

13. Ibid., 370–71.

14. Anna Viroubova, *Memories of the Russian Court* (New York: Macmillan, 1923), 358.

15. Vladimir Bekhterev, *Collective Reflexology* (New Brunswick, NJ: Transaction Publishers, 2001).

16. Mikhail Agursky, "An Occult Source of Socialist Realism: Gorky and Theories of Thought Transference," in *The Occult in Russian and Soviet Culture*,

ed. Bernice Glatzer Rosenthal (Ithaca, NY: Cornell University Press, 1997), 258–59, 263.

17. Current science explains the origin of arctic hysteria by a vitamin D deficiency in the bodies of native northerners, who are exposed to lengthy dark winter months; exposure to sunshine, on the contrary, stores vitamin D in human bodies.

18. Andreyev, *Vremya Shambaly*, 93–94 (see preface, n. 8).

19. Ibid., 111.

20. "Protokol doprosa A. V. Barchenko," 364–65.

21. Turar Ryskulov to Dmitrii Manuil'sky and Grigory Voitinsky, November 1927, RASPH, f. 495, op. 154, d. 24, p. 14.

22. Andreyev, *Vremya Shambaly*, 155 (see preface, n. 8).

23. Alexander Barchenko to Gombojab Tsibikov, May 24, 1927, in Shishkin, *Bitva za Gimalaii*, 323–24 (see preface, n. 10).

24. Ibid., 319.

25. Ibid., 337, 347.

26. Felix Dzerzhinsky (1877–1926) was a close comrade of Lenin, the creator and first head of the Bolshevik secret police, who simultaneously supervised the development of the Soviet economy.

27. Shishkin, *Bitva za Gimalaii*, 127–29 (see preface, n. 10).

Chapter Four

1. Tatiana Alekseeva and N. Matveev, *Dovereno zashchishchat revoliutsiiu* [Entrusted to Defend Revolution] (Moscow: Politizdat, 1987), 17.

2. Ibid., 59.

3. Tatiana Grekova, *Tibetskii lekar' kremlevskikh vozhdei* [Tibetan Healer of Kremlin Chiefs] (St. Petersburg and Moscow: Neva and Olma-Press, 2002), 188.

4. Georges Agabekov, *OGPU: The Russian Secret Terror* (New York: Brentano's, 1931), 264.

5. Christopher Andrew and Vasilii Mitrokhin, *The Sword and the Shield: The Mitrokhin Archive and the Secret History of the KGB* (New York: Basic Books, 1999), 26; I. S. Rat'kovskii, *Krasnii terror i deiatel'nost' VChK v 1918 g.* [Red Terror and Cheka Activities in 1918] (St. Petersburg: iz-vo St. Petersburgskogo universiteta, 2006), 185.

6. Particularly, Bokii suggested that a concentration camp be set up for class enemies on the Solovki islands in the northernmost part of Russia. It is symbolic that the steamboat that sailed between these islands and the mainland carried his name. It is also notable that the camp was established on premises confiscated from a Russian Orthodox monastery. In a switch to the secular religion of Communism, Christian icons on the monastery walls were replaced with portraits of Marx, Lenin, and Trotsky, and quotes from the Bible with slogans of the Communist Party. *Letters from Russian Prisons,* ed. Alexander Berkman (Westport, CT: Hyperion, 1977), 189.

7. Baberowski, *Der Rote Terror,* 38 (see chapter 3, n. 4).

8. McCauley, *Rise and Fall of the Soviet Union,* 56 (see chap. 3, n. 4).

9. "Iz protokola doprosa G. I. Bokia, May 17–18, 1937," in Andreyev, *Vremya Shambaly,* 209 (see preface, n. 8).

10. Ibid., 210.

11. Fyodor Chaliapin, *Maska i dusha* [Mask and Soul] (Paris: Sovremennyie zapiski, 1932), 281–82.

12. Bokii and his first wife, Sofia Doller, formally divorced in 1920. Doller, of mixed French-Russian Jewish origin, married Ivan Moskvin, a close college friend of Bokii. Moskvin similarly belonged to the elite of the Bolshevik Party. The former spouses maintained warm relations, and Bokii frequented Moskvin's apartment, where the chief cryptographer, Barchenko, and their friends conducted much of their esoteric talks about paranormal phenomena, Shambhala, and Tibetan medicine. The writer Lev Razgon, Bokii's son-in-law, who lived in this apartment for a few years, remembered constantly bumping into "doctors" who strove to locate "a certain something," such as finding a key to overcoming all illnesses and old age (Lev Razgon, *True Stories,* transl. John Crowfoot [Ann Arbor: Ardis, 1997], 44).

13. Ibid., 51.

14. Ibid., 281.

15. Andrew and Mitrokhin, *The Sword and the Shield,* 53. Bokii's section not only developed codes, intercepted radio signals, and listened to phone conversations of foreign ambassadors and the Bolshevik elite, but also forged ID documents and monitored how well various Soviet departments handled classified materials inside and outside the country.

16. David Kahn, *The Codebreakers: The Story of Secret Writing* (New York: Scribner, 1996), 642.

17. Grigory Bessedovsky, *Revelations of a Soviet Diplomat* (1931, reprint Westport, CT: Hyperion Press, 1977), 196. Bokii went very far in trying to keep his experts content and happy. In 1921, to Chicherin's chagrin, the chief cryptographer received special permission to procure regularly gourmet and delicatessen foods for his unit, as well as cognacs and wines from European countries, using hard currency and diplomatic channels of the Commissariat for Foreign Affairs. "Protokol zasedaniia prezidiuma VChK, July 8, 1921," in *Arkhiv VChK: sbornik dokumentov* [Archives of Cheka: Documents], ed. V. Vinogradov, A. Litvin, and V. Khristoforov (Moscow: Kuchkovo pole, 2007), 458. It is notable that the Special Section was showered with these outlandish perks amid the horrific mass famine that took the lives of more than a million Russians.

18. Grekova, *Tibetskii lekar' kremlevskikh vozhdei*, 188–89.

19. Shishkin, *Bitva za Gimalaii*, 133–34 (see preface, n. 10); Razgon, *True Stories*, 51.

20. Berkman, *Letters from Russian Prisons,* 192, 208, 210; Ann Applebaum, *Gulag: A History* (New York: Anchor, 2004), 38.

21. "Iz protokola doprosa G. I. Bokia, May 17–18, 1937," in Andreyev, *Vremya Shambaly*, 210 (see preface, n. 8).

22. Shishkin, *Bitva za Gimalaii*, 130 (see preface, n. 10).

23. Razgon, who was personally familiar with several officials who initiated this project, writes: "In an extraordinary short period of time an enormous institute with a vast staff and unheard-of privileges came into being" (Razgon, *True Stories*, 45).

24. "Protokol doprosa A. V. Barchenko," 365–67 (see chap. 3, n. 8).

25. Kahn, *The Codebreakers,* 640.

26. "Iz protokola doprosa G. I. Bokia, May 17-18, 1937," in Andreyev, *Vremya Shambaly*, 212 (see preface, n. 8).

27. Ibid., 210–11.

28. Svetlana Epifanova, "Maloizvestnie istochniki Mastera i Margarity," [Little-Known Sources of Master and Margarita] http://www.lebed.com/2000/art2076.htm (accessed April 14, 2010); A. G. Tepliakov, *Mashina terrora: OGPU-NKVD v Sibiri, 1929–1941* [Machine of Terror: OGPU-NKVD in Siberia, 1929-1941] (Moscow: Novyi Khronograf, 2008), 555–56.

29. Grekova, *Tibetskii lekar' kremlevskikh vozhdei*, 224.

30. Igor Simbirtsev, *VChK v Leninskoi Rossii, 1917–1923* [Cheka in Lenin's Russia, 1917–1923] (Moscow: Tsentrpoligraf, 2008), 337.

31. Agabekov, *OGPU*, 256.

32. Andreyev, *Vremya Shambaly*, 151–52 (see preface, n. 8).
33. Alexander Barchenko to Gombojab Tsibikov, May 24, 1927, and "Protokol doprosa A. V. Barchenko" (see chap. 3, n. 8).
34. Joseph Schneersohn, *The Heroic Struggle: The Arrest and Liberation of Rabbi Yosef Y. Schneersohn of Lubavitch in Soviet Russia* (Brooklyn, NY: Kehot, 1999), 135–36.
35. Ibid., 279.
36. Evgenii Moroz, "Kommunizm i evreiskaia magia; epizod istorii dvadtsatykh godov" [Communism and Jewish Magic: An Episode from the 1920s], *Neva* 6 (2005).
37. "Protokol doprosa A. V. Barchenko," in Shishkin, *Bitva za Gimalaii*, 375 (see preface, n. 10).

Chapter Five

1. Ossendowski, *Beasts, Men and Gods*, 92 (see chap. 2, n. 12).
2. About Communism as a surrogate secular religion, see David G. Rowley, *Millenarian Bolshevism, 1900 to 1920* (New York: Garland, 1987), and Igal Halfin, *From Darkness to Light: Class, Consciousness, and Salvation in Revolutionary Russia* (Pittsburgh: University of Pittsburgh Press, 2000).
3. Anthony Wallace, "Revitalization Movements," *American Anthropologist* 58, no. 2 (1956): 277.
4. Hélène Carrère d'Encausse, *L'Empire d'Eurasie: Une histoire de l'Empire russe de 1552 à nos jours* [Eurasian Empire: History of the Russian Empire from 1552 to the Present] (Paris: Fayard, 2005), 259.
5. Baberowski, *Der Rote Terror*, 28, 64–66 (see chapter 3, n. 4).
6. "The Baku Congress of the Peoples of the East," in *Soviet Russia and the East, 1920–1927: A Documentary Survey*, ed. Xenia Joukoff Eudin and Robert C. North (Stanford, CA: Stanford University Press, 1957), 165–72.
7. Sarkisyanz, *Russland and der Messianismus des Orients*, 630 (see preface, n. 1).
8. John Snelling, *Buddhism in Russia: The Story of Agvan Dorzhiev, Lhasa's Emissary to the Tzar* (Shaftesbury, UK: Element, 1993), 198–99.
9. Karl Ernest Meyer and Shareen Blair Brysac, *Tournament of Shadows: The Great Game and the Race for Empire in Central Asia* (New York: Basic Books, 2006), 272.

10. Hambo Agvan Dorzhiev, "Ustav o vnutrennei zhizni monashestvuiushikh v buddiiskikh hidanah Sibiri [1923]" [Life Guidelines for Monks in Siberian Buddhist Monasteries], RASPH, f. 89, op. 4, d. 162, pp. 33–36.

11. Hambo Agvan Dorzhiev, "V narodnii komissariat inostrannikh del RSFSR" [To the People's Commissariat for Foreign Affairs], May 6, 1923, in Ibid., p. 5.

12. Note the words of Khoren Petrosian, deputy chief of the Eastern Division of OGPU. In 1928, when the split of Buddhists into progressives and conservatives was complete, he stressed in a classified memorandum, "We need to continue working to further deepen the schism among conservative monks into smaller groups, thereby killing at birth all their attempts to make an organized stand" (Khoren Petrosian, "O buddiiskikh raionakh [On Buddhist Areas] [1928]," RASPH, f. 89, op. 4, d. 162, p. 68).

13. P. M. Nikiforov, "Dnevnikovie zapisi P. M. Nikiforova o rabote v Mongolii v kachestve polnomochnogo predstavitelia SSSR, July 1925–Seoptember 1927" [P. M. Nikiforov's Journal about His Work as a USSR Ambassador in Mongolia], RASPH, f. 144, op. 1, d. 7, p. 46 back.

14. Bina Roy Burman, Religion and Politics in Tibet (New Delhi: Vikas Publishing House, 1979), 41; Michael Jerryson, Mongolian Buddhism: The Rise and Fall of the Sangha (Bangkok: Silkworm Books, 2007), 58, 63.

15. S. M. Murgaev, "Uchastie kalmykov v Bol'shevistskom eksporte revolutsii v strankakh Dal'nego Vostoka (1920)" [Kalmyk Participation in the Export of the Bolshevik Revolution in the Far East], Novyi istoricheskii sbornik [New Historical Symposium] 1 (2006), http://www.nivestnik.ru/2006_1/index.shtml (accessed April 9, 2010).

16. Both Tuva and the Altai, the southernmost areas of Siberia located on the border with Mongolia, were populated by Turkic-speaking nomads (Buddhists and shamanists) closely related by language and culture.

17. Petrosian, "O buddiiskikh raionakh [1928], supplement 'Panmongolizm,'" p. 72.

18. Elbek-Dorji Rinchino, "Doklad E-D. Rinchino na zasedanii TsK MNRP June 25, 1925" [E-D. Rinchino's Report at a Meeting of the MNRP Central Committee], in Elbek-Dorji Rinchino o Mongolii, [Elbek-Dorji Rinchino on Mongolia], ed. B. V. Bazarov, B. D. Tsibikov, and S. B. Ochirov (Ulan Ude: institute mongolovedenuia, buddologii i tibetologii, 1998), 104.

19. R. N. Carew Hunt, A Guide to Communist Jargon (New York: Macmillan, 1957), 94.

20. Terry Martin, *The Affirmative Action Empire: Nations and Nationalism in the Soviet Union, 1923–1939* (Ithaca: Cornell University Press, 2001), 5.

21. Gerard M. Friters, *Outer Mongolia and Its International Position* (Baltimore: Johns Hopkins Press, 1949), 130–31.

22. Vladimir Pozner, *Bloody Baron: The Story of Ungern-Sternberg* (New York: Random House, 1938); Leonid Yuzefovich, *Samoderzhets pustiny: fenomenon sud'by barona R. F. Ungern-Shternberga* [Master of Desert: The Phenomenon of Baron R. F. Ungern-Sternberg] (Moscow: Ellis-lak, 1993); Boris Sokolov, *Baron Ungern: chernii vsadnik* [Baron Ungern: Black Horseman] (Moscow: AST-Press, 2006); Evgenii Belov, *Baron Ungern fon Shternberg: biografiiaa, ideologiia, voennye pokhody, 1920–1921* [Baron Ungern von Sternberg: Biography, Ideology, Military Campaigns, 1920–1921] (Moscow: Agraf, 2003); James Palmer, *The Bloody White Baron: The Extraordinary Story of the Russian Nobleman Who Became the Last Khan of Mongolia* (New York, Basic Books, 2008). Will Sunderland, a historian from the University of Cincinnati, is currently working on a book that promises to become the first comprehensive biography of the Mad Baron.

23. Belov, *Baron Ungern fon Shternberg*, 96.

24. In the 1920s, Toin Lama, a Mongol nationalist leader who fought against Chinese advances in southern (Inner) Mongolia, expressed well this widespread anti-Chinese hatred: "The past has taught us that only by the rattle of arms and savagery can we prevent the ploughman from violating the freedom of the steppe and the trader from contaminating our manners" (Henning Haslund-Christensen, *Men and Gods in Mongolia [Zayagan]* [New York: Dutton, 1935], 249).

25. "Predskazanie sviashchennosluzhitelia Lubsan Baldan Eshe" [Prophecy of Lobsang Yeshe], in *Baron Ungern v dokumentakh i materialakh* [Baron Ungern: Documents and Materials], vol. 1, ed. S. L. Kuzmin, (Moscow: KMK, 2004), 150–51.

26. Belov, *Baron Ungern fon Shternberg*, 120.

27. Sokolov, *Baron Ungern*, 284.

28. See the texts of these letters in Kuzmin, *Baron Ungern*, vol. 1: 126–35, 161–69.

29. Roman von Ungern-Sternberg, "Pis'mo glavnokomanduiushchego barona Ungerna, June 1921" [Letter of the Supreme Commander Baron Ungern], RASPH, f., 495, op. 152, d. 15, p. 53.

30. "Prikaz R. F. Ungerna No. 15 o nastuplenii na Sibir," in Kuzmin, *Baron Ungern*, vol. 1, 171. One of the people who composed this embarrassing text was Ossendowski. The amazed Shumatsky, who interrogated Ungern, asked if he was sure that it was the professor, known for his liberal and socialist leanings. Ungern answered, "I ordered him and he wrote it." It appears that Ossendowski was so terrified of the mad baron that he tried to render the baron's philosophy as best he could.
31. Boris Shumatsky, "Opros nachal'nika aziatskoi konnoi divizii generala Ungerna, 29 August 1921" [Interrogation of General Ungern, Head of Asian Cavalry Division], RASPH, f. 495, op. 154, d. 97, p. 46.

Chapter Six

1. No title [record of the minutes of the meeting of the Mongol-Tibetan Section, October 29, 1920], RASPH, f. 495, op. 152, d. 6, p. 13.
2. "Printsipy deiatel'nosti Mongolo-tibetskogo otdela sektsii vostochnikh narodov" [Guidelines for the Mongol-Tibetan Section of the Eastern Secretariat], RASPH, f. 495, op. 152, d. 6, pp. 25–26; "Instruktsia sotrudniku Mongolo-tibetskago otdela sektsii vostochnikh narodov" [Instruction for the Agents of the Mongol-Tibetan Section of the Eastern Secretariat], Ibid., pp. 33–33 back.
3. "Protokoly organizatsionnogo zasedania kollegii Mongolo-tibetskogo otdela sektsii vostochnikh narodov Sibburo [Minutes of an Organizational Meeting of the Mongol-Tibetan Section's Collegium of Eastern Department of the Siberian Bureau], August 20, 1920," RASPH, f. 495, op. 154, d. 7, p. 10; "Prikaz No. 3 upolnomochennogo III Kommunisticheskogo internatsionala na Dal'nem Vostoke [Order No. 3 Issued by a Representative of the Communist International in the Far East], February 18, 1921," RASPH, f. 495, op. 154, d. 93.
4. "V Montibotdel sekvostnara [To Mongol-Tibetan Section of the Eastern Secretariat], November 29, 1920," RASPH, f. 495, op. 152, d. 6, p. 18–18 back; "Nedelia ukrepleniia armii [A Weekly Campaign to Strengthen the Army], Kiahkta, June 3, 1920," RASPH, f. 495, op. 152, d. 2, p. 2.
5. Bumochir Dulam and Oyuntungalaq Ayushiin, "Transmission and Source of Prophecy in Contemporary Mongolia," *Mongolian History* (May 2007), http://mongolianhistory.blogspot.com/2007/05/transmission-and-source-of-prophecy-in.html (accessed November 1, 2009).

NOTES

6. Along with chunks of silver, Mexican dollars were the only valid currency in Inner Asia and China at that time.
7. "Obiasnitel'naia zapisaka k valiutnoi smete sektsii vostochnikh narodov na 1921," [Explanatory Note Regarding the Eastern Secretariat's Currency Budget] RASPH, f. 495, op. 154, d. 111, pp. 5–6.
8. "Torzhestvnnoe vstuplenie narrev. pravitel'stva v Urgu [Solemn Entrance of the People's Revolutionary Government into Urga], July 9, 1921," RASPH, f. 495, op. 152, d. 15, pp. 6–6 back.
9. Lomakina, *Groznie makhakaly Vostoka*, 363 (see chapter 2, n. 19).
10. Emanuel Sarkisyantz, "Communism and Lamaist Utopianism in Central Asia," *Review of Politics* 20, no. 4 (1958): 630.
11. Rebecca Empson, "The Repetition of Mongolian Prophetic Time," in Empson, *Time, Causality, and Prophecy*, 191–92 (see chapter 2, n.6).
12. Diluv Khutagt, *Memoirs and Autobiography of a Mongol Buddhist: Reincarnation in Religion and Revolution* (Wiesbaden: O. Harrassowitz, 1982), 167.
13. No title [guidelines for the Mongol-Tibetan Section], RASPH, f. 495, op. 152, d. 6, p. 30.
14. Khutagt, *Memoirs and Autobiography*, 122.
15. Boris Shumatsky to Mikhail Kobetskii, April 23, 1921, RASPH, f. 495, op. 154, d. 105, p. 33; Shumatsky to Kobetskii, May 20, 1921, Ibid., p. 39 back.
16. Lomakina, *Groznie makhakaly Vostoka*, 263 (see chapter 2, n. 19).
17. Elbek-Dorji Rinchino, "E-D. Rinchino o kharakteristike lichnostei nekotorikh deiatelei partii i pravitel'stva" [E-D. Rinchino about Several Personalities in Party and Government], in Bazarov, Tsibikov, and Ochirov, *Elbek-Dorji Rinchino o Mongolii*, 148 (see chapter 5, n.18); Caroline Humphrey, "Prophecy and Sequential Orders in Mongolian Political History," in Empson, *Time, Causality and Prophecy*, 85–86, 92, 96–97 (see chapter 2, n. 6).
18. Larry Moses, *The Political Role of Mongol Buddhism* (Bloomington: Indiana University, 1977), 180–81.
19. Nikiforov, "Dnevnikovie zapisi P. M. Nikiforova," entry for August 13, 1925 (see chapter 5, n. 13).
20. "Sektsiia vostochnikh narodov Sibburo [Department of Eastern Peoples of the Siberian Bureau], RASPH, f. 495, op. 152, d. 6, p. 11; no title [guidelines for the Mongol-Tibetan Section], RASPH, f. 495, op. 152, d. 6, p. 30.

21. Boris Shumatsky to Georgy Chicherin, S. I. Dukhovskii, and Meer Trilisser, July 1921, RASPH, f. 495, op. 154, d. 105, p. 40.
22. Boris Shumatsky to Georgy Chicherin, August 29, 1921, RASPH, f. 495, op. 154, d. 97, p. 43.
23. Agvan Dorzhiev, *Predanie o krugosvetnom puteshestvii, ili, Povestvovanie o zhizni Agvana Dorzhieva* [A Tale about a Round-the-World Journey, or a Life Story of Agvan Dorzhiev] (Ulan Ude: Buryatskoe kniznoe izdatel'stvo, 1994), 11.
24. Andreyev, *Vremya Shambaly*, 276 (see preface, n. 8).
25. Burman, *Religion and Politics in Tibet*, 62–63 (see chapter 5, n.14).
26. Batorskii [Sergei Borisov], "Sovremennii Tibet" [Modern Tibet], RASPH, f. 532, op. 4, d. 343, pp. 47, 59–60.
27. For more about Bailey, see Peter Hopkirk, *Setting the East Ablaze: Lenin's Dream of an Empire in Asia* (New York: Kodansha, 1995), 7–94.
28. Petrosian, "O buddiiskikh raionakh [1928]," 59 (see chapter 5, n. 12).
29. Andreyev, *Soviet Russia and Tibet*, 259 (see preface, n. 8).
30. C. R. Bawden, *Modern History of Mongolia* (New York: Preager, 1968), 262–63.
31. Andreyev, *Soviet Russia and Tibet*, 278 (see preface, n. 8).
32. Khutagt, *Memoirs and Autobiography*, 132.
33. Andreyev, *Soviet Russia and Tibet*, 281 (see preface, n. 8).

Chapter Seven

1. Sarkozi, *Political Prophecies in Mongolia*, 66 (see chap. 2, n. 10).
2. Robert C. Williams, *Russian Art and American Money, 1900–1940* (Cambridge, MA: Harvard University Press, 1980), 116.
3. Alexandre Andreyev, *Gimalaiskoe bratstvo: teosofskii mif i ego tvortsy* [Himalayan Brotherhood: Theosophical Myth and People Who Created It] (St. Petersburg: iz-vo St. Petersburgskogo universiteta, 2008), 146.
4. Zinaida Fosdick, *Moi uchitelia: vstrechi s Rerikhami (po stranitsam dnevnika, 1922–1934)* [My Teachers: Meetings with the Roeriches (Pages from the 1922-1934 Journal)] (Moscow: Sfera, 1998), 114, 188, 320–21; Andreyev, *Gimalaiskoe bratstvo*, 395–96.
5. Fosdick, *Moi uchitelia*, 87.
6. Andreyev, *Gimalaiskoe bratstvo*, 138.
7. Fosdick, *Moi uchitelia*, 117, 119, 122, 123.

8. Helena Roerich (Rerikh), *Pis'ma* [Letters], vol. 1 (1919–1933) (Moscow: MTR, 1999), 20.

9. Rosov, *Nikolai Rerikh vestnik Zvenigoroda*, vol. 1: 71 (see preface, n. 9).

10. Nicholas Roerich, *Shambhala* (New York: Frederick A. Stokes Company, 1930), 11.

11. Nicholas Roerich became Fuiama; Helena, Urusvati; George and Svetoslav Roerich, Udraia and Liumou; Morris Lichtmann, Avirakh; Sina Lichtmann, Radna; her sister Esther Lichtmann, Oiana; Louis Horch, Logvan; his wife Netty, Poruma; George Grebenstchikoff, Turukhan; and Frances Grant, Modra. All these names were derived from legendary and mythological Hindu and Buddhist characters. Henry Wallace, who joined the group in 1933 and became a trusted friend, was the only one in this group without a Hindu-Buddhist name; the politician was named Galahad after the seeker of the legendary Holy Grail.

12. Fosdick, *Moi uchitelia*, 105.

13. Nicholas Roerich, *Altai-Himalaya: A Travel Diary* (London: Jarrolds, 1929), 15.

14. Nicholas Roerich, *Shambhala*, 47, 5, 61.

15. Nikolai Kordashevsky (Dekroa), *Tibetskie stranstviia polkovnika Korda-shevskogo* [Tibetan Wanderings of Colonel Kordashevsky] (St. Petersburg: Dmitrii Bulanin, 1999), 80.

16. Helena Roerich, *Vysokii put'*, vol. 1: 45, 51, 65 (see preface, n. 7).

17. Ibid., 85–86, 95, 124, 154.

18. Fosdick, *Moi uchitelia*, 202.

19. Helena Roerich, *Pis'ma*, 38.

20. Roerich's friend the White émigré writer General Peter Krasnov might be another possible source of the Great Plan. In his novel *Beyond Thistle* (1922), he wrote that Russia's revival would come from Tibet.

21. Helena Roerich, *Vysokii put'*, 154.

22. Andreyev, *Gimalaiskoe bratstvo*, 241.

23. M. Dubaev, *Kharbinskaia taina Rerikha* [Roerich's Harbin Mystery] (Moscow: Sfera, 2001), 211.

24. Fosdick, *Moi uchitelia*, 197.

25. Depending on context, the Tibetan word *dorje* could mean "hard," "arrow," or "lightning."

26. Nicholas Roerich, *Altai-Himalaya*, 14.

NOTES

Chapter Eight

1. Fosdick, *Moi uchitelia*, 206 (see chap. 7, n. 4).
2. Helena Roerich, Tetrad' [Notebook], entries for May 22, 1924 and May 29, 1924, http://urusvati.agni-age.net/ (accessed April 10, 2010).
3. Andreyev, *Gimalaiskoe bratstvo*, 283 (see chap. 7, n. 3).
4. Ibid., 286.
5. Fosdick, *Moi uchitelia*, 242 (see chap. 7, n. 4).
6. Helena Roerich, "Pis'ma Eleny Roerich k sinu Svetoslavu [Helena Roerich's Letter to Her Son Svetoslav]," *Vestnik Ariavarty* [Messenger of Aryavarta] 1 (2001): 48.
7. Petrosian, "O buddiiskikh raionakh," p. 62 (see chap. 5, n. 12).
8. Helena Roerich, *Vysokii put'*, vol. 1: 479, 511 (see preface, n. 7).
9. Fosdick, *Moi uchitelia*, 206 (see chap. 7, n. 4).
10. Helena Roerich, *Vysokii put'*, vol. 1, 289, 322 (see preface, n. 7).
11. Rosov, *Nikolai Rerikh vestnik Zvenigoroda*, vol. 1: 135 (see preface, n. 9).
12. Viktor Brachev, *Okkultisty sovetskoi epokhi* [Occultists of the Soviet Age] (Moscow: Bystrov, 2007), 234–35.
13. Nicholas Roerich, *Altai-Gimalai* (Moscow: Sfera, 1999), 656. In the 1929 English edition, this episode with the OGPU agent was deleted (Roerich, *Altai-Himalaya*, 333 [see chap. 7, n. 13]).
14. Fosdick, *Moi uchitelia*, 265 (see chap. 7, n. 4).
15. Rosov, *Nikolai Rerikh vestnik Zvenigoroda*, vol. 1: 180 (see preface, n. 9).
16. This program was spelled out to Helena by Master Morya on March 18, 1926, during one of their spiritual talks (Helena Roerich, *Vysokii put'*, vol. 1: 462 [see preface, n. 7]).
17. Ibid., 465.
18. For more about the life of this daredevil, see Aleksei Velidov, *Pokhozhdeniia terrorista: odisseia Iakova Bliumkina* [Adventures of a Terrorist: Jacob Bliumkin's Odyssey] (Moscow: Sovremennik, 1998).
19. "Pokazania doktora K. N. Riabinina [Testimony of Dr. K. N. Riabinin], July 23-24, 1930," *Ariavarta* 1 (1997): 174.
20. Nicholas Roerich, *Shambhala* (see chap. 7, n. 10), 45; *Altai-Himalaya*, 336 (see chap. 7, n. 13).
21. Fosdick, *Moi uchitelia*, 262 (see chap. 7, n. 4).
22. Nicholas Roerich, *Altai Himalaya*, 353 (see chap. 7, n. 13).
23. Yu. L. Krol, "Boris Ivanovich Pankratov," *Strany i narody Vostoka* [Countries and Peoples of the East] 26 (1989): 90.

24. In 1929 Berlin was appointed the official controller of Boris Roerich (one of Nicholas's brothers), who remained in Red Russia and was blackmailed by the Bolshevik secret police into becoming a secret informant.
25. Fosdick, *Moi uchitelia*, 275-276 (see chap. 7, n. 4); Vladimir Rosov, "Arkhi-tekhtor B. K. Rerikh: Rassekrechennoe arkhivnoe delo N. 2538 [Architectural Designer B. K. Roerich: Declassified File No. 2538]," *Vestnik Ariavarty* [Messenger of Aryavarta] 10 (2008): 46. Moscow investigative reporter Oleg Shishkin came up with an unlikely argument that, dressed as a lama, Bliumkin actually joined the Roerichs and accompanied them to Tibet (Oleg Shishkin, *Bitva za Gimalaii*, 128–29 [see preface, n. 10]. There was no way for Bliumkin, an urbanite Jew from Odessa, to pose as a lama and be unnoticed. Even the indigenous Bolshevik "lama pilgrims" with Asiatic facial features, like Sergei Borisov (Oirot) and Arashi Chapchaev (Kalmyk), sent by the Soviets to Lhasa did not make it undetected. The Tibetans and Lt. Colonel Bailey quickly cracked the identity of all these "pilgrims." So, as attractive as it may sound, the story of Bliumkin posing as a lama should be put to rest.
26. The radiogram was intercepted by local White émigrés (Andreyev, *Gimalaiskoe bratstvo*, 330 (see chap. 7, n. 3).
27. Nicholas Roerich, *Shambhala*, 295 (see chap. 7, n. 10).
28. Nicholas Roerich, *Altai-Himalaya*, 107 (see chap. 7, n. 13).
29. Kordashevsky, *Tibetskie stranstviia*, 90 (see chap. 7, n. 15).
30. Helena Roerich, *Vysokii put'*, vol. 1: 512, 513, 519 (see preface, n. 7).
31. Ibid., 528.
32. Pavel Portniagin, "Sovremennyi Tibet: missia Nikolaia Rerikha [Modern Tibet: Nicholas Roerich's Mission]," *Ariavarta* 2 (1998): 53, http://ay-forum.net/1/Ariavarta_2/2_11.pdf (accessed April 10, 2010).
33. Kordashevsky, *Tibetskie stranstviia*, 282 (see chap. 7, n. 15).
34. Meyer and Brysac, *Tournament of Shadows*, 472 (see chap. 5, n. 9).
35. Kordashevsky, *Tibetskie stranstviia*, 301 (see chap. 7, n. 15).
36. Konstantin Riabinin, *Razvenchannyi Tibet* [Tibet Debunked] (Samara: Agni, 1996), 672. The couple severed ties with their former travel companions, whom they no longer found useful. The fate of Dr. Riabinin was tragic. Caught into the sophisticated blackmail game the Bolshevik secret police played with Nicholas Roerich and his brother Boris, he was arrested twice and pressured by Stalin's secret police to admit their Tibetan party was a spy ring headed by the "English agent" Nicholas Roerich. Despite various physical and mental tortures, the doctor demonstrated

incredible courage, refusing to slander his former friend. Riabinin miraculously survived nineteen years of Stalin's concentration camps and was released in 1949. Before his death in 1953, he worked as a pediatric physician. The young Theosophist Portniagin settled at Harbin in China, graduated from a Catholic college, and became a Catholic missionary. After World War II, he was also arrested by the Soviet secret police and was confined from 1948 to 1956 in a concentration camp for "anti-Soviet activities." After his release, Portniagin settled in Samarkand, Soviet Central Asia, where he worked as an English translator. He died in 1977. Like Portniagin, Colonel Kordashevsky found his spiritual niche, turning to Christianity and becoming a Catholic monk. He died an impoverished man in Jerusalem in 1948; his novel about Joan of Arc remained unfinished.

37. Nicholas Roerich, *Altai-Himalaya*, 29 (see chap. 7, n. 13).

38. Nicholas Roerich, *Shambhala*, 164 (see chap. 7, n. 10).

39. For more on the Roeriches' contacts with Wallace and FDR, see Meyer and Brysac, *Tournament of Shadows*, 474–91 (see chap. 5, n. 9); Williams, *Russian Art and American Money*, 136–43 (see chap. 7, n. 2); John C. Culver and John Hyde, *American Dreamer: The Life and Times of Henry A. Wallace* (New York: Norton, 2000), 130–46.

40. Helena Roerich, *Pis'ma* [Letters], vol. 3 (Moscow; MTR, 2001), 351 (my reverse translation of text that was translated from English into Russian).

41. Fosdick, *Moi uchitelia*, 609 (see chap. 7, n. 4).

42. C. R. Bowden, *Modern History of Mongolia* (New York: Praeger, 1968), 205.

43. Samdin, "O Banchen-lame [On Panchen Lama, 1934]" RASPH, f. 532, op. 4, d. 335, p. 102–102 back.

44. Fosdick, *Moi uchitelia*, 659 (see chap. 7, n. 4).

45. Ibid., 623.

46. Rosov, *Nikolai Rerikh vestnik Zvenigoroda*, vol. 2: 79–80 (see preface, n. 9).

47. Rosov, *Nikolai Rerikh vestnik Zvenigoroda*, vol. 1: 59–61 (see preface, n. 9).

48. Culver and Hyde, *American Dreamer*, 143.

Notes

Epilogue

1. Dubaev, *Kharbinskaia taina Rerikha*, 230–31 (see chap. 7, n. 23); Rosov, *Nikolai Rerikh vestnik Zvenigoroda*, vol. 2: 169 (see preface, n. 9).
2. Meyer and Brysac, *Tournament of Shadows*, 488 (see chap. 5, n. 9).
3. Rosov, "Arkhitekhtor B. K. Rerikh," 43 (see chap. 8, n. 25).
4. Ibid., 46.
5. Andrei Yudin, *Tainy Bol'shogo doma* [Secrets of the Big House] (Moscow: Astrel, 2007), 15.
6. Shishkin, *Bitva za Gimalaii*, 27–40, 51–63, 72–75, 105–125 (see preface, n. 10).
7. Andreyev, *Vremya Shambaly*, 176 (see preface, n. 8).
8. Oleg Shishkin, "Nachalo okkultnogo i paranormalnogo proekta OGPU [The Beginning of the OGPU Occult and Paranormal Project]" (2006), http://www.harrimaninstitute.org/MEDIA/00787.pdf (accessed April 29, 2010).
9. His real name was Abraham Levin (1889–1941). Before joining the Cheka/OGPU in 1918, he was an activist in the Jewish Socialist Bund Union.
10. "Iz protokola doprosa G.I. Bokia," in Andreyev, *Vremya Shambaly*, 218 (see preface, n. 8).
11. Ibid., 216–17, 219–20.
12. The girl did not survive anyway. As a relative of an "enemy of the people," she was shipped to a concentration camp and perished on the way.
13. Razgon, *True Stories*, 282 (see chap. 4, n. 12).
14. Grekova, *Tibetskii lekar' kremlevskikh vozhdei* (see chap. 4, n. 3).
15. Shishkin, "Nachalo okkultnogo."
16. Andreyev, *Vremya Shambhaly*, 182–83 (see preface, n. 8).
17. Hopkirk, *Setting the East Ablaze*, 207 (see chap. 6, n. 27).
18. Sergei Roshchin, *Politicheskaia istoriia Mongolii* [Political History of Mongolia] (1921–1940) (Moscow: Institut vostokovedeniia, 1999), 292.

Illustration Credits

Figures 1.1: Burnette D. Conlan, *Roerich* (Riga: Roerich Museum, 1939): 158; figures 1.2, 1.3, 2.1: Albert Grünwedel, *Mythologie des Buddhismus in Tibet und der Mongolei* (Leipzig: F.A. Brockhaus, 1900): 54, 173, 69; figures 2.2, 2.6, 2.7, 2.8: Hermann Consten, *Weiderpltze der Mongolen im Reiche der Chalcha* (Berlin: Dietrich Reimer, 1920), vol. 2, plate 9, plate 49, plate 54, vol. 1, plate 47; figure 2.3: David MacDonald, "Where a Lama Leads the Way," *Asia Magazine* 19, no. 2 (1929):101; figure 2.4: photo by J. Erickson and M. Pode, *Asia Magazine* 30, no. 9 (1930): 649; figure 2.5: Sven Hedin, "Living God and King-Priest of Tibet," *Asia Magazine* 25, no. 4 (1925); figure 3.1: © Oleg Shishkin, Viktor Brachev; figure 4.1: © Kuchkovo pole; figure 4.2: photo by the author; figure 4.3: courtesy David King Collection, London; figure 4.4: Galina Ol and N. N. Lansere, *N. N. Lansere* (Leningrad : Stroiizdat, 1986); figure 5.1: © Ch. Moenhbayar, moenhbayar. blogspot.com; figure 5.2: © Alexandre Andreyev; figure 5.3: Boris Volkov, "A Motor Deal with the Living God in Urga," *Asia Magazine* 31, no. 4 (1931): 238; figure 5.4: Ferdinand Ossendowski, "With Baron Ungern in Urga," *Asia Magazine* 22, no. 8 (1922): 616; figure 5.5: Boris Volkov, "A Descendent of Genghis Khan," *Asia Magazine* 31, no. 11 (1931): 702; figure 5.6: Boris Volkov, " A Motor Deal with the Living God in Urga," *Asia Magazine* 31, no. 4 (1931): 233; figure 6.1: courtesy Russian Archive of Social and Political History, Moscow; figure 6.2: Ernestine Evans, "Looking East from Moscow," *Asia Magazine* 22, no. 12 (1922): 973; figure 6.3: William Henry Chamberlin, "The Soviet Shadow in the East," *Asia Magazine* 26, no. 3 (1926): 238; figure 6.4: © Deutsch-Mongolische Gesellschaft; figure 6.5: Owen Lattimore, "Ordeal by Snow," *Asia Magazine* 19, no. 1 (1929): 41; figures 7.1 through 8.6, 8.8, and E.1: courtesy of Nicholas Roerich Museum, New York City; Figure 8.7: Burnette D. Conlan, *Roerich* (Riga: Roerich Museum, 1939): 47; figure E.2: © Leonid Naumov.

Index

ciphers, 71
classless society, 64
class warfare
  in Mongolia, 111–12
  in Tibet, 146
collectivism, 167
colonization, 22
Comintern (Communist International)
  Eastern Division of, 106
  Eastern Secretariat and, 127
  end of, 232
  four sections of, 129–30
  Mongol soldiers and, 135–36
  Mongol-Tibetan Section of, **128**
  purpose of, 104
  Roerich and, 184
  Tibet and, 142–43
Commissariat for Foreign Affairs, **78,**
  79, 92–93, 131, 195, 234
Committee for the Study of Mental
  Suggestion, 57
communes
  of Barchenko, 60–61
  of Bokii, 88–90, 229
Communism
  merged with Buddhism, 189,
    225–26
  nationalism and, 232
  as secular prophecy, 102–5
Communist International. *See* Comintern
Communist University of the Toilers of
  the East (KUTV), 146
concentration camps, 73, 81
Constantine the Great, 176
Crane, Charles R., 164
cryptography, 71, 75, 79

D
Dalai Lama, 20
Dalai Lama, Fifth
  Roerich as, 167, 177–78, **178**

Dalai Lama, Thirteenth, **31**
  Bogdo-gegen death and, 150–51
  Borisov and, 147–49
  death of, 208–9
  diplomacy of, 144, 152–53
  Dorzhiev and, 108
  military concerns of, 145
  modernization and, 33–34, 145–46
  "Mongol Embassy" and, 149–53
  Panchen Lama and, 30–31, 155–56
  political skills of, 182
  Red Russia and, 143, 185
  Roerich and, 166
  weapons for, 195
d'Alveydre, Alexandre Saint-Yves,
  48–54, 91
Dambi-Dzhamtsyn. *See* Ja-Lama
Danzan, 133, 135
Darjeeling, 176–77, **177**
David-Neel, Alexandra, 107–8
deities in Tibetan Buddhism, 12–16
Dhammapada (Gautama Buddha), xxvi
dharmapalas (deities), 13–16
Dimanshtein, Semen, 87
Doctor Chernii (Barchenko), 49
Doller, Sofia, 87, 230
Dorzhiev, Agvan
  as double agent, 151–52
  life and death of, xxiii, 233
  Shambhala war and, 227
  temple of, 61–62, 160, 196, 233
  as Tibetan ambassador, 108–10,
    143–44
Drepung monastery, 147
drumming, 96–97
Dunkhor, 63
Dzerzhinsky, Felix, 65–66, 82, **83**

E
East, 105–9, 168
Eastern Secretariat (Siberia), 106, 127,
  129

About the Author

Andrei Znamenski, a native of Russia, has studied history and anthropology in both Russia and the United States. Formerly a resident scholar at the Library of Congress and then a visiting professor at Hokkaido University in Japan, he has taught at Alabama State University and the University of Memphis in Tennessee.

Znamenski's major fields of interests include shamanism, the history of Western esotericism, Russian history, world civilizations, and the history of religions as well as well as indigenous religions of Siberia and North America. He has lived and traveled extensively in Alaska, Siberia, and Japan. His field and archival research among Athabaskan Indians in Alaska and native people of the Altai (Southern Siberia) resulted in the books *Shamanism and Christianity: Native Responses to Russian Missionaries* (1999), *Through Orthodox Eyes: Russian Missionary Narratives of Travels to the Dena'ina and Ahtna* and *Shamanism in Siberia* (both in 2003).

Between 2003 and 2004, Znamenski resided in Japan, where along with his Japanese colleague, Professor Koichi Inoue, he worked with *itako*, blind female healers and mediums from the Amori prefecture. Endeavoring to answer why shamanism has become so popular among Western spiritual seekers, he then edited the three-volume anthology *Shamanism: Critical Concepts* (2004) and wrote *The Beauty of the Primitive: Shamanism and Western Imagination* (2007).

Quest Books

encourages open-minded inquiry into
world religions, philosophy, science, and the arts
in order to understand the wisdom of the ages,
respect the unity of all life, and help people explore
individual spiritual self-transformation.

Its publications are generously supported by
The Kern Foundation,
a trust committed to Theosophical education.

Quest Books is the imprint of
the Theosophical Publishing House,
a division of the Theosophical Society in America.
For information about programs, literature,
on-line study, membership benefits, and international centers,
see www.theosophical.org
or call 800-669-1571 or (outside the U.S.) 630-668-1571.

Related Quest Titles

Nicholas and Helena Roerich, by Ruth A. Drayer

Shambhala, by Victoria LePage

Theosophy, by Robert Ellwood

The World of the Dalai Lama, by Gill Farrer-Halls

To order books or a complete Quest catalog,
call 800-669-9425 or (outside the U.S.) 630-665-0130.

Praise for Andrei Znamenski's

RED SHAMBHALA

"The lines between mystical seekers, secret policemen, spies, and charlatans constantly cross and blur in this fascinating, and at times astounding, story about the interplay of mysticism and politics in the shadow of Stalin's Russia."
> —Richard Spence, Professor of History, University of Idaho

"An amazing story, told by a fine scholar but written accessibly. It has larger-than-life characters against the background of a myth of Shambhala that haunted the Russian imagination as it did the Western, but with rather different consequences."
> —Mark Sedgwick, author, *Against the Modern World: Traditionalism and the Secret Intellectual History of the Twentieth Century*

"This groundbreaking investigation makes us aware that the sacred and the profane can share the same mythical milieu. A must-read book for people interested in the fuzzy area among mystique, esotericism, and politics."
> —Marcello De Martino, Ph.D., Istituto Italiano per l'Africa e l'Oriente, Rome, and author of *Mircea Eliade Esoterico*

"Reads like the best of thrillers."
> —Willard Sunderland, Professor of History, University of Cincinnati